Using Young Adult Literature:

Thematic Activities Based on

Gardner's Multiple Intelligences

Using Young Adult Literature:

Thematic Activities Based on

Gardner's Multiple Intelligences

Editor: Jacqueline Glasgow

Christopher-Gordon Publishers, Inc.

Norwood, Massachusetts

CREDITS

Every effort has been made to contact copyright holders for permission to reproduce borrowed material where necessary. We apologize for any oversights and would be happy to rectify them in future printings.

Endorsement by Howard Gardner reprinted by permission of Howard Gardner.

"Implication of the Theory of Multiple Intelligences for Assessment" by Linda Campbell, 1994, from the 1994 ASCD Multiple Intelligences Series Facilitator's Guide #2, pp. 5–8. Copyright © 1994 Linda Campbell. Adapted with permission.

Overhead 21. "A Developmental Self-Assessment of the Multiple Intelligences," by Linda Campbell, from the 1994 ASCD Multiple Intelligences Series Facilitator's Guide, #1, p. 73. Copyright © 1994 Linda Campbell. Reprinted with permission.

Excerpt entitled "Table 4:1 Four Stages of Reading Literature" from *Bridging English* by Joseph O'Bierne Milner and Luch Floyd Morock Milner, 1993, (page 86). Upper Saddle River, New Jersey: Prentice-Hall, Inc. Pearson Education. Copyright ©1993 by Prentice-Hall, Inc. Reprinted with permission.

"Overview of Gardner's Multiple Intelligence" adapted from "Different Child, Different Style" by K. Fagella and J. Horowitz, 1990, (pp. 49–54), Instructor, September 1990 issue. Copyright ©1990 by Scholastic. Reprinted with permission of Scholastic.

Excerpt titled Learning Difficulties Checklist from *7 Kinds of Smart* (pp. 172–175), by Thomas Armstrong, 1993, New York: Penguin Putnam Inc. Copyright ©1993 by Thomas Armstrong. Used by permission of Plume a division of Penguin Putnam Inc.

Excerpt titled Glossary of Film Terms from "Producing Student Films: Shakespeare on Screen" by Mark Franek, 1996, *English Journal,* p.52. Copyright 1996 by Heinemann Boynton/Cook Publishers. Reprinted with permission. Also from *Reel Conversations,* (p. 20 figure 2.2) by Ann Wilder and Alan Teasley, 1996, Portsmouth, New Hampshire: Heinemann. Copyright ©1996 by Heinemann and the authors. Reprinted with permission.

Characterization Activity used with permission of Colleen Ruggieri.

Figure 3:2, Teacher Observation Sheet from *The Complete Guide to Thematic Units: Creating the Integrated Curriculum,* (p. 69), by Anita Meinbach, Liz Rothlein, and Anthony Fredericks, 1995, Norwood, Massachusetts, Christopher-Gordon Publishers, Inc. Copyright ©1995 by Christopher-Gordon Publishers, Inc. Reprinted with permission.

Multiple Intelligences Survey from Surfacquarium Consulting by Walter McKenzie. Used by permission of Walter McKenzie.

All student work used with permssion.

Christopher-Gordon Publishers, Inc.
1502 Providence Highway, Suite 12
Norwood, MA 02062
800-934-8322
781-762-5577

Printed in the United States of America

10 9 8 7 6 5 4 3 2 1   06 05 04 03 02

Library of Congress Catalog Card Number: 2001095880

ISBN: 1-929024-36-3

ENDORSEMENT

"The idea of multiple intelligences has the most educational power when it is used to promote deep understanding in one or more disciplines. Jackie Glasgow and colleagues have achieved just such power; they have produced well-designed materials and thoughtful analyses which promise to enhance the teaching of literature."

—Howard Gardner

DEDICATION

To my parents:

Jack and Thelma Neill
who taught me to love life and to live it to the fullest.

To my children:
Stephen, JoEllen, Andrew, Deborah, Mary Beth, Judy

and their children:
who are already reading and finding the life found in great stories, great books!
Devin, Keith, Jessica, Braham, Braden

and

To Howard Gardner:
Thank you for your contributions to
our teaching and learning;
You have taught us to recognize and nurture our intelligences
and those of our students.

Acknowledgments

Teaching and learning is a collaborative, interactive process. I am indebted to all of my students who challenge me to meet both their needs and interests to learn, and who provoke me to take risks in doing so. I wish to thank Mike Conrath, Carol Marino, and Vickie Giovangnoli from the Trumbull County Educational Service Center for providing the opportunities to present workshops for developing curriculum based on Gardner's Multiple Intelligences. I give special thanks to all the English teachers who attended these workshops, inspired me to explore and implement Gardner's theory, and contributed many of the chapters for this book. Thanks to Samantha Nesbitt and Vickie Dellinger for their careful editing of the works in progress. Writing about the multiple intelligences would not be possible without Stephen Spencer, my husband, who believes in and supports my inquiry into the intelligences. I owe tremendous gratitude to Howard Gardner who taught us to know ourselves and our students in unique ways.

Many thanks to the reviewers and editors at Christopher-Gordon for their creative talents in the production of this book. Sue Canavan paved the way with strong guidance and technical support. Kathryn Liston assisted in the fine details of rights and permissions. Laurie Maker carefully attended to details that made for a much stronger manuscript. Carol Treska attended to artistically formatting the text. Thanks to all the people working behind the scenes at Christopher-Gordon to make this book a success.

BRIEF TABLE OF CONTENTS

CONTENTS

**Chapter 2: "The Holocaust: Poignant Memories
Preserved" with Young Adult Literature**

**Chapter 3: "Surviving the Civil War in Cambodia Through
Immigration" with Crew's *Children of the River***

Chapter 4: "Heroes, Heartbreak, and Healing: What Was it like in Vietnam?"

Joyce Rowland with Jackie Glasgow 93

Chapter 7: "Building Tolerance and Empathy Toward Others" with Harper Lee

Chapter 8: "New Ties, Unconventional Relationships" with M. E. Kerr

Chapter 9: "Conformity vs. Individuality" in Cormier's *The Chocolate War*

Chapter 10: "Preservation of Self and the Environment" with Will Hobbs

Chapter 11: "Confronting Environmental Threats" with Robert O'Brien

LIST OF TABLES

LIST OF FIGURES

PREFACE

"Literature is what people get *passionate* about" declares Peter Elbow in his book, *What is English?* (1990, p 101). English teachers are often polarized about the literature that stimulates their passion as they wrestle with canon selections versus other texts, but I get *passionate* about Young Adult Literature. I realized very soon that my mission in teaching secondary English classes was not merely to meet the needs of future English majors, but particularly to convince the average student—given all the other interesting things in life—to engage in literary texts. I quickly abandoned traditional lectures of standard interpretations of literary works in favor of a more personal and subjective approach to reading and responding to texts. As I encountered resistance to reading and formalistic analysis of the classics, I searched for alternative texts to meet students' needs. That collection of alternative books has now grown into a recognized body of literature known as Young Adult Literature. Since the 1960's, my classrooms have been filled with works by S.E. Hinton, Paul Zindel, Robert Lipsyte, Stephen Dunning, Virginia Hamilton, Judith Guest, Robert Newton Peck, and Robert Cormier, to name a few of the Young Adult authors on my original reading list. Through the years, my students have made personal connections with these books that have changed their views about reading, writing, and the world in general. They, too, have become passionate about the lives of the characters in the books with whom they identified. Even reluctant readers have joined the throng and read beyond the requirements. While not all my stories ring with success, young adult literature has brought truth and meaning to my life, as well as to the lives of hundreds of students throughout my career.

While this literature has increased students' reading beyond the trickle, Gardner's theory of multiple intelligences opened the floodgates to meeting the needs of all students. My teaching changed dramatically from traditional, subject-centered teaching to subversive, student-centered teaching; from common notions of a single intelligence to multiple intelligences as multiple ways of knowing and learning. Along with exploring ways to make English more meaningful to even the most reluctant at-risk student, I began conducting staff development workshops for English teachers in the area to share ideas, create activities, and implement them. As interest in these workshops continued and changed teachers' and students' lives, we were encouraged to begin developing thematic units incorporating our best instructional strategies. This book is a testament of our best practice, our best understanding of Gardner's theory, our best student progress.

In the end, you as the professional must judge what works best in your particular instructional context. You must determine your curriculum goals and ways you will meet professional standards. You know your students' needs and abilities and your personal interests. Partake of the literature and activities in this book to develop and nurture your own intelligences and the intelligences of your students. Enjoy the feast!

OVERVIEW

Developing Students' Multiple Intelligences
in Response to Young Adult Literature

Written for English language arts educators, this book offers practical classroom applications based on Gardner's Multiple Intelligences and his Principles for Teaching for Understanding. Each chapter presents a thematic unit based on award-winning young adult novels that allow students to identify and assimilate different world views (Cooter, 1989). Since the themes developed through literature transcend traditional content-area boundaries, they quite naturally lend themselves to a curriculum incorporating disciplines represented by the multiple intelligences. Gardner suggests that society as a whole would be better served if disciplines could be presented in a number of ways. Gardner is convinced that schools attempt to cover far too much material and that superficial understandings—or nonunderstandings—are the result. Instead, schools should help students reach vocational and avocational goals that are appropriate to their particular spectrum of intelligences (1993, p. 9). Since not all students exhibit the same intelligence profile, nor do they share the same interests, the activities in the thematic units provide ample choices for both teachers and students to make-meaning and construct knowledge from the suggested literature.

This book was written to assist teachers in acquiring "intelligent fair" methods of designing curriculum and assessment approaches, and in nurturing individual capacities so that each student may experience the pleasure of successful learning in areas of strength, while exploring and nurturing areas that are weak. This book is filled with effective teaching strategies that would be useful for teachers seeking to enrich their classroom activities, regardless of their interest in Gardner's Multiple Intelligences theory. As one reviewer said, "It provides multiple entry points for teachers with strong linguistic or logical intelligences to reach non-traditional learners." This book provides engaging and educative opportunities for all kinds of readers and writers in the English language arts classroom. Pre-service English Education students will find many ideas for strengthening their repertoire of classroom strategies to assist them in their first years of teaching. Experienced teachers will benefit from the new, creative ideas for enriching their classroom experiences.

The units in this book were prepared by Trumbull County English and Language Arts teachers during curriculum development workshops, which I facilitated at Kent State University. Some of the units are developed for middle school students, while others are designed more specifically for secondary students. In most cases, the units are flexible and adaptable for either age group interested in the topics. The units are not intended to be implemented in their entirety; rather activities are described to trigger creativity and interest in each of the multiple intelligences. In keeping with Gardner's Principles for Teaching for Understanding, most of the units suggest ways to utilize community resources in relating learning to life beyond school. Gardner believes that connection to the community helps students feel more engaged and competent, and therefore more inclined to serve society in a constructive way.

Engaging Students in Meaningful Reading Experiences

Unless students can find meaningful experiences in their reading, they will more likely turn off the English teacher and turn on the television. Teachers must maintain high expectations for students while engaging them in the story. In return, students must learn to articulate their feelings, opinions, and thoughts about books they read. Students must learn to think rationally about the issues evoked in the text with which they become emotionally involved. Both cognitive and affective components of the mind should be utilized in making meaning of the reading experience. Louise Rosenblatt insists on the term *transaction* as "a means of establishing the active role of both reader and text in interpretation and ensures that we recognize that any interpretation is an event occurring at a particular time in particular social or cultural context" (1995, p. 295). In Rosenblatt's reader response theory, the reader is recognized not only as active, but also as carrying on "a continuum from predominantly nonliterary, or *efferent*, reading, to predominantly literary, or *aesthetic*, reading" (p. 292). The purpose of *efferent* response is to carry away information and reproduce it to fulfill a specific task, such as a plot summary or character analysis. However, reading to find the answer to a factual question requires attention mainly to the public aspects of meaning and excludes, or pushes into the periphery, personal feelings or ideas activated. Rosenblatt believes that the reader must first adopt the *aesthetic stance*—that is, attention to the personal associations, feelings, and ideas being lived through during the reading. She posits that once the work has been aesthetically evoked, it then can become the object of reflection and analysis, according to the various critical and scholarly approaches (p. 295). Traditional and formalist methods of teaching literature treat it as a body of information to be transmitted, rather than as experiences on which to reflect. Reader–response methods encourage students to relive, predict, evaluate, connect, and link text with their own lives. In both kinds of reading, *efferent* and *aesthetic*, the reader focuses attention on the stream of consciousness, selecting out the particular mix of public and private linkages with the words dictated by the purpose of the reading. But if students know they will be tested primarily on factual aspects of the work, a full aesthetic reading is prevented, and the mix swings toward the efferent end of the continuum. In a day when students resist reading books, reader response methodology is "essential to the survival of the reading of literature as an active part of our American culture" (p. 293). Therefore, this book provides teachers with a plethora of ideas for evoking the aesthetic stance toward reading and responding to young adult literature.

Four Stages of Reading Literature

In order to conceptualize responses to literature in a developmental sequence from the personal *aesthetic* stance to the public, *efferent* reading of the text, we need a comprehensive framework for literature instruction. *The Four Stages of Reading Literature* developed by Milner and Milner (1993) provides such a framework (See Table 0.1). This four-stage construct begins with the reader's personal reaction to the text, moves toward a public sharing and interpretation of meaning, and then progresses to formalistic study and critical understanding of the text. The student progresses from individual reader, to participant in a community of learners, to researcher of ideas. Even though each stage builds on the work of the preceding stage and prepares for the next, the movement is recursive. The students are always analyzing and evaluating ideas as they emerge from personal connections, associations and experiences made in the reading. The stages begin with the students' concrete interpretations of the text, move to collective understandings and end with abstract and critical insights, to the extent that a text is pursued beyond the reader response level.

As students first engage in the text, they are invited and encouraged to take the aesthetic stance in their *reader responses*. They should be free to choose from a range of good books, literature which brings them pleasure and meets their need and interests as they enter into the human experience that literature presents. As Louise Rosenblatt suggests, "the reader seeks to participate in another's vision—to reap knowledge of the world, to fathom the resources of the human spirit, to gain insights that will make his own life more comprehensible" (1995, p. 7). Readers should derive satisfaction from literature either by identifying with a character who possesses qualities similar to their own or by merely escaping from their stressful lives into the story. Books must be provided that hold out some link with the young reader's past and present preoccupations, anxieties, and ambitions. Students should be encouraged to reflect on their own lives, as well as come to see human beings and society in a broader context of emotions and ideas. Establishing an atmosphere of informal, friendly exchange is essential for students to feel comfortable in revealing their emotions and judgments. Writing strategies such as freewriting, associative recollections, and journal responses tend to capture personal meaning students have made from literary experience.

TABLE 0.1: FOUR STAGES OF READING LITERATURE

Stages	Purpose in Reading	Primary Task	Distance from Text	Questions about the Text (Formal Elements and Areas of Study)
Reader Response	Pleasure	Read	Immediate	***Thatness*** (Unmediated) Humor/wit (Sociological) Insight (Psychological) Beauty (Aesthetic)
Interpretive Community	Understanding	Conceptualize	Reflective (Responsive)	***Whatness*** Event (Plot) Person (Character) Meaning (Theme)
Formal Analysis	Appreciation	Formalize	Self-conscious (Investigative)	***Howness*** Form (Structure) Style (Imagery) Intent (Point of View)
Critical Synthesis	Expansion	Reconstruct	Multiconscious (Exploratory)	***Whyness*** Context (History) Text (Bibliography) Metatext (Criticism)

Reprinted by permission of Prentice-Hall, Inc., Upper Saddle River, NJ. Taken from *Bridging English* by Milner and Milner, 1993, p. 86.

After students have made their personal journey into the text and excited their passion for the story, they bring their insights to share in the class *interpretive community*. Through sharing their responses in the larger group, students learn to listen with understanding to others and to respond in relevant terms. With class members acting as sounding boards, students can share experiences, ask questions, and present judgments they have made from their reading. In turn, classmates can clarify, dispute, and elaborate the interpretations they have construed from the text. When the classroom is viewed as a safe haven for exploring ideas and sharing opinions, students are free to respond intimately and spontaneously to literature. "When students begin that communal sharing, the multiplicity of interpretations widens individual perspectives and unseats the idea that any one reading is the definitive reading" (Milner and Milner 1993, p. 100). Through public discussion of literature, students gain confidence in their ability to respond to literature personally and collectively. Having examined the basic concepts of the particular literary work, students are prepared to move on to the next stage.

In the third stage, *formal analysis*, students address the formal elements of the text and examine the author's craft. The purpose of formal analysis is "to give [students] terminology and techniques to use in sharing [their] insights . . . to evaluate books and assist readers in moving up in developing their skills . . . and to read reviews, articles, and critical analyses with greater understanding" (Donelson and Nilsen 1997, p. 44). Although literary techniques can be addressed in many different ways, literature is often studied by classification of genre and by analysis of such essential literary elements as plot, theme, character, point of view, tone, setting, and style. Students focus on how these specific aspects of texts fit together to form a coherent whole. This technical focus alone would omit the personal and communal reader responses so necessary to assure strong engagement in the text, but in order to understand literature as an art form, students must engage in formal analysis of literature. Even though some students resist this level of response, connecting personal meaning with formal matters is important in learning to appreciate literature in deeper and more enduring ways.

As students develop the ability to analyze and interpret different kinds of literary criticism, they make meaning through *critical synthesis*. Critical synthesis invites students to see a text from the perspective of those "who are personally and professionally engaged in the study of literature and who have developed strong positions and theories about it" (Milner and Milner 1993, p. 116). The purpose of this stage is to make students aware of diverse perspectives other than their own which come through examination of historical, biographical, formalist, feminist or Freudian interpretations of the work. Traditional literary theory usually focused exclusively on "literary" or canonical texts—novels, stories, poems, essays, or drama. Recently, theorists such as Robert Scholes have broadened our conceptions of texts to include a range of modes, genres, and media forms. In the context of Young Adult Literature, students might reach critical synthesis through research of the social, political and historical context of their literary work and by examining the growing body of literary criticism for this body of literature.

Thus, the *Four Stages of Reading Literature* provides a framework for preserving and enhancing the meaning-making process. The student constructs meaning of the text by first evoking the *aesthetic* stance which then grows, builds and develops toward the *efferent* reading of the text in the analytical and critical approaches to the text. If we shortcut this developmental process, we jeopardize the aesthetic reading and risk losing the reader altogether. Applebee (1993) has amply documented excessive use of analytic approaches to thinking about literature in the English classes he observed. His research indicates that teachers tend to minimize the reader response stage of making meaning. If personal connections to the text are encouraged, the freedom to construct and express meaning in the most appropriate format must also be given. When I think about the time I first learned the importance of providing opportunities for students to make meaning on their terms, I think of the story about Pete.

Construction of Meaning Through Reader Response Projects

My classes had always been activity oriented, but it was not until I met Pete in a General English 12 classroom some years ago that I changed my approach to teaching. Pete was a handsome Swede with blond hair and blue eyes. He was friendly enough, but totally *uninterested* in reading the short stories in the twelfth grade anthology. He hunched down in his seat, wanted to sleep through English and dared me to make him read. I began wondering what to do about Pete. What English did he really need to know to work effectively in the local General Electric plant? Did I know any literature that he'd be *interested* in reading? How in the world was I going to get Pete through the required research paper? I selected Jessie Stuart's *The Thread That Runs So True* as a book that might capture Pete's imagination. This book describes the school experience of a group of boys who live in the hills of Kentucky just across the Ohio River from Portsmouth, Ohio. The boys like to hunt, trap, and skip school when they can, just like Pete and his friends. I was so relieved when the students actually began to read this book in class. They even took their books home and brought them back to class the next day with a chapter read.

Then I began talking about the research paper required by the board of education. I still remember the groans. They wanted to know their options. Options? Would the school board go for projects as evidence of competency for graduation? Reluctantly, they did permit me to break the long-standing tradition. That's all Pete and his friends needed to begin the construction of the log cabin school house they envisioned in Jesse Stuart's book. They worked diligently on it with the help of the industrial arts teacher. It was the first constructive project he'd seen them do! When they finished the one room school house, it was complete with a pot belly stove, smoke coming out of the chimney, a slate at each student's desk, and a wash bowl in the back of the room. I was so proud of their work that I not only shared it with the board of education, but also took this project to the OCTELA (Ohio Council of Teachers of English and Language Arts) Spring Conference. I had heard that Jesse Stuart was to be there as the banquet speaker. I set up a table in the back of the hall and placed all my students' projects and papers from the book on it. After his presentation, I invited him back for a look. Needless to say, he was moved. He understood my purposes and was delighted to see that young people understood his book and his message.

By constructing these projects, the students had become both tremendously imaginative and acclimated to an environment that valued the generation of non-written "texts" as a vehicle to construct meaning. In the following years, in addition to the core of writing I required, I increasingly encouraged students to represent their understanding of literature through unconventional types of compositions. My rationale for emphasizing multiple forms of compositions was that the students were, like Pete, highly engaged in the projects, far more so than when they were being evaluated through conventional writing. The at-risk readers often became the most enthusiastic and productive workers in the class. Above all, the students, besides being engaged, were clearly demonstrating an understanding of literature in ways not accessible through their writing. The project approach elicited a personal, aesthetic stance of reader response from them as they demonstrated their knowledge and understanding of the young adult novels we were reading. Even though I felt good about what I was doing, I did not become totally comfortable with this project approach until I met Howard Gardner and learned about his theory of multiple intelligences.

Multiple Intelligences

Several years ago, I attended a teacher in-service seminar where Howard Gardner was the keynote speaker. I not only listened attentively to his lecture, but I found myself avidly taking notes. He referred to his seminal work, *Frames of Mind* (1983) and exclaimed his surprise at the interest educators were taking in his psychological theory of multiple intelligences. Since that meeting with Howard Gardner, I have continued to read his works as he focuses on educational applications of his theory: *The Unschooled Mind: How Children Think and How Schools Should Teach, Multiple Intelligences: The Theory in Practice* (1991 and more recently, *Creating Minds: An Anatomy of Creativity Seen Through the Lives of Freud, Einstein, Picasso, Stravinsky, Eliot, Graham, and Gandhi* (1993). His latest book, *The Disciplined Mind: What All Students Should Understand* (1999), articulates his ultimate goal for an educated citizenry that understand the physical world, the biological world, and the social world—in a personal context as well as from a broader social and cultural perspective. Gardner's theory of multiple intelligences has provided a strong psychological foundation to support the pedagogical approach to meaning construction that I had been developing in my English classes. I now have theoretical grounding for the projects students create in responding to literature that often incorporates nonlinguistic activities such as models, video tapes, skits, musical productions, and artistic responses. Armed with Gardner's theory, I know that we are not just "playing games" as some have intimated, but that we are, in fact, enabling students to construct meaning and develop their intelligences in ways they choose and value. Gardner's research on human intelligence breaks away from the common notions of intelligence and challenges us to consider the multiple intelligences as multiple ways of knowing and learning.

Beliefs about Intelligence

Beliefs about intelligence have changed drastically throughout this century. In the early 1900s, Alfred Binet developed a test to measure learners with disabilities. During World War I, the army utilized the Standford-Binet test to determine who would carry a gun. From that day on, the IQ test has looked like psychology's biggest success—a genuinely useful scientific tool. The most popular test developed by David Wechsler has been revised and renormed a number of times over the years to reflect the changing demographics of the country. What these tests have in common is that one's intelligence, which was more or less determined by heredity, could be tested and quantified as an intelligence quotient (IQ). This idea of fixed intelligence could then be used to sort the population according to one's intelligence capacities by plotting the I.Q. scores on a bell-shaped curve. By definition, most of us are average, a few are gifted, and a few are mentally retarded. This bell curve mentality of intelligence has pervaded other areas of assessment such as norm-referenced standardized tests like the S.A.T. and A.C.T.. With these scores, students are sorted into various colleges, universities, and graduate schools. Within public school institutions, the bell curve mentality is used to sort students within classrooms, academic programs, and graduate classes. It tells us little about what students have learned and understood in such classes. At best, it describes that about 10 percent of the students do very well on these types of tests, 10 percent do poorly, and about 80 percent get average results. While the bell curve may be useful for research purposes, it does not accurately portray students' learning, understanding, and knowing.

Instead of looking for a bell-shaped curve to describe students' learning, Lazear (1994) suggests that the J-curve gives a far more accurate picture of the growth of knowledge. This curve suggests that knowledge grows in a compounding fashion. The student may know very little at the beginning or bottom of the J-curve, but as knowledge is enhanced, expanded, and deepened, the student does nothing but grow and the curve rises upward. If our assessment practices are to reflect this growth, we must ground ourselves in a theory that embraces development and rejects limitations.

Howard Gardner's research offers an alternative to this narrowly defined concept of intelligence that limits human growth and development. Instead of viewing human knowledge in terms of a score on a standardized test, Gardner defines intelligence as:

- The ability to resolve genuine problems or difficulties that one encounters in real life
- The ability to find or create new problems to solve
- The ability to make something or offer a service that is valued within one's culture

Gardner states that human intelligence must be genuinely useful and important in at least one cultural setting with problem-solving and product-making the most important elements (1983, p. 60–61).

Through his work with brain damaged patients at a Boston hospital, Gardner realized that the kind of damage which was suffered was dependent upon the location of the injury in the brain. He began to consider the possibility that our brain possesses many distinct potentials and abilities. Gardner developed a set of criteria to determine what exactly constitutes an intelligence (1983, pp. 62–66). Here are eight "signs" of an intelligence:

- Potential isolation by brain surgery
- Existence in special populations, such as prodigies or idiot savants
- An identifiable core operation or set of operations
- A distinctive developmental history, along with a definable set of expert "end-states" performances
- An evolutionary history and evolutionary plausibility
- Support from experimental psychological tasks
- Support from psychometric findings
- Susceptibility to encoding in a symbol system

These are the criteria by which any candidate for intelligence can be judged. Gardner shows that intelligence is not just a matter of academic achievement, but that it must promote the ability to function effectively in life outside of schools.

Rather than having just one fixed intelligence, Gardner holds that all human beings are capable of at least eight different ways of knowing the world. According to Gardner's research, we are all capable of knowing the world through language, logical-mathematical analysis, spatial representation, musical thinking, the use of the body to solve problems or to make things, an understanding of nature, an understanding of other individuals, an understanding of ourselves, and understanding our role in the world. See Table 0.2 *Overview of the Multiple Intelligences* for a description of the nine intelligences that Gardner has identified so far. This table gives examples of what each type of learner likes to do, is good at, and learns best.

TABLE 0.2: OVERVIEW OF GARDNER'S MULTIPLE INTELLIGENCES

TYPE	LIKES TO	IS GOOD AT	LEARNS BEST BY

LINGUISTIC LEARNER
 	
"The Word Player"
	read
	write
	tell stories
		memorizing names, places,
		   dates and trivia
			saying, hearing and seeing
			   words

LOGICAL/ MATHEMATICAL LEARNER "The Questioner"	do experiments figure things out work with numbers ask questions explore patterns and relationships	math reasoning logic problem solving	categorizing classifying working with abstract patterns/relationships
SPATIAL LEARNER "The Visualizer"	draw, build, design and create models daydream look at pictures/slides watch movies play with machines	imagining things sensing changes mazes/puzzles reading maps/charts	visualizing dreaming using the mind's eye working with colors/pictures
MUSICAL LEARNER "The Music Lover"	sing, hum tunes listen to music play an instrument respond to music	picking up sounds remembering melodies noticing pitches/rhythms keeping time	rhythm melody music
BODILY/ KINESTHETIC LEARNER "The Mover"	move around touch and talk use body language	physical activities (sports/dance/acting) crafts	touching moving interacting with space processing knowledge through bodily sensations
INTERPERSONAL LEARNER "The Socializer"	have lots of friends talk to people join groups	understanding people leading others organizing communicating manipulating mediating conflicts	sharing comparing relating cooperating interviewing
INTRAPERSONAL LEARNER "The Individual"	work alone pursue own interests	understanding self focusing inward on feelings/dreams following instincts pursuing interests/goals being original	working alone individualized projects self-paced instruction having own space

NATURALIST
LEARNER
 	
"The Nature Lover"
	spend time outside
	explore nature
	observe natural phenomenon
	collect natural artifacts
	listen to natural sounds
		finding patterns in nature
		naming natural
		phenomenon
		noticing changes in wind,
		   stars, weather, etc.
		able to discern, identify and
		   classify plants and animals
			exploring nature
			having time to observe
			conducting hands-on
			   scientific experiments
			landscaping and creating
			sanctuaries (Hoerr, 1996)

EXISTENTIALIST LEARNER "Why are we here?"	think and meditate ponders questions about life, death and ultimate realities; likes to explore religious questions	asking philosophical questions "What is our role in the world?" "Why is there evil?"; pursue truth, beauty, peace in nature or in the fine arts	learns in the context where humankind stands in the "big picture" of existence; learning new things is easier when I understand their value.

Adapted from Faggella, K. and Horowitz, J. (September 1990). Different Child, Different Style. Instructor. 49-54. Reprinted by permission of Scholastic, Inc.

Underlying Assumptions of Gardner's Theory

The eight intelligences reinforce Gardner's cross-cultural perspective of human cognition. The culture into which one is born partly influences the capacities one develops. Each intelligence provides tools for learning, problem-solving, and creating that all human beings can use. The following are some of the underlying assumptions of Gardner's theory (1983):

1. *Each person is born with a unique combination of intelligences that form a distinct cognitive profile.*

Gardner believes that every normal individual possesses a unique blend of the eight intelligences that he has identified to this date. He acknowledges that while genetic factors set some kind of upper boundary on the extent to which an intelligence may be realized, it is unlikely that this biological limit is rarely, if ever, approached. Given enough exposure to the materials of the intelligence, nearly anyone who is not brain damaged can achieve quite significant results in that intellectual realm. (Note the Suzuki violin program where four-year-olds play the Vivaldi Violin Concerto.) By the same token, no one—whatever his or her biological potential—is likely to develop an intelligence without at least some opportunities for exploration of the materials that elicit a particular intellectual strength (Walters & Gardner, 1987). In sum, the culture plays a potent role in determining the extent to which an individual's intellectual potential is realized. It is no accident that an individual develops strengths in one area as opposed to another.

2. *Everyone relies on one or more intelligences for successful daily living.*

There are several ways to be intelligent within each of the eight intelligences. None of us is proficient at all of the subcomponents of an intelligence when we consider our strengths. For example, if someone is strong in linguistic intelligence, she may want to specify in what ways she uses that intelligence. Perhaps she is a professional writer, speaker, or literary critic. However, she may not be skilled at writing poetry or formal business proposals. Because the intelligences seldom work in isolation and usually work in tandem with other intelligences, Gardner is opposed to categorizing or labeling learners according to specific intelligences. At the same time, he acknowledges that we all have preferences. Gardner suggests that where individuals differ is in the strength of these intelligences and in the ways in which such intelligences are invoked and combined to carry out different tasks, solve diverse problems, and progress in various domains.

3. *Each intelligence is modifiable and can be nurtured and developed.*

Even though we each possess all eight of the intelligences that Gardner has identified at this time, we have not all developed them to the same extent. Based on Gardner's research, Linda and Bruce Campbell (1992) developed a self-assessment rubric for recognizing levels of development for each intelligence: novice (learns from observer), apprentice (experimenter), practitioner (user), expert (master), inventor (creator). Since none of us have *all* the intelligences well developed, our intelligence profiles are most likely jagged. It would be perfectly normal to be expert in the intelligences we use in our professional lives and be novice in the intelligences that we seldom exercise. Use Table 0.3—*A Developmental Self-Assessment of the Multiple Intelligences* to create your cognitive profile. Make a vertical bar graph by filling in each column to the level of development of each intelligence that you feel is appropriate. For instance, if you enjoy listening to music, but don't sing or play an instrument, you would fill in the bottom square of the music column indicating that you are at the novice level. However, if you have played or sung music professionally, you would fill in the music column from the bottom square up through the expert square. If you compose and publish music, you might fill in the whole music column. Continue filling out the chart for each of the intelligences to create your personal profile.

To help students understand their unique palette of intelligences, ask them to complete McKenzie's Multiple Intelligences Survey found in Appendix A or on the internet at http://surfaquarium.com/MIinvent.htm. On the other hand, the *Multiple Intelligences Developmental Assessment Scale (MIDAS)* by C. Branton Shearer is the most sophisticated instrument designed to assess one's multiple intelligences. According to Shearer, the purpose of the MIDAS is to "help identify each student's natural raw materials so they may be provided with support and challenged to develop these gifts into personally rewarding and meaningful work that is valued within their community" (1996, p. viii). For more information go to http://www.angelfire.com/OH/themidas/themidas4.html.

Implications for Education: Teaching for Understanding

If our belief that lifelong learning is necessary for success in a complex and interdependent world, we must teach for understanding. In his 1991 book, *The Unschooled Mind: How Children Think and How Schools Should Teach*, Gardner contrasts the concept of understanding with that of knowledge. When a person knows something, the statement usually means she has mentally stored the information and can readily retrieve it. By contrast, when a student understands something, it is assumed that her skills surpass stored information. *Understanding* refers to what people can do with information, rather than what they have memorized. Insight involves action more than possession. When students understand something, they can explain concepts in their own words, use information appropriately in new context, invent fresh analogies, and make

TABLE 0.3: A DEVELOPMENTAL SELF-ASSESSMENT OF THE MULTIPLE INTELLIGENCES

Levels of Learning	Linguistic	Logical/ Math	Spatial	Naturalist	Bodily-Kines-thetic	Musical	Inter-personal	Intra-personal
Inventor (Creator) Invents new forms of communication through the intelligence or creates original works. Moves human knowledge forward.								
Expert (Master) Demonstrates mastery of the concepts and practices of the intelligence in professional or avocational activities. May be viewed as a specialist. Enhances skills through interaction with other specialists, through self-critique and intuition.								
Practitioner (User) Develops proficiency in the intelligence's symbol system. Understands the concepts, skills, and principles of the intelligence's discipline and applies such knowledge in numerous contexts and new situation. Refines skills and knowledge through formalized instruction, as well as through self-critique. Knows how to learn additional skills.								
Apprentice (Experimenter) Perceives relationships between symbols and the objects or events they represent. From exposure to role models or through formal instruction, learns the symbol system, concepts, skills, and disciplinary body of knowledge of the intelligence.								
Novice (Observer) Learns about the intelligence through sensorimotor exploration of the environment and interaction with others. Observation, imitation, interaction, and experimentation instill knowledge, tools, and skills.								

Adapted from Linda Campbell (1992). A Developmental Self-Assessment of the Multiple Intelligences. In *Understanding Multiple Intelligences Facilitator's Guide*. ASCD. Reprinted with permission from ASCD.

generalizations. Memorization and recitation are not indicative of understanding. Gardner suggests the following principles for teaching for understanding:

- Include rich, time-worthy material. Focus on generative topics that are
  central to the discipline.
- Identify important goals and essential skills.
- Use multiple intelligences entry points into content.
- Relate learning to life beyond school.
- Assess learning authentically with portfolios, exhibitions of learning,
  and projects.

Schools with a multiple intelligences perspective grapple with how better
to teach their students so that they truly understand and can apply what they
have learned. Gardner distinguishes between "surface" and "deep" application
of the theory (Dec. 1995, p. 16). Surface applications include describing every
activity in terms of the putative intelligences that it entails, or every child in
terms of her/his alleged intellectual strengths and weaknesses. "Deep"
applications of the theory go beyond surface applications of the theory and
ultimately bring about a different way of thinking about children and their
education. See Table 5:1 for *Multiple Intelligences Activities and Bloom's Taxonomy
for Children at Work*. Schools that teach for deeper understanding focus on
three aspects:

- Personalizing learning by striving to reach each child through engaging
  his or her individual learning potential and personal interests through
  increased student choices
- Blending assessment and instruction by asking students to apply their
  knowledge in real-world ways
- Engaging the local community in K–12 schooling through programs
  that offer apprenticeship, mentoring, or enrichment opportunities

Teaching for understanding means engaging students in meaningful experiences
where they are asked to explore their intelligences and relate learning to real
life situations. To teach for understanding, we must know our students in new
ways and think about curriculum, instruction and assessment differently from
traditional practice.

Teaching for Understanding in English/Language Arts Classrooms

Multiple intelligences theory says that there are nine different intelligences,
but schools are typically organized around only the linguistic and logical/
mathematical intelligences. If a learner is strong in these intelligences, success
comes easily; but not all learners are strong in these areas. English and language

arts teachers are by profession experts in verbal/linguistic intelligence. If we confine our curriculum and instruction to just this one intelligence, then we tend to best reach those students who likewise prefer linguistic intelligence. If, on the other hand, we allow students to learn and make-meaning in the intelligences of their strengths, their linguistic intelligence is more likely to develop. This does not mean that every lesson must have eight different options. It does mean, however, that teachers need to consider all of the intelligences in planning instruction and assessment.

Gardner challenges educators to engage all students in meaningful inquiry: "Can we draw on our expanding knowledge of human development, individual differences, and cultural influences as we seek ways of enhancing the understandings of large numbers of students?" (1999, p. 186). How can we draw on constructivist approaches to teaching that are both developmentally appropriate and respectful of individual differences so that we teach for deep understanding of important concepts in a diverse classroom? In order to do so, Gardner advocates that education should be based on two foundations: (1) educators need to recognize the difficulties of students in attaining genuine understanding of important topics and concepts, and, (2) educators need to take into account the differences among minds and, as far as possible, fashion an education that can reach the infinite variety of students (p. 186). Gardner contends that a "multiple intelligences perspective" can enhance understanding in at least three ways (pp.186–187):

- *By Providing Powerful Points of Entry.* Since people of all ages find stories inviting, Gardner suggests the most effective ways to involve a large number of learners is through vivid, dramatic narratives (p. 189). See Table 4:1 for *Multiple Intelligences Activities for Entry and Development Approaches to Multiple Perspectives of the Heroes, Heartbreak, and Healing in Vietnam.*

- *By Offering Apt Analogies.* Analogies serve as gateways to connect unfamiliar topics or themes to prior experience or knowledge. Once interested, students are ready for full contact with the principal content of rich topics through various comparisons, analogies, and metaphors. In addition to the linguistic intelligence, analogies activate the logical/mathematical and visual/spatial intelligences.

- *By Providing Multiple Representations of the Central or Core Ideas of the Topic.* The extent to which students grasp these core ideas comprises effective teaching. Accommodating the meaningful construction of knowledge from a diverse population of students is more likely to occur if students are presented with multiple representations of the central ideas of the topic. Multiple representations of core ideas activate all the multiple intelligences by giving students choices to represent ideas in forms that are meaningful to them. In short, school must be individualized and personalized to be effective. We need to understand the specific mental representations of each student in as much detail as possible. And, insofar as is feasible, we ought to configure education to allow two outcomes: (1) students encounter materials in ways that allow them access to their content, and (2) students have the opportunity to show what they have learned, in ways that are comfortable for them, yet also interpretable by the surrounding society (1999, 72-73). See Table 1, Chapter 1, for *A Multiple Intelligences Perspective for Teaching for Deep Understanding of Riding the Freedom Train*. Instead of promoting a single literacy, this model causes us to think in terms of multiple literacies, where various ways of knowing and being are encouraged and enhanced.

Promoting Multiple Literacies.

Applebee (1981) argues that English educators should consider "writing as a tool for exploring a subject ... for discovering meaning rather than just transcribing an idea ... [We] tend to overlook the extent to which these devices help us generate new ideas 'at the point of utterance'" (p. 100). Also overlooked is the potential that other tools have for enabling similar processes. A tool can be used in many ways, not all of which are compatible with a learner's goals. To use writing as an example, a student may or may not value writing as a tool for constructing meaning in response to literature. Writing can come in many forms, each being valued by or useful to writers in different situations. In order to respond to literature, for instance, a student ideally has many writing options, including keeping a journal, retelling the story from a different point of view, writing a formal essay or a letter, or composing a poetic response. The student may even prefer other modes of expression than writing to demonstrate understanding of the text, such as a drawing or musical composition. However, the response to literature in the English classroom has usually been limited to written texts. The use of non written texts as tools for meaning construction has rarely been sanctified in English language arts classrooms.

Applebee (1981, 1993) has documented the ways in which schools privilege analytic writing over other functions and constrain student expression through their imposition of analytic form, a form not always valued by students. The degree to which a particular tool enables meaning construction, therefore, depends on the disposition of the learner and the prevailing communication genres of the learning context (Smagorinsky and Coppock, 1994). An alternative to current practices would be to endorse writing as one of many types of composition allowed for the construction of meaning: that the composition of other kinds of texts (music, art, dance, drama) can potentially enable students to construct meaning in the media they value. Gardner's theory of the Multiple Intelligences supports this broadened notion of students' response to text. Gardner has argued that students' most potent means of thinking may come through areas other than the logical and linguistic realms. Thus, students who are stronger in other areas are disadvantaged in a classroom where writing has established exclusive rights as a unique mode of learning. Gardner argues that different intelligences are fostered by different cultures and, that as schools become less dominated by students of Western descent, the focus on logical linguistic assessment will become a more questionable practice (1993). By defining literacy as the use of language, art, music, movement, and other sign systems to explore and expand our world, each of these underlying processes is enhanced as a potential of schooling to serve a democratic multicultural society. According to Short, Harste and Burke, the extent to which art, music, mathematics, movement, and so forth, are seen as legitimate ways of knowing, determines the kind of democracy we have as these decisions affect who participates and whose voice gets heard (1996, p. 53). So, if the goal of learning is meaning construction, then we must empower all students in the English classroom by shifting the emphasis from single literacy to multiple literacies. See Table 2:1 for an *Overview of Holocaust Unit Activities that Nurture the Multiple Intelligences* and Table 6:2 for an *Overview of Multiple Intelligences Activities for "Living in an Outsider Society."*

Use Literacy Activities to Develop Multiple Intelligences

Within the verbal/linguistic framework, literacy activities can be incorporated into the English/Language Arts curriculum to help students develop and explore their multiple intelligences. By first making meaning of the text using the intelligence of their choice, students are able to represent knowledge in areas of their strengths. By giving students choices of reader-response activities within the verbal/linguistic framework, they can select activities which enable them to be successful. Students having strong verbal/linguistic intelligence can be encouraged to nurture and develop other intelligences that might not be as highly developed. Through these experiences, students learn to make sense of and think differently about the books they read. See Table 0.4 for *Literacy Activities to Develop Multiple Intelligences within a Verbal/Linguistic Framework.*

Gardner's work helps us to see that in many classrooms, students are not developing rich understandings because they are limited to traditional forms of linguistic interaction. When interactions and intelligences are supported by more open contexts of learning, such as the activities listed above, students reveal abilities and understandings that surprise both their teachers and themselves.

TABLE 0.4: LITERACY ACTIVITIES TO DEVELOP MULTIPLE INTELLIGENCES
WITHIN A VERBAL/LINGUISTIC FRAMEWORK

Intelligence	Literacy Activities
Verbal/Linguistic—sensitivity to the order and meaning of words	Book Summary, Dependent Authors Biopoem, Found Poem, I Am Poem
Logical/Mathematical—the capacity to manipulate objects and notice patterns	Maps, Timelines, Budgets, Graphic Organizer, Character Mapping, Character Continuum
Visual/Spatial—the ability to produce a graphic likeness of forms or objects perceived	Story Portrait, Storyboard, Collage Coat of Arms, Painting, Murals, Webs Visualizations, Image-Freewriting
Musical/Rhythmic—sensitivity to tone, pitch and rhythmic patterns	Soundtrack, Choral Readings, Backgrounds, Create Raps, Songs, Rhythms, Sounds
Bodily/Kinesthetic—the ability to use one's body for expressive purposes	Tableaux, Gestures, Role Plays, Simulations, Dances, Monologues, Impersonations, Dramas, Video-taping, Movement Activities
Naturalist—sensitivity to the natural world, comfortable with plants and animals	Projects with plants, animals, seasons, rocks, weather conditions, night life, wilderness, geographic features, science experiments
Interpersonal—the ability to understand the moods and emotions of others	Report Sack, Buddy Journals, Scrapbooks, Character Probe, Polar Appraisal, Interviews, Reader's Theater, Collaborative Writing
Intrapersonal—ability to understand one's feelings and emotions	Freewriting, Associative Recollection, Book Review, Reflection Papers, Diaries, Self-Directed Learning Contract

Use Authentic Assessment Strategies

Gardner says that assessment should genuinely benefit students: "In my own view, psychologists spend far too much time ranking individuals and not nearly enough time helping them. Assessment should be undertaken primarily to aid students" (1993, p. 178). If assessment is to benefit students, then we must devise and use means of assessment that paint a whole picture of students' learning that go beyond—but may include—traditional standardized and paper-and-pencil tests. In teaching for understanding, Gardner recommends that we assess learning authentically with portfolios, scrapbooks, exhibitions of learning, and projects. He suggests that an important aspect of assessing learning should include the individual's ability to solve problems or create products using the materials of the intellectual realm (1993, p. 31). When students have the opportunity to contract for their projects, they also learn to manage their own learning, become self-directed, and demonstrate their knowledge through whatever expression they choose. The thematic units in this book suggest that Gardner's three dimensions be the basis for assessment:

- Content and skill assessment (most often used in schools today)
- Interpersonal assessment (where students receive feedback from their peers, teacher, parents, community members, and knowledgeable experts in the field)
- Intrapersonal assessment (where students reflect on the quality and process of their work)

Assessment in this paradigm is used to enhance and celebrate student learning, to deepen understanding, and to expand students' ability to transfer learning to life beyond formal schooling. For an example of this paradigm for a thematic unit, see Table 11:1 *Activities to Assess Student's Learning about Environmental Threats.*

Managing the MI Classroom

In *The Disciplined Mind* (1999), Gardner argues that the purpose of K-12 education should be to enhance students' deep understanding of truth (and falsity), beauty (and ugliness), and goodness (and evil) as defined by their various cultures. See Table 10.1 for *Activities for Deep Understanding of the Environment Using the Multiple Intelligences for Seeking Truth, Inspiration by Beauty, and Making Moral Decisions.* With this stance, Gardner transforms the tired debate between "traditionalists" and "progressives." Gardner states his philosophy of education this way:

"I favor depth over breadth, construction over accumulation, the pursuit of knowledge for its own sake over the obeisance to utility, an individualized over a uniform education, and an education that is public in character. I favor student-centered education over teacher-centered education, and I support an education attentive to developmental and individual differences" (p. 39).

Since all students possess all intelligences and since intelligences can be nurtured and strengthened, the curriculum should provide opportunities for students not only to represent knowledge in their preferred, comfortable intelligences, but also to develop and nurture those intelligences that are used less frequently. See Table 3:1 *Four Stages to Nurture and Develop Students' Multiple Intelligences for "Surviving the Civil War in Cambodia Through Immigration."* With these goals firmly in mind, here are some teaching suggestions to implement the thematic units in this book:

Whole Group Instruction
Since each of the thematic units has a Young Adult Novel at the core, all

students are expected to read the work. If the book is read out of class, class time can be used to introduce various reader-response activities suggested within the unit (character mapping, polar appraisal, story discussion, grids, etc.). Each day they might try a different activity for the chapter(s) they read the night before. Teachers can also use whole group instruction to teach mini lessons that would be appropriate for all learners.

Cooperative or Flexible Learning Groups
Once students become familiar with the activities, they engage in more interpersonal relationships as they work together to complete the task. Many of the activities suggested in the units are designed for cooperative learning groups. Groups can be working on the same project or each group could be working on a different one. Use flexible grouping to arrange students according to interest, skill level, or random pick.

Independent Learning Centers
Learning Centers can be set up according to the different intelligences, or they can be designed for various projects. If the tasks are such that all students would benefit by completing them, then plan a rotation so that each group cycles through each learning center.

Learning Contracts
Personalized instruction is at the heart of education according to Gardner. By providing students with learning experiences that revolve around their interests, talents, and needs, they generally have better motivation and achievement. Given a list of projects for the unit, ask students to contract for their learning. See "Contracting as a Means of Celebrating Individuality" in Chapter 9, for a sample contract.

Community Involvement
MI classrooms often extend beyond the four walls of the classroom. Local libraries, labs, businesses, hospitals, museums, government offices, homes and parks offer alternative learning environments. Frequent field trips clarify and enhance topics of study. Parents, community experts, visiting artists, and other special instructors are invited to teach subjects from gardening to architecture to strengthen students' talents and build upon their interests. Service projects and participation in community activities provide a way for students to give back to the community. See "Making a Difference Project" in Chapter 5 and "Walk in My Shoes Project" in Chapter 7.

Character Development
An important goal of Gardner's followers is to equip students with the skills necessary to contribute and participate meaningfully in the world. These

teachers not only promote core values of respect, compassion, stewardship, integrity, responsibility, but also strive for high standards and excellence. See Table 7:1 for *Using the Multiple Intelligences to Build Tolerance and Empathy* and Table 8:1 for *Activities to Explore Unconventional Relationships and Build the Personal Intelligences*.

References

Applebee, A. N. (1981). *Writing in the secondary school.* Urbana, IL: NCTE.

Applebee, A.N. (1993). *Teaching literature in the secondary school.* Urbana, IL: NCTE.

Campbell, L., & Campbell, B. (1995). *The multiple intelligences series facilitator's guide.* Alexandria, VA: ASCD.

Cooter, R. B. (1989). Thematic units for middle school: An honorable seduction. *Journal of Reading, 32* (8), 76-81.

Donelson, K., & and Nilsen, A. (1997). *Literature for today's young adults.* (5th ed.). New York: Longman.

Gardner, H. (1983/1993a). *Frames of mind: The theory of multiple intelligences.* New York: Basic Books.

Gardner, H. (1991). *The unschooled mind: How children think and how schools should teach.* New York: Basic Books.

Gardner, H. (1993b). *Multiple intelligences: The theory and practice.* New York: Basic Books.

Gardner, H. (1993). *Creating minds: An anatomy of creativity seen through the lives of Freud, Einstein, Picasso, Stravinsky, Eliot, Graham, and Gandhi.* New York: Basic Books.

Gardner, H. (1995, December). "Multiple intelligences" as a catalyst. *English Journal, 84* (8), 16-18.

Gardner, H. (1999). *The disciplined mind: What all students should understand.* New York: Simon and Schuster.

McKenzie, W. (1999–2000). *Multiple intelligences survey.* Surfaquarium Consulting. http://surfaquarium.com/MIinvent.htm.

Milner, J., & Milner, L. (1993). *Bridging English.* New York: Merrill.

Lazear, D. (1994). *Multiple intelligence approaches to assessment.* Tucson, AZ: Zephyr Press.

Rosenblatt, L. (1995). *Literature as exploration.* (5th ed.). New York: Modern Language Association.

Shearer, C. B. (1996). *The MIDAS: A guide to assessment and education for the multiple intelligences.* Columbus, OH: Greyden Press.

Short, K., Harste, J., & Burke, C. (1996). *Creating classrooms for authors and inquirers*. (2nd ed.). Portsmouth, NH: Heinemann.

Smagorinsky, P., & Coppock, J. (1994). Cultural tools and the classroom context: An exploration of an alternative response to literature. *Written Communication 11* (3), 283-310.

Smagorinsky, P. (1995, February). Constructing meaning in the disciplines: Reconceptualizing writing across the curriculum as composing across the curriculum. *American Journal of Education 103*, 160-185.

Smagorinsky, P. (1995, December). Multiple intelligences in the English class: An overview. *English Journal 84* (8), 19-26.

Walters, J., & Gardner, H. (1987, April). Managing intelligences (Tech. rep. no. 33). Cambridge: Harvard University, Project Zero.

Young Adult Titles

Cormier, R. (1974). *The chocolate war*. New York: Pantheon.

Crew, L. (1991). *Children of the river*. New York: Laurel-Leaf Books.

Cushman, K. (1995). *The midwife's apprentice*. New York: Clarion.

Cushman, K. (1995). *Catherine, called Birdy*. New York: Harper Trophy.

Hamilton, V. (1984). *The house of Dies Drear*. New York: Macmillan.

Hamilton, V. (1997). *The mystery of Drear House*. New York: Scholastic.

Hamilton, V. (1995). *Many thousand gone: African Americans from slavery to freedom*. New York: Knopf.

Hinton, S. E. (1997). *The outsiders*. New York: Puffin.

Hobbs, W. (1996). *Beardance*. New York: Camelot.

Hobbs, W. (1997). *Bearsong*. New York: Camelot.

Kerr, M. E. (1989) *Night kites*. New York: HarperTrophy.

Kerr, M. E. (1995). *Deliver us from Evie*. New York: HarperTrophy.

Kerr, M. E. (1997). *"Hello," I lied*. New York: Harpercrest.

Krisher, T. (1994). *Spite fences*. New York: Delacorte.

Lee, H. (1988). *To kill a mockingbird*. New York: Warner Books.

Levine, E. (1993). *Freedom's children: Young civil rights activists tell their own stories*. New York: G. P. Putnam's Sons.

Myers, W. D. (1991). *Fallen angels*. New York: Scholastic.

O'Brien, R. (1987). *Z for Zacharia*. New York: Aladdin Books.

Paterson, K. (1991). *Lyddie*. New York: Lodestar Books.

Speigelman, A. (1991). *Maus*. New York: Pantheon Books.

Stuart, J. (1976). *The thread that runs so true.* New York: Simon & Schuster.

Voigt, C. (1995). *Jackaroo.* New York: Turtleback.

Wiesel, E. (1982). *Night.* New York: Bantam.

Yolen, J. (1988). *The devil's arithmetic.* New York: Penguin.

PART I

Growing Up and Surviving in a Chaotic World of War and Work

Part I of this book contains thematic units about *Growing Up and Surviving in a Chaotic World of War and Work*. In a day of nuclear bomb testing, terrorist acts, environmental threats, and global sweatshops, young adults must learn to deal with the impending, potential chaos. By taking an historical approach to the survival of young adults through personal and political crises at home and work, students will have the opportunity to examine and personalize characteristics, attitudes, and strategies that enable people to cope with chaotic times.

Chapter 1: "Riding the Freedom Train on the Underground Railroad" is based on Virginia Hamilton's *House of Dies Drear, The Mystery of Drear House,* and *Many Thousand Gone: African Americans from Slavery to Freedom*. Students stitch a freedom quilt based on their research and reading about the Underground Railroad as a culminating activity for this unit.

Chapter 2: "The Holocaust: Poignant Memories Preserved" is based on personal accounts of the young adult Holocaust literature by Anne Frank, Jane Yolen, Lois Lowry, Carol Matas, Han Nolan, and others. The culminating activity for this unit will be a Holocaust Exhibition where students share the legacy of the Holocaust through their final projects. Students also plan and plant a flower garden in remembrance of holocaust victims.

Chapter 3: War experiences are captured in the Asian conflicts in Cambodia through *Children of the River* by Linda Crew. In this unit, the culminating activity is a Cambodian Culture Fair featuring student exhibits, storytelling, Khmer art and sculpture, Khmer cuisine, classical dance and music, CNN News and a monologue of a Buddhist Monk.

Chapter 4: Heroes, Heartbreak, and Healing: What was it like in Vietnam? In this unit, students utilize their multiple intelligences to examine the human element of the Vietnam experience by responding to young adult literature that gives voice to those who sacrificed and served in the war. In addition to participating in a readers' theater and enacting a class reunion of 1969, students join with their family members and each group constructs a Family Scrapbook that portrays the war experiences for various perspectives.

Chapter 5: "Children at Work: From Paterson's Textile Mills to Global Sweatshops" features *Lyddie* by Katherine Paterson. The culminating activity for this unit is the "Child Labor/Global Sweatshop: Making a Difference Project." Students choose the form of the project, adhering to only one requirement: they must take their project outside the walls of the classroom into the real world.

Chapter 1

Riding the Freedom Train on the Underground Railroad with Virginia Hamilton

Carolyn Suttles

Introduction

The Underground Railroad was perhaps the most dramatic protest action against slavery in United States history. It was a clandestine operation that began during the colonial period, later became part of organized abolitionist activity in the 19th century, and reached its peak in the period 1830-1865. The story of the Underground Railroad is one of individual sacrifice and heroism in the efforts of enslaved people to reach freedom. This thematic unit, *Riding the Freedom Train,* introduces students to the history, meaning, significance, and legacy of the Underground Railroad. Students will come to realize the high costs people paid for freedom in the past, as well as come to value the freedom they enjoy today. Both abolitionists and fugitives lived a life of danger, suspense, lawlessness, and mystery. As young adults seek their independence in a chaotic world, they, too, must consider the price of freedom. Would they have helped out on the Underground Railroad if they had lived during those times? What is it like to run for your life? What is it like to be your brother's keeper? This unit can also be extended to include current issues that cause people to flee for their lives. Families from Haiti and Central America still seek freedom and refuge in Canada. Through the study of civil conflict a century ago, themes of tolerance, empathy, and social justice can be examined along with present day pursuits for freedom.

How can we convey these important concepts in a multicultural context that engages all students in meaningful inquiry that goes beyond a surface knowledge or cursory reading of the texts? Howard Gardner's educational vision is clear. Deep understanding should be the central goal for effective education. In the case of this unit, *Riding the Freedom Train*, students should acquire a deep understanding of the fugitives' fight and flight for freedom captured in the underground railroad movement of old, as well as present day applications of this theme. Through young adult literature, picture books and nonfiction sources, students will examine laws, lives, and literature that expose both the oppression of the fugitives and their pursuit of freedom. Works by such authors as Virginia Hamilton, Paula Fox, Jim Haskins, Joyce Hansen, Raymond Bial, and Ann Petry reveal the risks taken by oppressed people seeking their freedom and by those who chose to help them. This unit is designed to provide students with a deep understanding of a desperate quest for freedom. See explanation of Gardner's challenge to teaching for understanding in the Overview, p. 16. See Table 1.1 for a Multiple Intelligences Perspective for Teaching for Deep Understanding of *Riding the Freedom Train*.

Activate Verbal/Linguistic, Interpersonal, and Other Intelligences Depending on the Response Project

Collaborative Reading of Young Adult Literature

The entry point for activating verbal/linguistic intelligence is based on reading Virginia Hamilton's books and other related literature, that explore the extreme risks and strong measures taken by the "passengers," "conductors," and "station masters" on the Underground Railroad to obtain freedom for all. She is a distinguished young adult author, who grew up in a southern Ohio community that was part of the network of the Underground Railroad system. Her ancestors were among the fugitives who fled from the south in the first half of the nineteenth century. Hamilton believes her books grew out of her childhood wonder about these fleeing people. "I had a longing as a child," she has said. "I needed to know how men, women and children could travel hundreds of miles on foot through enemy land. I found out that they were brave and clever almost beyond belief." In her books, *The House of Dies Drear*, and its sequel, *The Mystery of Drear House: The Conclusion of the Dies Drear Chronicle*, she writes a story about a Black family that tries to unravel the secrets of their new, haunted home which was once a stop on the Underground Railroad. In a recent book, *Many Thousand Gone*, Hamilton chronicles the lives of 35 famous former slaves and their struggle for freedom. The anecdotal fragments are masterfully chosen to illustrate the commonplace cruelty, as well as to rehearse pivotal events and to record triumphs of freedom. For

TABLE 1.1: A MULTIPLE INTELLIGENCES PERSPECTIVE—TEACHING FOR DEEP UNDERSTANDING
OF *RIDING THE FREEDOM TRAIN*

Multiple Intelligences	Multiple Entry Points	Comparisons, Analogies, Metaphors	Multiple Representations
Verbal/Linguistic	Study vocabulary: House of Dies Drear The Mystery of Drear House Many Thousand Gone	Read other slave narratives: Harriet Tubman, Nightjohn, Slave Dancer	Read an Essay on Fugitive Slaves Act; write: Biopoem, Diary entries, Congressional letter, Chapter summaries
Logical/Mathematical	Find Freedom code words and passwords used on the Underground Railroad; Calculation of fugitives; Haskins' Get on Board	Discuss Navaho codes used in WWII against Japanese; calculation of oppressed groups today; Escape methods used by prisoners	Map the UGRR; Map escape routes; Map escape tunnels; Map town; Create timeline of the period; Make character Map
Visual/Spatial	View film: House of Dies Drear; Follow the Drinking Gourd picture book; Bial's UGRR; Artifacts of the UGRR	Read Sweet Clara and the Freedom Quilt; Study meanings captured in Amish Quilts; Oppression shown in paintings from UGRR	Create a visual for vocabulary; Reproduce Pluto's Cave; Make Freedom Quilt, Handbills, Freedom Collages
Musical/Rhythmic	Play recordings of spirituals and freedom songs from UGRR	Find and listen to freedom songs from WWII, Vietnam, Civil Rights movements	Perform spirituals and freedom songs; create sounds in the haunted house and sounds of the night; compose music or songs that convey oppression and/or freedom
Bodily/Kinesthetic	Visit an underground railroad station; visit a museum with artifacts from UGRR	Compare hiding strategies of holocaust victims; prisons; drug dealers; collect artifacts from the Holocaust	Make a Tableau; Run for freedom plan; survival plan night; take a hike or backpack; adopt a station; give service to social agencies
Intrapersonal (Knowledge about ourselves)	Write journal entries: a dangerous moment, plans thwarted, a time to hide, all alone, "scared to death", cruelty in the world	Discuss fear tactics used by slave owners; Complete character probe; Find passages that reflect characters' feelings and emotions	Record evoked responses to readings; write reflection papers, diary entries; impersonate a fugitive; do a reader's theater; give oral interpretations
Interpersonal (Knowledge about others)	Collaborative Reading	Polar Appraisal	Family Scrapbook; Character Map; Interview Tubman; Debate laws
Naturalistic	North star and big dipper constellation	Other natural phenomena that facilitate or obstruct escape	Life in a Cave; Traveling at night; hiding in a cave; nightlife; hike at night following the gourd; support National Park Service in preserving historic areas
Existential (proclivity to pose and ponder questions about life, death and ultimate realities (1999, p. 72)	Hamilton's purpose in writing about her heritage; themes of tolerance, empathy, and social justice during UGRR	Current issues that cause people to flee for their lives; examples of oppression today; equity issues in school and society	Research current issues; create skits based on themes of social justice; freedom debate; personal essays on oppression and social justice

more information on Virginia Hamilton, an internet "key word" search using her name will guide teachers to her award-winning home page.

Since books and reading time can be scarce, here is a method for maximizing both. By tearing a book apart and distributing different chapters to different groups, the whole book can be read in one class period. For this unit, take two copies of the book, *The House of Dies Drear* by Virginia Hamilton and separate the pages from the binding organizing them into chapters. Pages from the second book are used to complete chapters when the first page of a new chapter is double-sided. Then, laminate the pages and place a rubber band around one or two chapters depending on lengths. Each group should have about the same amount of reading. Give each group of three or four students a chapter(s) to read aloud within their group, but withhold the closing chapter(s) to avoid giving away the ending. Students can designate a particular reader or they can pass the chapter around and read it round-robin style. Since the pages are laminated, they can use grease pencils to highlight important passages which can later be wiped clean. After reading the chapter, each group is responsible for retellings, musicals, or whatever else they can imagine.

Even though students are sometimes confused by reading only part of the story without knowing the details presenting their chapter(s) to the class. They can choose to represent their part of the story in any type of performance they would like: projects, skits, visuals, poems, that preceded their section, many are motivated and interested in reading the novel in its entirety after class. Of course, this strategy can be used for any other of the books in this unit where there is a limited supply of books and when time for reading a book is also limited.

Invite students to read other young adult novels from the annotated bibliography at the end of the chapter and compare them with Hamilton's works. What are common themes? How do fugitives survive? What values do they hold? What do oppressors gain? Why do they resort to such cruelty? What changes the situation? What hope is there for social justice?

Activate Logical/Mathematical, Visual/Spatial, Verbal/Linguistic Intelligences

Freedom Codes and Passwords

The Underground Railroad has been described as "silent and secret" and "running on silent rails in the dark of night." People developed codes, passwords, and secret signals for runaways and "investors" in the railroad to use. To activate logical/mathematical intelligence, ask students what codes and passwords they have discovered in their reading so far. Brainstorm and write possible definitions for the following Underground Railroad code words and terms, then tell students how they were historically used. See Table 1.2 for suggested codes and passwords.

TABLE 1.2: CODES AND PASSWORDS

Abolitionist—person who demanded immediate emancipation of slaves
Agent—coordinator, plotting course of escape, making contacts
Bales of Wool (large and small)—adults and children ready for transport
Conductors—people directly transporting fugitives
Drinking Gourd—North Star
Freedom Train—Code for UGRR
Gospel Train—Code for UGRR
Hams—large hams are adults, small hams are children
Heaven—Canada
Load of Potatoes, Parcels, Bundles of Wool—code word meaning fugitives to be expected
Paradise—Canada
Preachers—leaders, speakers for UGRR
Promised Land—Canada
Shepherds—people escorting escaping slaves
Station—place of safety and temporary refuge, safehouse
Station Master—keeper of safehouse
Stockholder—donor of money, clothing, food, etc. to UGRR
"The wind blows from the South today"—warning of slave catchers nearby
"A friend with friends"—code, password used to signal arrival of fugitives with UGRR
    conductor
"The friend of a friend sent me"—code used by fugitives traveling alone to indicate they were
    sent by UGRR network

To compare code words and passwords used on the Underground Railroad with other meaningful codes, ask students to research Navaho codes used in WWII against the Japanese (Hunter, 1996). Students might also research the Morse Code, "pig latin," and teen jargon that uses symbols for communicating various purposes among designated populations.

Activate Visual/Spatial, Logical/Mathematical, Verbal/Linguistic Intelligences

Film Viewing

After discussing various film-making techniques, students will watch the PBS movie of *The House of Dies Drear*. While watching the movie, they should focus on one or more of the topics found on the Film Viewing Guide. See Table 1.3.

After discussing the movie, students write a critical response focusing on the aspect of the film they have chosen. They are encouraged to support their analysis with specific examples from the movie. This analysis also reinforces writing necessary to students in states that have high stakes testing. Other documentaries are available through PBS Video such as "Roots of Resistance: a Story of the Underground Railroad" released in 1990 and through CBS News, "Harriet Tubman and the Underground Railroad" released in 1972.

The Tubman video reenacts one of her most dangerous trips leading slaves out of Maryland and explores the Fugitive slave law. It presents arguments for and against slavery.

TABLE 1.3: FILM VIEWING GUIDE

- Do you feel there's an opinion expressed by the filmmaker? What is it? How do you know this? Do you agree? Why or why not?
- Use the thoughts and feelings the film evokes and critique the realism, violence, content, point of view, moral.
- Reflect on the title. Is it or isn't it appropriate or significant? If it's not, come up with another title. Explain.
- Reflect on the film techniques:
  - Lighting (high key, high contrast, low key)
  - Color (cool, warm, subdued, intense, symbolic)
  - Sound (how sound and music is used to underscore, parallel, or counterpoint an image or scene)
  - Editing (how shots are used to establish a scene, effects achieved through sequencing, cuts and dissolves)
- Compare the book to the movie, analyzing changes and why they were made.

Activate Musical/Rhythmic, Bodily/Kinesthetic, Verbal/ Linguistic, Interpersonal Intelligences

Spirituals

Bring in books of spirituals from the library or use the songs found in Jim Haskins' *Get on Board* and Petry's *Harriet Tubman*. The lyrics and music for *Follow the Drinking Gourd* are found in the book by that title by Jeanette Winter. Listen to the tape of *Music of the Underground Railroad* sung by Kim and Reggie Harris. The Harris' present the history of the Underground Railroad from a nationwide perspective interspersed with songs and spirituals once used as "code songs" within the Underground Railroad and slave communities. For purposes of comparison, ask students to bring in recordings of freedom songs from WWII, Vietnam, or the Civil Rights Movement to play for the class.

In groups of four, have students research a spiritual and prepare to perform it for the class. They should also be prepared to explain any words with double or code-like meanings. Students have the option of giving an oral dramatization, creating a dance, singing, or performing an instrumental rendition of their spiritual. They may choose to bring in a CD, tape, or cassette of the piece to contrast or assist with their performance. Also ask students to find at least five selections of music that create the mood of particular scenes from one of the novels. Some students might write the lyrics to a song about the importance of either some aspect of the Underground Railroad or other important historical event in which people are searching for freedom.

Activate Logical/Mathematical Intelligence

Timeline for the Underground Railroad

Building and extending the vocabulary lesson, students work in groups of three or four to create a time-line of the Underground Railroad. This project is linear and sequential, but the information can be represented in various, creative formats. Some students prefer to use posterboard, ruler, and ink. Other students will add pictures, photos, and magazine clippings to enhance the visual effects. Ideas for timelines include making dioramas or mobiles identifying key events. Artistic enhancement might involve using maps for the background, creating symbols to represent people and events, and color-coding abolitionists, fugitives, and legal activities. Students learn a lot from each other as they share their projects with the class. To get students motivated, they can get a basic overview of a timeline from 1518-1865 found in *Get on Board* by Jim Haskins. In the back of *The Underground Railroad* by Raymond Bial, there is a Chronology of the Antislavery Movement in America. For an alternative assignment that nurtures the logical/mathematical intelligence, ask students to make a timeline of the events in *The Mystery of Drear House* by Virginia Hamilton, *Harriet Tubman* by Ann Petry, or *Which Way Freedom?* by Joyce Hansen.

Activate Visual/Spatial, Logical/Mathematical, Interpersonal Intelligences

Model of Pluto's Cave or Drear House

After reading Virginia Hamilton's *The House of Dies Drear* and the *Mystery of Drear House*, students will either reproduce Pluto's cave or design the blueprints of Drear House. Pluto's cave may be represented as a model or blueprint. The Drear House blueprint or model should include the various tunnels and secret doors. Another alternative would be to draw a map of the Drear, Carr, and Darrow properties, labeling all of the important places. The map should include all known buildings or residences on those properties. They may work with up to two other people or choose to work alone. After completion, students will present their project and identify important features. Art materials are placed on tables in the back of the room to facilitate the cave making. They can make blueprints, drawings or models. There is graph and drawing paper, as well as papier-maché and cardboard materials. Students should document their projects with excerpts from the novel.

Activate Logical/Mathematical, Interpersonal, Visual/Spatial Intelligences

Escape Routes from Slavery to Freedom

There were many routes taken by slaves traveling on the Underground Railroad. Harriet Tubman began many of her journeys near the plantation in Bucktown, Maryland, where she was born, traveling north through Wilmington, Delaware, and on to Niagara Falls and St. Catharines in Canada. As an entry point for this activity, read one or more of the following picture books to set the stage for students becoming slaves running for freedom and mapping their escape routes. *Follow the Drinking Gourd* by Jeanette Winter is a beautiful picture storybook that captures the harrowing escape of one family who finds its way to Canada by following the Big Dipper. *Aunt Harriet's Underground Railroad in the Sky* by Faith Ringgold is another excellent picture book that tells how Cassie learns of her great-great-grandparents' long journey from slavery to freedom, guided by the voice of Harriet Tubman. In *The Drinking Gourd* by Monjo, a Quaker family helps slaves escape to one of the stations along the way. *Meet Addy* tells about the risks Addy and her mother take to escape to Philadelphia via the Underground Railroad. For this activity, students become slaves running for freedom and map their escape route. Provide students with maps of the eastern United States and Canada obtained from donations, xeroxed copies, or computer programs. Maps can also be obtained from the U.S. National Park Service publication, *Underground Railroad: Special Resource Study*, or call the Denver Service Center (303) 969-2100. For a basic map to show trends throughout the United States see the map in Haskins' *Get on Board* or the map in Ringgold's *Aunt Harriet's Underground Railroad in the Sky*. After dividing students into groups of three or four, have them choose one of the origination/destination choices in Table 1.4.

TABLE 1.4: ESCAPE ORIGINATION/DESTINATION CHOICES

- Bucktown, Maryland to St. Catharines Ontario
- Florence, S. Carolina to Thorold, Ontario
- Jackson, Tennessee to Lincoln, Ontario
- Covington, Georgia to Port Colborne, Ontario
- Leland, Mississippi to Windsor, Ontario
- Mansfield, Louisiana to Hamilton, Ontario
- Alexander City, Alabama to Hamilton, Ontario
- Lynchburg, Virginia to Sutton, Quebec
- Pineville, Kentucky to Windsor, Ontario
- Hendersonville, N. Carolina to Abercorn Plain, Quebec

Groups need to map their escape route, remembering that they can only travel at night. Each day's resting spot must be marked on the map, and a nightly mileage log must be kept. Total mileage to the destination must also be determined. This will be more difficult than it sounds as slaves often could not travel "as the crow flies" because of impassable rivers, lakes or towns. Each student is responsible for a reflection paper about the escape, which also reinforces metacognition and writing skills. It should include the thoughts and feelings of the slave during the route to freedom. An extension of this lesson would be a creative writing assignment in which they create their own imagined stories of escape. They could also write and perform a play telling this story. Another idea would be to assign a personal essay about the meaning and value of freedom. Students might ponder whether or not they would have helped out on the Underground Railroad if they had lived during those times.

Activate Intrapersonal, Interpersonal, Visual/Spatial, Bodily/Kinesthetic, Musical/Rhythmic Intelligences

Oral Interpretation: Dramatic Performance

The goal of oral interpretation is to convey meaning and understanding of the passage from literature to the audience. Even though the primary instrument for delivering the interpretation is through the effects of the voice, consider other ways to enhance the delivery as well. For instance, costumes, props, sets, lighting, background music, and movement help to create the mood, tone, and emotional effects that add meaning to the presentation. The teacher may use a short film clip to show students how these effects add to interpretation. This project might be done individually as a monologue or impersonation. It might also be a collaborative presentation such as an interview, dialogue, reader's theater, or puppet show. Although the performance is generally live for the class, another option would be to show the videotape. The following are ideas for dramatic performance of the literature for *Riding the Freedom Train*:

- Read a slave narrative and give a book talk on it
- Interview a slave descendant and present a narrative of that family's history
- Impersonate one of the slaves in *Many Thousand Gone* and tell your story
- Impersonate a slave catcher, abolitionist, or congressman giving their perspectives on the Underground Railroad
- Role play the discovery of the treasure with Mattie, River Lewis, Pluto and Mr. Small in *The House of Dies Drear*

- As a reporter, cover and videotape the story about the discovery of the treasure for your news station
- Recreate live or on video the discovery of the secret room by Thomas
- Prepare a monologue for Grandmother Jeffers of all that has transpired since she moved to Ohio that she would want to tell to Silva and Beau in *The Mystery of Dies Drear*
- Prepare a reader's theater for one of the moving passages in *Get on Board, Which Way Freedom?, Harriet Tubman, or the Dies Drear Chronicles*
- In *The Mystery of Dies Drear*, Thomas said, "We should know about the past, but we shouldn't let the past take us over." Give a persuasive speech (5 minutes) agreeing or disagreeing with Thomas.

These dramatic presentations require students to utilize overlapping intelligences within the verbal/linguistic framework. The assignments provide students with the opportunity to both stimulate their creativity and to show their strengths as they interpret and present the meaning they have made of these texts.

Activate Visual/Spatial, Interpersonal, Intrapersonal Intelligences

Freedom Collage

To help students connect the oppression of the people in the Underground Railroad with current world problems, ask them to create a collage. Students should collect pictures from current news magazines and newspapers of oppressed people around the world who need freedom from their circumstances. See *The Underground Railroad* by Raymond Bial for images representing that period of time. Other picture books in the reference list are useful for inspiring collage ideas. A discussion or paper might accompany the collage to explain the situations and arguments for freedom which the students choose to portray. For instance, very surprising similarities exist between arguments given by pro-slavery advocates in the 19th century and reasons used today to advocate abortion. In addition, arguments against women's suffrage and against emancipation of slaves are similar.

Students might also choose to research and represent the Overground Railroad/Sanctuary Movement. When the U.S. Immigration and Naturalization Service refused to grant refugee status, a contemporary effort was launched on the part of churches and humanitarian groups to help Central Americans reach sanctuary in Canada. Churches in your community may have been involved in the Sanctuary Movement. Periodicals in the 1970s, 1980s and 1990s have discussed this issue in detail. *Grab Hands and Run* by Frances Temple is an excellent fictionalized story of such a family's flight.

Another extension of this lesson would be to discuss and research current civil disobedience issues. Organizations like Amnesty International, Operation Rescue, ACT-UP, Greenpeace, and groups opposed to nuclear armament are examples of civil disobedient individuals and groups in recent history. Collages portraying their activities would give different perspectives of freedom issues.

Activate Visual/Spatial, Logical/Mathematical, Bodily/Kinesthetic, Verbal/Linguistic Intelligences

Stitching the Freedom Quilt

Read *Sweet Clara and the Freedom Quilt* by Deborah Hopkinson aloud to your class as an entry point for this activity. Create your own Underground Railroad quilt by assigning each student to research one of the people, places, or events from the following tables. Students write a paper or paragraph telling what happened, where events occurred, who was involved, and why this person, place or event was important in the history of the Underground Railroad and/or abolition movement. Raymond Bial has taken beautiful photographs in his book *The Underground Railroad* that might inspire student creations. For more information about what it was like to be a slave trying to escape to freedom on the Underground Railroad, see Levine's . . . *If You Traveled on The Underground Railroad*. Virginia Hamilton's *Many Thousand Gone* tells the story of many of the slaves listed below who are appropriate for research and inclusion as quilt squares. *Our Song, Our Toil: The Story of American Slavery as Told by Slaves* is particularly well designed and contains full-color and black-and-white photographs that illustrate a collection of vivid narrative passages from the diaries, letters, and autobiographies of slaves that would be useful in this project. Students then create a "quilt square" with symbols, illustrations of events and a map related to their research topic. You may want them to submit a sketch before beginning on the final piece. "Quilt squares" may be computer-generated or hand-drawn on paper to make a bulletin board or wall mural. The squares can be mounted on colored butcher block paper to give a background and border for the squares. The squares may also be stitched or embroidery-painted on ten-inch squares of white fabric (I cut up a double-sized sheet) to make a real quilt keepsake to hang in the school. Ask members of a local quilting club to visit your class, set up a loom, and instruct the students in the art of quilting. See Table 1.5 for people, places and events for quilt research.

Students can collect scraps of fabric from family and friends to make borders and strips between the squares to look like rivers, railroad tracks, or wagon trails. Fabric remnants, thread, and trim materials can also be donated or purchased for low fees at local fabric stores. Dedication of the quilt is an excellent opportunity to show off the students' work at a school assembly, open house, or program that parents and community members might attend.

TABLE 1.5: PEOPLE, PLACES AND EVENTS FOR QUILT RESEARCH

Levi and Catherine Coffin
Dies Drear
Thomas Garrett
Harriet Tubman
William Still
Frederick Douglass
Lucretia Mott
Harriet Beecher Stowe
William and Ellen Craft
Henry "Box" Brown
Jermaine Loguen
William Lloyd Garrison
Jonathan Walker
John Brown and Harpers Ferry
Eliza Harris
Sojourner Truth
John Rankin
Dred Scott
Elijah Lovejoy

Activate Verbal/Linguistic, Logical/Mathematical, Intrapersonal, Interpersonal Intelligences

Freedom Debate

The laws passed in Congress during the time of the Underground Railroad affected the lives of slaves in the south as well as those who gained freedom in the north. After having read *Harriet Tubman: Conductor on the Underground Railroad* and excerpts from *The Freedman's Record* about Harriet Tubman, ask students to read about the Fugitive Slave Act of 1850 in an encyclopedia, at the library, or by using on-line resources. Why was it passed? How did this law help keep the country from splitting? What happened to escaped slaves because of this law? What happened in Kansas because of this law? Was the human cost of this law worth the fact that it postponed The Civil War? In order to prepare students for their part in the debate, assign half of the students to be a congressman and half to be Harriet Tubman. They are to write three journal entries as that person in conjunction with their position in the Fugitive Slave Act. Then, in the voice of the assigned character, argue either for or against The Fugitive Slave Act of 1850. After the debate, students write a persuasive essay from the materials they have collected and heard in class.

Activate Musical/Rhythmic, Naturalist, Bodily/ Kinesthetic, Visual/Spatial Intelligences

Follow the Drinking Gourd

After listening to the song or reading the words for "The Drinking Gourd," assign students to take a nighttime walk with friends or family by finding and following the north star. They could practice walking silently, hiding from "slave catchers," and taking a "nap" in a comfortable spot. For more ambitious groups, a backpacking adventure could be planned to simulate the experience. For more information about the practical aspects of walking to freedom, see the web page for Anthony Cohen, historian and author, who walked from Maryland to Ontario as part of his research for the National Parks and Conservation Association. He describes his route, clothes, food, shoes, and people who made it possible. Students can even send messages and ask him questions from this web page called *The North Star*.

Another activity would be to ask students to look around their own homes and neighborhoods and list ways and places where fugitive slaves might hide. Students might "invent" hiding places, describing and illustrating them for classroom display. Students should tell how and with what materials hiding places could be constructed and hidden. They should be able to describe why this hiding place would not be found when the slave catchers come. Would these hiding places be appropriate for the homeless people today? Ambitious groups might even plan a weekend retreat where students spend a night sleeping in the shelter they have created.

For students living in the Northeastern and Midwestern states, plan a field trip to some of the homes or "stations" that were once a part of the Underground Railroad. Today, many of these homes have been converted to museums that are open to the public. As well as touring the grounds, students will see a lot of memorabilia such as slave logs, pictures, and diaries. Follow-up activities to the field trip might include either a musical or poetic response. They might write a biopoem about either one of the station owners or slaves that stopped there on their trip north. An alternative assignment would be to write lyrics to an existing piece of music about the history of the station they visited. For more information, see the U.S. National Park Service publication, *Underground Railroad: Special Resource*. It contains sketchy, but accurate history and maps showing documented routes and stops on the Underground Railroad, slave population by region, and period transportation routes. These maps are very useful in the classroom, especially to show how the Railroad functioned as an organized network. Copies of the maps may be obtained from the Denver Service Center at (303) 969-2100. The entire publication may be obtained by interlibrary loan through any library.

Activates All of the Multiple Intelligences

Underground Railroad Freedom Scrapbook

The scrapbook is the culminating activity for this unit providing students the opportunity to create a picture in order to experience the life and times of the Underground Railroad. The scrapbook is designed to elicit multigenre writing: letters, journal entries, headlines, news articles, handbills, songs, poems, explanations, descriptions, and narrations. Students select names of characters who belong to families that represent slaves, slave owners, abolitionists. (Families can be constructed according to the characters in the Picture Books suggested at the end of the chapter.) Each family member will construct a scrapbook using information from the novels and historical documents. Students should show evidence of understanding their heritage through the eyes of their character, much more than just reproducing the information in the book. The scrapbook produced by each family must be historically accurate (like you've been there), emotionally moving (develop a voice), and artistically appealing (take time). See Table 1.6 for sample scrapbook families.

TABLE 1.6: SAMPLE SCRAPBOOK FAMILIES

Rural Ohio Family *Dies Drear Chronicles*	Neighboring Family *Dies Drear Chronicles*	Protector of Treasure *Dies Drear Chronicles*
Mr. Small (History Professor) Mrs. Small Thomas Buster Bill Great-Grandmother Jeffers	River Swift Darrow Sr. River Lewis Darrow Jr. Mattie Darrow Pesty Mackey Wilbur Russell River Ross	Mr. Pluto (Henry Skinner) Myhew Skinner
Ohio White Abolitionist Jacob Aarons Sarah Aarons Ben Aarons	**Georgia Plantation Owner** John Manns Elise Manns James Rachel	**Canadian Free Slave** John Lewis Kathryn Lewis Benjamin

After putting character names on index cards, have students select a card and join together in family groups. During the first group meeting, students should create a history for their family and a description of the town where they choose to reside. The rest of the assignments they should either be able to do on their own or work along with other students. See Table 1.7 for Scrapbook Assignments.

TABLE 1.7: SCRAPBOOK ASSIGNMENTS

- Tell the story of the family (who you are, how you came to be where you are, personal character information
- Describe the town description (maps, demographics, size, location, attitudes toward slavery, descriptions of townspeople)
- Create headlines and news articles (at least four created, but accurate articles about historical events relevant to your character)
- Make handbills about slavery (at least two handbills posted by or about your character, that would have been posted at this time)
- Write letters (at least four letters written to or from family/group members, friends, etc.)
- Write a letter to Congressman (one letter to state or national congressman concerning a true event, written from your character's perspective, of course). This must be typed and written in formal language
- Write a response letter from the Congress person, typed on letterhead
- Find or write song lyrics (at least three spirituals which affected your character)
- Write a poem (the words to one poem which affected your character)
- Write a journal entry (at least one entry concerning your thoughts about slavery and the Underground Railroad)
- Find a photo (picture of a family heirloom and explanation of why it's important to your family)
- Write a biopoem about your character
- Create a memorial (blueprint, sketch, or picture) dedicated to the slaves and abolitionists who lost their lives while escaping or while helping slaves escape
- Write a journal entry (about a historical person from this period whom your character would have (or does) admire(d).
- Write or find code words (include code words you have learned or that you create to help keep family members safe)

Before students submit their scrapbooks, they should complete a self-reflection paper. Students should comment on the strengths of their project and the obstacles they overcame in completing it. They should discuss the interpersonal aspects of the group process as well as progress. What advice would they offer next year's students to assist in their successful completion of the scrapbook? They might indicate their best entry or piece of work. What was least successful? Why? What was the most difficult part of the assignment to complete? What grade do you expect to receive? The student's reflection on the project can be a valuable part of the assessment process. While providing student examples for all the assignments would be desirable, the following Tables and Figures contain examples of four assignments from the scrapbooks. Jennifer Halstead's poetry is found in Table 1.8, and Table 1.9 displays Katy Pemberton's family heirloom. Table 1.10 contains Handbills about a Character by Jen Weaver. Figure 1:1 and Figure1:2 consist of Memorials designed by Steph Wisniewski and Amy Boorn.

TABLE 1.8: POETRY BY JENNIFER HALSTEAD

Say, have you heard the story Of a little colored town, Way over in the Nation On such a lovely sloping ground? With as pretty little houses As you ever chanced to meet, With not a thing but colored folks A-standing in the streets? Oh, 'tis a pretty country And the Negroes own it, too With not a single white man here To tell us what to do! —Uncle Jesse, town poet	Dies Considerate, discrete, depending, honest Lover of freedom, God, children Who feels forgotten, hopeful, unheard Who needs equality, independence, and support Who fears slavery, punishment, and rebellions Who gives shelter, love, and safety Who would like to see peace, freedom, and friendship Resident of Portsmouth, Ohio Drear

TABLE 1.9: FAMILY HEIRLOOM BY KATY PEMBERTON

Family Heirloom (Picture of a Powder Horn)
This powder horn was carried by a Darrow ancestor during the Civil War. It has been passed down many generations. It is made of ivory from the tusk of an elephant. Its use was to carry gunpowder to be loaded into the gun of a soldier. We are very proud to have it, and the fact that it was awarded to a black man says how good of a soldier he was when so few were recognized at that time.

TABLE 1.10: HANDBILLS ABOUT A CHARACTER BY JEN WEAVER

$150 Reward	100 DOLLARS REWARD!
Ranaway from the subscriber, on the night of Monday the 11th of July, a negro man named, **TOM,** about 30 years of age, 5 feet 6 or 7 inches high; of dark color; heavy in the chest; several of his jaw teeth out; and upon his body are several old marks of the whip, one of them straight down the back. He took with him a quantity of clothing and several hats. A reward of $150 will be paid for his apprehension and security, if taken out of the State of Kentucky; $100 if taken in any county bordering on the Ohio River; $50 if taken in any of the interior counties except Fayette; or $20 if taken in the latter county. John A. Manns	Ranaway from the subscriber on the 27th of July, my Black Woman, named **EMILY,** Seventeen years of age, well grown, black color, has a whining voice. She took with her one dark calico and one blue and white dress, a red corded gingham bonnet; a white striped shawl and slippers. I will pay the above reward if taken near the Ohio river on the Kentucky side, or THREE HUNDRED DOLLARS, if taken in the State of Ohio, and delivered to me near Lewisburg, Mason County, Kentucky. July 28, 1842 John A. Manns

FIGURE 1.1: MEMORIAL
BY STEPH WISNIEWSKI

FIGURE 1.2: MEMORIAL
BY AMY BOORN

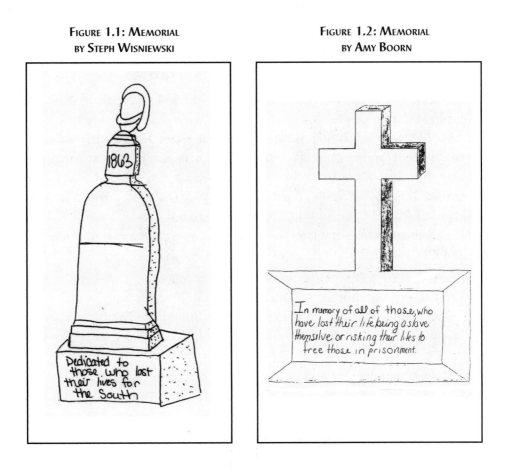

Assessment for the scrapbook should be negotiated with the students before the project begins. The point values are arbitrary and can be adjusted by the teacher and the class, but should be agreed upon before the project begins.

Conclusion

Having invested the time in reading and writing about the Underground Railroad, students are well-grounded in this period of time when civil disobedience prevailed. They have acquired a deep understanding of the risks taken by both fugitives and abolitionists for freedom through a multiple intelligences perspective. Given powerful points of entry, offering comparisons, and providing multiple representations of core ideas, students have looked, not only to the past, but to modern day issues that cause people to rebel against the system and to find refuge and peace. They value the freedom they enjoy in their homes and in their work.

References

Primary Source Material on Slave Narratives

Blockson, C. L. (1994). *The Underground Railroad.* New York: Berkeley Publishing Group.

An excellent and well-respected compilation of letters, diaries and narratives of Underground Railroad stories organized by state and region with 16 pages of photographs.

Coffin, L. (1997). *Reminiscences of Levi Coffin, The reputed president of the Underground Railroad.* Richmond, IN: Friends United Press.

Excellent collection of stories about many escaping slaves in both Indiana and Ohio who passed through Coffin's home.

Drew, B. (1968). *A northside view of slavery the refugee: or narratives of fugitive slaves in Canada.* Westport, CT: Greenwood Publishing Group.

In 1955, Boston educator and journalist Benjamin Drew went to Canada to collect narratives from among the estimated 30,000 fugitive slaves there and published their stories which described the horrors of slavery and the runaways' escape.

Hansen, E. (Ed.). (1993). *The Underground Railroad: Life on the road to freedom.* Carlisle, MA: Discovery Enterprises, Ltd.

Collection of narratives, newspaper articles and readings about the slaves who ran for freedom.

Stepto, M. (1994). *Our song, our toil: The story of American slavery as told by slaves* (ed.). Brookfield, CT: Milbrook Press.

Full-color and black-and-white photographs illustrate a collection of vivid narrative passages from the diaries, letters, and autobiographies of slaves.

Music of the Underground Railroad

Harris, Kim and Reggie. *Music of the Underground Railroad.* Chatham Hill Games, Box 253, Chatham, NY 12037. (800-554-3039)

The cassette tape of songs is sold in a set with a well-conceived board game and video.

Picture Books on the Underground Railroad

Armstrong, J. (1993). *Steal away to freedom.* New York: Scholastic.

Beatty, P. (1992). *Who comes with cannons?* New York: Morrow Junior Books.

Connell, K. (1993). *Tales from the Underground Railroad.* A. Haley, (Ed.).

Autin, TX: Raintree Steck-Vaughn.

Elish, D. (1993). *Harriet Tubman and the Underground Railroad*. Brookfield, CT: Milbrook Press.

Ferris, J. (1989). *Go free or die: A story about Harriet Tubman*. Minneapolis, MN: Carolrhoda.

Hopkinson, D. (1993). *Sweet Clara and the freedom quilt*. New York: Knopf.

Johnson, D. (1993). *Now let me fly: The story of a slave family*. New York: MacMillan.

Johnson, L. W. (1995). *Escape into the night: The riverboat adventures, no. 1*. Minneapolis, MN: Bethany House.

Kristof, J. (1993). *Steal away home*. New York: Scholastic.

Lawrence, J. (1997). *Harriet and the promised land*. New York: Aladdin Paperbacks.

Levine, E. (1992). *If you traveled on the Underground Railroad*. New York: Scholastic.

Monjo, F. N. (1993). *The drinking gourd: story of the Underground Railroad*. New York: HarperCollins.

Porter, C. (1993). *Meet Addy: An American girl*. Middletown, WI: Pleasant Company.

Rappaport, D. (1991). *Escape from slavery: Five journeys to freedom*. New York: HarperCollins Juvenile Books.

Ringgold, F. (1993). *Aunt Harriet's Underground Railroad in the sky*. New York: Crown.

Smucker, B. C. (1979). *Runaway to freedom: A story of the Underground Railroad*. New York: Harper & Row.

Stein, C. (1997). *The story of the Underground Railroad*. Chicago: Children's Press.

Winter, J. (1992). *Follow the drinking gourd*. New York: Knopf.

Picture Book of the Navajo Code Breakers

Hunter, S. H. (1996). *The unbreakable code*. Flagstaff, AZ: Northland Publishing Company.

Young Adult Literature for *Riding the Freedom Train*

Bial, R. (1995). *The Underground Railroad*. New York: Houghton Mifflin Publishers.

An engaging exploration of the Underground Railroad and the effect of slavery on American life, it is full of photographs, newspaper clippings, and excerpts from documents of the period.

Fox, P. (1991). *The slave dancer.* New York: Yearling Books.
This powerful story of slavery tells the tale of thirteen-year-old Jesse, snatched from the docks of New Orleans and thrown aboard a slave ship to play his fife so the captured slaves will dance and keep their muscles strong. Jesse yearns for an end to the horrors.

The Fugitive Slave Law of 1850
The law required "all good citizens" to help Federal marshals return captured runaway slaves to their masters.

Hamilton, V. (1984). *The house of Dies Drear.* New York: Macmillan.
A Black family tries to unravel the ghosts, mysteries and secrets of their new home which was once a stop on the Underground Railroad.

Hamilton, V. (1997). *The mystery of Drear House.* New York: Scholastic.
A Black family living in the house of long-dead abolitionist, Dies Drear, must decide what to do with his stupendous treasure, hidden for one hundred years in a cavern near their home.

Hamilton, V. (1995). *Many thousand gone: African Americans from slavery to freedom.* New York: Knopf.
This book features 35 inspiring stories about famous former slaves such as Nat Turner, Harriet Tubman, Frederick Douglass, and others living from 1619 through the Civil War.

Hansen, J. (1986). *Which way to freedom?* New York: Avon Books.
The story of escaped slaves seeking the Underground Railroad but being drawn instead into the Civil War.

Haskins, J. (1993). *Get on board: The story of the Underground Railroad.* New York: Scholastic Publishers.
From the first Blacks brought to this country in chains, slaves came up with ingenious ways to escape to freedom. Haskins tells many courageous stories of both the slaves and the people who helped lead them to freedom.

Paulsen, G. (1995). *Nightjohn.* New York: Laurel-Leaf Books.
A former slave returns to slavery to teach others to read and pass on the vision of freedom. Twelve-year-old slave, Sarney, risks dismemberment for learning to read.

Petry, A. (1983). *Harriet Tubman: Conductor on the Underground Railroad.* New York: HarperTrophy.
Born a slave, Harriet Tubman not only escaped herself, but also delivered hundreds of others from the drudgery of slavery, thus earning the title of the legendary "Moses."

Temple, F. (1993). *Grab hands and run*. New York: Orchard Books.
After his father disappears, twelve-year-old Felipe, his mother, and his younger sister set out on a difficult and dangerous journey, trying to escape their home in El Salvador to Canada.

CHAPTER 2

The Holocaust: Poignant Memories Preserved with Young Adult Literature

Rita Elavsky

Introduction

A *Diary of Anne Frank* unit which originally took about three weeks has grown to a nine-week, in-depth study of the Holocaust. Since the school's textbook supplied very little background about Anne Frank's life or historical information about World War II, students raised many questions about the time period. Students did not even have a map with which to reference Germany, Amsterdam, or Bergen-Belsen. Most students' awareness of the years 1933-1945 did not extend past Hitler, concentration camps, and one gentile popularized in Hollywood by Steven Speilberg. So, this unit has emerged through inquiry into the Holocaust by both students and teacher. Although this unit has been used with eighth graders, it can easily be adapted to fit any time frame and grade levels from 6-12. The following are student goals attainable through the course of the unit:

- To understand important terms and ideas related to the Holocaust, such as Aryan Race, Final Solution, anti-Semitism, and others
- To be exposed to literature that has emerged from the Holocaust
- To draw inferences from historic and current events
- To identify the major leaders and groups of World War II
- To understand tragic characters, plots, and themes in literature
- To identify major perpetrators, bystanders, and victims of WWII

- To identify with a time line important events of the Holocaust and Anne Frank
- To nurture the students' multiple intelligences by giving them opportunities to chose various ways of constructing meaning of Holocaust experiences.

A larger goal from the study of the Holocaust and Anne Frank is to foster in students the need to learn from past mistakes, to make an effort to fight against bigotry and prejudice, and to develop an awareness of the danger such indifference may mean for future cultures.

Nurturing Gardner's Multiple Intelligences While Preserving Poignant Memories of the Holocaust

The activities in this unit provide students with opportunities to nurture and develop their multiple intelligences through a variety of choices they may make in responding to literature of the Holocaust. While the intelligences required to complete an activity are not discrete, they often overlap in that more than one intelligence is utilized in completing the assignment. Table 2.1 gives an overview of the intelligences and activities suggested for this Holocaust Unit

TABLE 2.1: OVERVIEW OF UNIT ACTIVITIES THAT NURTURE THE MULTIPLE INTELLIGENCES

Intelligence	Activities
Linguistic Intelligence: "Focus on words— saying them, hearing them, reading them, looking at them, feeling them" (Haggerty, 1995, p. 59).	• Write a memoir • Create an original Holocaust short story or poem • Explore Jewish holiday traditions • Make a Bingo review game • Compare/contrast a video to a book • Research projects of the Holocaust • Holocaust Diary Project • Critique Holocaust videos • Read Holocaust literature • Listen to oral readings of the Holocaust
Logical-Mathematical Intelligence: "Focus on concept formation and searching for relationships and patterns" (Haggerty, 1995, p. 59).	• Study geography of Holocaust • Make maps of Europe in the 1940s • Organize important terms list • Crosswords/Word Searches for Holocaust • Create floor map of concentration camp • Recipes for potato latkes • Clothesline time line of Holocaust

cont.

Music/Rhythmic Intelligence: "Focus on rhythm, melody, tone quality" (Haggerty, 1995, p. 59).	• Select and listen to music of the 1940s • Create new anthem for fighting prejudice • Collect songs of the Ghetto • Write song to accompany art pieces • Put a poem to music or dance a poem • Listen to and sing Hanukkah songs
Visual/Spatial Intelligence: "Focus on images, pictures, color" (Haggerty, 1995, p. 59).	• Slide show or picture diary of a memoir • Study artifact poster set • Create virtual reality of the Holocaust museum • Create art for a school Holocaust Museum • Create a Holocaust movable mural • Visit US Holocaust Museum Memorial Website and critique the art, sculpture, artifacts • Create a bulletin board to represent your research
Bodily/Kinesthetic Intelligence: "Focus on touching, manipulating objects, bodily movement" (Haggerty, 1995, p. 59).	• Share artifacts from WWII • Design 3-D representation of secret annexe • Spin the Dreidl game • Act out scenes of the play • Visit Daniel's story exhibit
Naturalist Intelligence: Focus on making distinctions in the natural world and using this ability productively.	• Initialize a recycling program • Organize a march to support non-racial violence • Demonstrate survival tactics for those persecuted by the Nazis • Plant a tulip garden dedicated to the memory of victims of the Holocaust
Interpersonal Intelligence: Focus on "collaboration and dynamic interaction" (Haggerty, 1995, p. 59).	• Contact a survivor • Small group discussion of Holocaust readings • Role play a character from the readings • Interview with an historian • Group research project
Intrapersonal Intelligence: Focus on self-reflection, self-monitoring and self-assessment. Independent reading and project	• Visit various Holocaust websites and reflect on the information • Create a website of your reactions to the Holocaust • Create a picture diary of your life. • Write a memoir of a momentous even in your life. • Complete independent study of the Holocaust

All the Multiple Intelligences

Building on Background Knowledge / Motivating

Begin the unit with a memoir by Hazel Shelton Abernethy (1994) entitled "The Home Front: 1941-1945." Abernethy's memoir begins when she was fourteen years old in Nacogdoches, Texas. Her first recollection is the bombing of Pearl Harbor, which affected not only the U.S. military forces, but also civilian life on the home front.

Students learn about the sacrifices American soldiers and civilians selflessly made during World War II and the U.S. involvement on the home front during 1941-1945. They are invited to explore how outside events (local, national, and international news stories) can effect an individual. Ask them to think about their personal experiences. Have they ever experienced any sudden changes in their home life such as a major family move? Ask them to reflect on a momentous event in their lives and write their own memoir about the experience. Instead of writing a memoir, spatial learners can have the option of presenting their memoir in a picture diary, slide show, or other visual means. If students choose to use a slide show, they can set the presentation to music to help set the tone. An excellent 5-pack PBS video on America's involvement on the Home Front during the war can be viewed to build additional background about the era, *America Goes to War: The Home Front—WWII* (1989).

Ask students if any national events in their lifetime had a large impact on them. Do they think that Americans could make the same sacrifices today as were made in 1941? If the same shortages occurred again today, students would most likely be giving up a lot of extracurricular activities unless they were willing to walk! Discuss the impact that a limited gas supply during the war would have on students' social life, as well. "Make it do, wear it out, and do without" was a World War II slogan which encompassed the attitude that the American public took in an effort to ration products like gasoline, metal, tires, and food that was important to the war effort. Generally students see a similarity between the rationing of World War II and the recycling movement today. If a recycling program does not exist in the school, this is an opportunity to initiate a program and enlist the assistance of parents and community organizations to make it work.

By eighth grade most students have been exposed to Ogle's (1986) KWL chart (What you Know, What you Want to Know, What you Learn), so the next ice-breaking activity is familiar to them. Students are given a blank chart for their notebooks and a large version is placed on a bulletin board or wall for the entire unit. After reviewing how to label the chart and the meaning of the K, W, and L, students write WWII, the Holocaust, and Anne Frank at the top of their papers. With these three ideas in mind, students are given 5-10 minutes to jot down some items in the first two columns. Even students who know nothing of the Holocaust or have never even heard of Anne Frank, successfully manage to list some details about WWII based on the Abernethy memoir. Individual knowledge varies widely depending upon each student's own reading and personal interest.

The teacher should walk around the room looking at students' responses to this assignment. Supply some students with 3" x 5" notecards and a marker to write some examples of what they know and questions they have for the "K" and the "W" columns. The "L" column is reserved for what they learn throughout the course of the unit. I like to use different colored index cards for each column. Students place the cards on the bulletin board KWL chart as they complete them. When there is an adequate representation of cards in the first two columns, volunteers go up to the chart to read them. The teacher can add any details that seem necessary, or answer any questions at this time. See Table 2.2 for some typical examples of items that students supply for this activity.

TABLE 2.2: KWL CHART

K		W	
Great Britain was an ally with the U.S. during WWII	Anne Frank hid in an attic during the war to avoid being captured by the Nazis	Did Anne Frank survive the Holocaust?	How did the war end?
Hitler was the leader of Germany during WWII	Anne Frank was a young Jewish girl	What does Holocaust mean?	How did America get involved?
The U.S. entered WWII when the Japanese bombed Pearl Harbor	WWII took place in the 1940s	Why did the people want to follow Hitler?	What was it like in a concentration camp?
Hitler sent millions of innocent people to concentration camps	Supplies and food were rationed during war time	How long did Anne Frank hide and what happened after she was found?	How many died in the Holocaust?

Intrapersonal, Interpersonal, Verbal/Linguistic, Rhythmic/Musical, and Visual/Spatial Intelligences

Resources, Literature, Video Viewing, and Group Discussion

The KWL chart activity shows that the majority of the eighth graders know little to nothing about the period from 1933–1945 in Europe known as the Holocaust. Show the documentary *Survivors of the Holocaust 4* on the very next day after the KWL chart to give the students a basic overview of the Holocaust from several survivors' points of view.

The first segment of the video, *Survivors of the Holocaust* (1996), documents what life was like in Europe prior to the Holocaust. Students are able to see some actual footage of the diverse European culture through situations like holidays, schooling, and daily life. Background accompanying music also gives students a feel for the cultural differences of the Jews growing up and living in the 1930s and 40s. Through this visualization experience, students can better identify and empathize with the survivors and the victims of this unforgettable time in history.

The one-hour video is produced by the Survivors or the Shoah Visual History Foundation and Turner Original Productions and it is directed by Steven Spielberg. As Spielberg reminds us, "the testimonies of the survivors reveal that the devastating events of the Holocaust didn't happen to faceless numbers, they happened to . . . men and women and children with names and faces and families and dreams. People just like us."

An on-line study guide is available to reproduce and use prior to, during, and after the viewing of the documentary. It can be obtained at the Survivors of the Shoah Visual History Foundation website, http://www.vhf.org/.

Indeed, Holocaust survivors were hesitant to reveal their personal experiences for many years after World War II ended. It wasn't until after war criminal Adolf Eichmann's trial in the 1960s that survivors finally started retelling their painful stories of internal struggles and harrowing experiences. Survivors who are willing to share their stories today can be located through a number of national and local agencies including the following:

- The National Conference, 71 Fifth Avenue, New York, NY 10003. 800-352-6225
- Anti-Defamation League, 823 United Nations Plaza, New York, NY 10017. Braun Center for Holocaust Studies. 800-343-5540
- Holocaust Memorial Center (Detroit) 6602 W. Maple Rd., West Bloomfield, MI 48033, 313-661-8040
- United States Holocaust Memorial Museum, 100 Raoul Wallenberg Pl. SW, Washington, DC 20024-2150. 202-488-0400

Students with strong interpersonal skills can be encouraged to contact a survivor in their local area, interview him or her, or arrange for a school visit. One survivor of the Holocaust who regularly tours the nation telling her story in an effort to educate today's youth is Gerda Weissmann Klein. Gerda has an interesting story to tell about her life before the Holocaust with her family; her exile from the city of Bielsko, Poland where she grew up; her painful memories of forced labor in a textile factory; and a death march which claimed the life of two of her best friends. She has published her story as a memoir entitled *All But My Life* (1995). Her poignant story is also the basis for *One*

Survivor Remembers (1996), an award-winning documentary produced by Home Box Office and the United States Holocaust Memorial Museum. After viewing and discussing the videos, introduce students to a library of books related to the Holocaust. Visit the local libraries and scour the shelves for suitable books that correspond to your students' reading levels. Encourage students to select a book for independent reading, and suggest they begin with a narrative or diary because these genres personalize the events that victims experienced. The students become more actively involved in the reading and feel a greater connection to the characters when reading survivors' stories. See a Holocaust Selected Reading List recommended for the middle school classroom at the end of this chapter.

It isn't until about the second week into the Holocaust unit that the students actually do any independent historical background reading. The United States Holocaust Memorial Museum web site has an excellent historical summary. Ask students to visit the site http://www.ushmm.org because in addition to the required reading, there are numerous links that the ambitious student will find interesting. Devise questions for students to answer that correspond with the historical summary. This becomes a basis for later class discussion and questions.

Student interest broadens as they learn more about this significant period in history. Optimally, discussion will reveal that students' relatives were involved in the war; ask them to bring rare artifacts to class. Ask students to share treasures: ration books and coins, photographs of concentration camp liberations, or perhaps a Nazi flag torn from a German government building that they might be able to collect.

One way to share literature of the Holocaust and WWII with students is through oral reading. *Rose Blanche* (1985) by Roberto Innocenti is a very touching, dramatic look at a young Aryan girl who experiences the realities of the Holocaust's atrocities. The picture book has wonderful illustrations and is an excellent source for initiating productive class discussion and questioning about perpetrators, bystanders, and victims.

Daniel's Story (1993) by Carol Matas provides a good story for oral reading. Although this piece of historical fiction is longer, it is a powerful story told from a young boy's perspective. Through personal accounts of his survival in the Lodz ghetto and Auschwitz, young adolescents can find inspiration for their own personal journey through life. In 1992, Matas was asked to write the book as a companion to the exhibit "Daniel's Story: Remember the Children" which is now open to the public in the United States Holocaust Memorial Museum in Washington, D.C. Daniel represents the millions of children who suffered or died in the Holocaust.

Inspired by the unforgettable horrors of Nazi tyranny and the children that survived them, Matas wrote another novel, *After the War* (1996). The drama chronicles the life of Ruth, a 15-year-old survivor, as she struggles to come to the aid of illegal immigrants to Palestine.

Perhaps the most eminent and often read memoir of the Holocaust aside from *The Diary of Anne Frank* (1967) is the book, *Night* (1986), written by Nobel Peace Prize novelist Elie Wiesel. Wiesel's account of his experiences in Nazi death camps as a young boy make this work an excellent choice to describe the tragedy to today's youth. Wiesel has dedicated his life to fighting against indifference which he says is "the worst enemy to humankind."

Logical/Mathematical, Visual/Spatial, Linguistic, and Bodily/Kinesthetic Intelligences

Map Study

Some map study is essential for students to learn and understand Holocaust history and its impact on European geography. Students utilize their logical/ mathematical intelligence by analyzing and classifying the allies, neutrals, and axis countries. Through labeling major cities and death camps, students can visualize the context for reading the Anne Frank story. *The Historical Atlas of the Holocaust* (1996) is an indispensable tool for reference when studying maps of the Holocaust. It is available in hardback or on CD-Rom.

Given a blank map of Europe in the early 1940s, all students label the countries and bodies of water, the allies, neutrals, and axis countries. In addition, they label some major cities that are part of our study of the Holocaust like Nuremberg, Amsterdam, and Berlin. Also, they label sites of major ghettos, concentration camps and death camps that are mentioned in the Anne Frank story and in our discussions and their research. For bodily/kinesthetic learners, this map can also be done as a large-scale floor map, which helps students understand the geography of the time period and the relationship between countries involved in World War II.

For logical/mathematical learners, other, more specific maps can be done in conjunction with the Holocaust unit. For example, students interested in further research in the area of Rescue and Resistance may develop maps of escape routes from German-occupied Europe. As Germans sought to deport Jews and other non-Aryans to concentration camps and death camps in Poland between 1941 and 1944 to carry out their "Final Solution," a few brave individuals helped by hiding the victims or aiding in their escape. Neutral countries, such as Spain and Sweden, were havens for thousands of refugees. The rescue of Danish Jews involved a cooperative rescue operation by boat across the Oresund, the narrow body of water between Denmark and Sweden.

This rescue is brought to life in Lois Lowry's Newbery Award Winning historical fiction novel *Number the Stars* (1990).

Verbal/Linguistic, Logical/Mathematical, Visual/Spatial, and Interpersonal Intelligences

Group Research Project

For this project, students develop their interpersonal intelligence through collaborative research, peer editing of written work and presentation of information to the class. Students sign up for one of the assignment choices and must do research and cover the necessary material. Students develop their verbal/linguistic intelligence as they learn how to choose effective resources including books, pamphlets, and internet sites. Works cited pages are required, students learn the importance of proper quotation and paraphrasing, and they practice how to properly document various kinds of sources. They primarily utilize web sites, and books, but some go as far as interviews or AV resources to obtain information. In-class time is devoted to reading, notetaking, organization of materials, all of the steps of the writing process, peer sharing and editing, and working with others in their group in the decision-making process regarding how the final product presentation will appear artistically. Students with strong visual/spatial intelligence can add appropriate pictures, graphs, maps, graphics or other enhancements for the project.

Students choose their own groups of no more than four people. See Table 2.3 for Team Project assignment choices. They determine which group member will be responsible for each required research topic and if there will be collaborative writing on any of the parts. All information must be documented with a works cited page in proper format. Students also make choices about the artwork that will accompany their writing on the final project. They receive a group grade for this project. See Table 2.4 for Assessment Guidelines.

TABLE 2.3: HOLOCAUST TEAM PROJECT ASSIGNMENT CHOICES

Anne Frank	Cruel and Inhumane	The Victims	Axis Leaders
• Anne's early years/family • Anne's years in hiding/Miep Gies • Anne Frank House today • Westerbork and Bergen-Belsen	• Babi Yar • Mobile killing squads • Death marches • Forced labor camps	• Jehovah's Witnesses • Jews • Gypsies: Sinta and Roma • Polish • Soviet POWs • Homosexuals • Handicapped	• Benito Mussolini • Adolph Hitler • Emperor Hirohito • Gen. Hideki Tojo
Ghettos	**Resistance**	**Nazi Racism**	**Nazi Propaganda**

• Deportation of Jews to
  • Lodz
  • Kovno
  • Warsaw
  • Terezin
    (Theresienstadt)
	• Escape from Sobitor
	• The White Rose
	• Warsaw ghetto uprising
	• Mordecai Anielewicz
		• Anti-semitism
		• Burning Books
		• Boycott of Jewish businesses
		• Kristallnacht (Night of Broken Glass)
			• 1936 Olympics
			• Hitler Youth (Jugend)

Location of the Victims	**Concentration Camps**	**Extermination (Death) Camps**	**Auschwitz—Birkenau**
• Hollerith machine • Aryan Race • Nuremberg Laws	• Typhus & other diseases • Liberation of camps • Location of and general description: Dachau, Mauthausen, Treblinka	• The "Final Solution" • Zyklon B gas • Gas chambers • Crematoriums • Kapos, Mass graves, • Living conditions	• Josef Mengele • Medical experiments • T-4 program • Handicapped Appell • Daily life • Forced Labor
Rescues and Escapes	**Punishment**	**Nazi Officials**	**Allied Leaders**
• Danish rescue boats • The St. Louis • Oskar Schindler • Raoul Wallengberg	• Nuremberg Trials • Simon Wiesenthal	• Rudolph Hess • Adolf Eichmann • Hermann Goehring • Heinrich Himmier • Heydrich Reinhard	• Joseph Stalin • Franklin Delano Roosevelt • Winston Churchill
Jewish Customs and Religious Practices	**The Nazis**	**Important Events/ Dates**	**Homefront**
• Hanukkah • The Menorah • Judaism • Star of David • Yom Kippur/The Seder • Passover	• Gestapo • SS • SA • SD	• Pearl Harbor Day (Dec. 7, 1941) • D-Day (Normandy) • VE-Day • Nagasaki and Hiroshima (August 6 and 9, 1945)	• Women in the military • Women in the work force • Rationing/shortages • Civilian efforts • Japanese interment camps

TABLE 2.4: TEAM PROJECT ASSESSMENT GUIDELINES

Rating Scale: 5 = Excellent, 4 = Good, 3 = Average, 2 = Weak, 1 = Poor
Grading weights are given for each section to total 100%

Content, Structure, and Style	5	4	3	2	1
1. Ideas are clear and coherent; all reports are factual					
2. Ideas are logical and well-chosen; they are adequately developed and presented with suitable transitions and paragraphing					
3. Ideas are unified; they don't stray from the subject or ramble					
4. Papers are informative and interesting					
5. Papers use a variety of sentence structures and effective, mature wording that is clearly that of the student writers. **Subtotal _____ X 2 = _____**					
Grammar, Usage, and Mechanics					
6. Uses standard grammar, including proper punctuation and capitalization					
7. Contains no more than 2 or 3 minor errors in spelling **Subtotal _____ X 1 = _____**					
Other					
8. Project is neat and attractive; appropriate pictures, graphs, etc.					
9. Follows directions, including spacing and format, blue/black pen or typed in 12 pt. lettering and shows evidence of apparent proofreading/revision					
10. In-class work and team co-operation					
11. Works Cited pages in proper format, are attached to the back of the project for each report **Subtotal _____ X 2 = _____**					

Total Score _____%   Assignment Grade _____
Comments:
The strongest aspect of this project is:

Skill(s) to work on for future group assignments is/are:

Verbal/Linguistic, Logical/Mathematical, Spatial, Bodily/Kinesthetic, and Interpersonal Intelligences

Time Lines, Plot Lines, and Key Terms

As students are conducting their Holocaust research, they will undoubtedly stumble across terminology, geographical and biographical names which they will not be able to pronounce. These words can be collected in a box in the classroom. A couple of students strong in the area of verbal/linguistic intelligence can find out how to correctly pronounce each of the terms. A list of terms with their phonetic pronunciations can be compiled by categories. These lists can be typed and given to students for their notebooks. Additionally, the terms may be audiotaped as songs or raps by students with strong musical intelligence.

Students with strong logical/mathematical intelligence can create crossword puzzles or word searches as alternative methods to study these important concepts.

Instead of creating a time line in a traditional, linear fashion, the bodily/kinesthetic and spatial learners of the class can develop a "clothesline" of important events and dates of the holocaust history or literature which can be strung across the classroom and easily changed and manipulated.

Students are given an incomplete plot line on which only key words of the Freytag Pyramid (1846) appear. There is a large reproduction of this plot line (exposition, rising action, climax, falling action, conclusion) in the room that remains up for the duration of the *Diary of Anne Frank* (1967) play. At various stopping points like the end of certain scenes, students add details to the plot line on strips of tagboard, a different colored marker for each class. By the end of the play, the entire plot line is complete. Students enjoy seeing what their peers in other classes have contributed to the plot. See Table 2.5 Anne Frank Plot Line.

TABLE 2.5: ANNE FRANK PLOT LINE

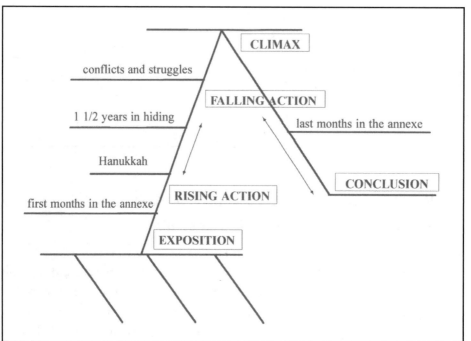

Intrapersonal, Verbal/Linguistic, and Visual/ Spatial Intelligences

Independent Study

For the students with strong intrapersonal intelligence who do not do their best work in groups, there is an option of independent research. The idea for an independent study unit stemmed from the opportunity for students to enter various Holocaust contests, both locally and nationally. Our local Holocaust contest is divided into categories: research writing, creative writing, creative multi-media, and visual art. See Table 2.6 for excerpts from *Holocaust Promise* by Amy Spencer (8th grade), a poem written for her independent study. This poem received recognition in local and state writing competitions.

TABLE 2.6: HOLOCAUST PROMISE

Living in the horror of the unknown,
Hearing death and seeing life,
Drafted in the home of death,
Slowly removed—one by one,
My people are exterminated
Like the rats in the sewers of Budapest.
Living in darkness
And having contentment only when
    the stomach
Has food.

Even still, I'm marked, branded,
Like an animal they claim me to be:
J for Jew
1 for being alone
5 for who had been in my family
3 for the number alive
0 for the oven my brother tends, and
1 for my single life—
The mark of shame upon my arm.

Removed from a family,
Scattered like mice running
Running from the Nazi cats,
separated from emotions,
Isolated by my faith,
I realize the unfathomable truth.

The frail, the weak, and the light of head
Are chosen to be the first ones burned.
They choose me out of all my friends.
They choose me to die first—0
All because I am so thin.
I am starving and staggering
When they call me to the oven,
And I see how the stronger survive.
Burning from the rage and fear
Of the German ego, I turn to ashes.
Tightly compacting in the rising smoke
When they ran their fingers across their
    throats,
The uncaring world had rejected me—
Stop after stop, place after place.
And with each rejection,
They summoned my annihilation.

But as I rise in the darkened cloud, my vision
    clears:
The smoke from the oven stops smoking,
The Jews on the way to the camp stop
    coming;
The war is over;
The Jews are free;
Israel is a state; and
In America—Jews!
They flourish in numbers there
As they do in the rest of the world.
And I hear a voice say:
"Look now toward heaven,
And tell the stars,
If thou be able to number them
So shall thy seed be."

Students who elect to do independent study must be self-motivated and ambitious to handle the reading and research required for the independent study. These students are encouraged to read several of the books listed on the Holocaust Selected Reading List. They must be strong in intrapersonal intelligence because they have to evaluate their own progress on a daily basis. They have to take responsibility for completing given tasks and maintaining a schedule. Generally, this project is appropriate for gifted students or those in an enriched program. See Table 2.7 for suggestions for Independent Study Projects.

TABLE 2.7: INDEPENDENT STUDY PROJECTS

- Design a web page for your book or theme
- Organize a march to support non-racial violence (like the march of the living)
- Listen to "We Are the World;" use song to create another "anthem" for fighting prejudice/ teaching tolerance and acceptance
- Make a scrapbook of your life
- Put a poem to music or dance
- Create a bulletin board to display your research
- Represent victims in visual way (like the chart or graph or different dyed pastas)
- Paint a mural to be broken down and displayed
- Design a virtual reality Holocaust museum
- Compare Terezin to other concentration camps using the book, *I Never Saw Another Butterfly* (1993)
- Research other efforts in history where Gentiles have risked their lives to help others. Present them in the form of a slide show presentation or web page.
- Create a 3-D representation or model of Anne Frank's secret annexe, a ghetto, or a concentration camp.

At the onset of the project, an Independent Study Contract is drawn up between the teacher and the student. Other agreements are discussed with the students involved such as duration of the project, determination of grades, and the goal to be achieved. See Table 2.8 for Independent Study Contract to be signed by teacher, student, and parents.

TABLE 2.8: INDEPENDENT STUDY CONTRACT

- Independent study will be done during the student's regular academic class on days determined by the teacher.
- It may be necessary for the student on independent study to spend time out of school working on research, preparation, and writing associated with the independent study unit.
- The student who elects an independent study will be exempt from most regular classroom activities, homework, quizzes, and assignments as deemed reasonable by the teacher. Some missed assignments may need to be completed as homework.
- A schedule for independent study will be determined by the teacher at the onset of the project.
- It is the student's responsibility to record a daily log of the activities accomplished during the time allotted for independent study.
- The grade/value of the project will be determined by the teacher and discussed with the student at the onset of the project.
- It is the student's responsibility to adhere to the schedule devised by the teacher. This is part of the student's overall grade for the project.
- Any student who fails to meet preliminary deadlines may be dismissed from the independent study program.
- It is the student's responsibility to meet with the teacher to discuss and evaluate progress at various stages of the independent study program. This can take place before or after school or during study hall.

Verbal/Linguistic, Visual/Spatial, Intrapersonal Intelligences

Holocaust Diary Project

While reading *The Diary of Anne Frank* play orally in class, which takes about two and a half weeks, students are working in and out of class on the next project of the unit, which is the Holocaust Diary. Through the diary, students develop their intrapersonal intelligence by reflecting on the reading and study of the unit in a personal way. See Table 2.9 for some of my instructional goals at the time of this assignment.

TABLE 2.9: INSTRUCTIONAL GOALS FOR HOLOCAUST DIARY PROJECT

Students are to:
- Read and decide which entries to both write about, and respond to, using appropriate prompts in a clear and coherent way
- Gain an understanding of the concept of tragedy including tragic characters, plot and theme
- Distinguish between what is directly stated and what might be inferred from a passage
- Develop and support interpretations of text using background knowledge and inferences
- Locate information in the play or other supplemental materials to support their interpretation

The teacher can devise a series of suitable prompts or obtain prompts from various resources, teacher texts, and student suggestions. Holocaust resource materials helpful in designing prompts for this Diary Project for students are:

- Isaacman, Clara (1988). *Pathways Through the Holocaust: An Oral History by Eye-Witnesses.* KTAV Publishing House.
- Cusenza, Daniel P. and Merle Davenport (1997). *Holocaust.* Grand Rapids: Instructional Fair.
- Kassenoff, Miriam Klein and Anita Meyer Meinbach (1994). *Memories of the Night: A Study of the Holocaust.* Torrance, CA: Frank Schaffer Publications.
- *Teacher's Educational Poster Set* (1993). Washington, DC: United States Holocaust Memorial Council.

See Table 2.10 for a sample prompt for the diary project and a typical average eighth grade student response written by Amy Price.

TABLE 2.10: SAMPLE PROMPT AND RESPONSE FOR DIARY PROJECT

Diary Entry #34:
   The Anne Frank House in Amsterdam is now a museum and foundation committed to promoting Anne's ideals. What are these ideals? If Anne were alive today, what would she want people your age to understand? Write an entry that might have been Anne's message to the youth of today.

Response:
   Anne Frank was a person who always had hope. She was in a bad situation, worse than any I could even imagine, yet she still stayed positive. It must have been very hard for her to keep her head up and to keep smiling, but she did it. Anne is a person who never looks on the down side of things. She always looks on the bright side. She says, "In spite of everything, I still believe that people are really good at heart." I wish I could learn to be like her. I really admire her and her attitude.
   If Anne was alive today she would want teenagers to appreciate what they have. She would want teenagers to realize that it is not right to complain about the little things when you have your freedom. She had so much more to complain about than any one who is a teenager today. I think Anne would tell us to be thankful for what we have and to listen to our parents. She would not want us to be angry when they gave us a curfew because at least we have our freedom to go out for a little while and return safely. Anne would also tell us to appreciate our families because you never know when you could be separated from the people you love. They could be there with you one minute and gone the next. I guess the biggest message would be to stay positive, appreciate what you have and be thankful for your family.

All the Multiple Intelligences

Closure Activities for the Unit

Two major motion pictures have been made based on Anne Frank's famous diary. The original *Diary of Anne Frank* starring Millie Perkins as Anne was made in 1959 by 20th Century Fox Film Studios. It is a black and white version and has a running time of 180 minutes, but students prefer the version starring Melissa Sue Gilbert. This one has a shorter running time and students like this color version; also, since it is does not differ from the play by Albert Hackett and Francis Goodrich, which they have already read, they are completely familiar with the plot. Taking students to see a stage version of *The Diary of Anne Frank* adds a dramatic interpretation of this work. *Anne Frank Remembered* is another video worth watching as a way to bring closure to the unit. The video explores Anne Frank and her family's daily life before going into hiding. Then, through emotional interviews with childhood friends and acquaintances whom Anne and Margot befriended in the camps, the film documents events of Anne's life beyond the diary including experiences in Westerbork, Auschwitz, and Bergen-Belsen, where Anne died in April of 1945, just weeks before its liberation. This critically acclaimed Oscar winner for Best Documentary of 1995 is successful in painting a memorable picture of Anne Frank's final months, showing how her diary, with the help of family friend Miep Gies, went from a personal notebook to world-renowned literature.

"Anne Frank in the World: 1929-1945" is a photographic exhibit that has been touring the world since its June 12, 1985 premier in Amsterdam, Frankfurt, and New York City. The exhibit, which was created by the Anne Frank House in Amsterdam, continues to visit communities across the country. The North American Tour is sponsored by the Anne Frank Center USA, Inc. which is located in New York City. They coordinate "Anne Frank in the World" with various other local Holocaust educational programs to include distinguished speakers and even Holocaust survivors who talk about anti-Semitism, discrimination, and other dehumanizing social stereotypes.

If these options are not feasible, ask students to act out the play, or even just one scene of the play. The bodily-kinesthetic, musical, and spatial learners could collaborate to design a set, costumes, and sound effects. The musical learners could personalize the production by creating their own song or anthem for fighting prejudice and for teaching tolerance and acceptance to others.

The United States Holocaust Memorial Museum located in Washington, DC houses the world's largest collection of Holocaust-related artifacts. The museum, which was dedicated in 1993 is a memorial to the millions of victims of the Holocaust. Visitors will find numerous educational opportunities within its aesthetically-appealing architectural framework. The permanent exhibition houses documents, photographs, and displays that illuminate the visitor's mind with the dark, genocidal events of 1933-1945 in Europe. Educational programs are available for adults and students; the Wexler Learning Center and Holocaust Research Institute, both within the museum, are open for archival study and research.

Naturalist Intelligence; Bodily/Kinesthetic Intelligence; Interpersonal and Intrapersonal Intelligences

Planning and Planting a Garden

A culminating activity that involves students, teachers, administrators, parents, community members, and local businesses is planting a vegetable or flower garden. This cooperative horticultural project is a hands-on opportunity for students to nurture their naturalist intelligence as they learn about how plants grow; they also develop a sense of pride and ownership in remembrance of holocaust victims.

At the onset of this project, students will have to make several decisions. Should the garden be placed on the school lot, or should it be somewhere else in the community? Will it be a vegetable or flower garden? Who will be responsible for tending the garden? Exactly what will be planted? Perhaps a certain color flower will be selected to represent a group of victims of the Holocaust. Climate and growing seasons depending on your locale will also determine the care and maintenance the garden will require.

The purpose of the garden can be manifold. According to the Center for Health Design, gardening has therapeutic benefits for the mind, body, and soul. Aside from the personal growth that one can gain from growing a garden, it can be a source of beauty, recreation, and food. People from the community can share in the harvest, and food donations can be made to local hunger organizations. Flowers can be given to hospitals, elderly care facilities, and churches.

For students, cultivating a garden brings them closer to nature and helps them to debrief and to work through emotions of grief, sorrow, and compassion from studying the holocaust. They enjoy the physical activity of working outside with their hands; they enjoy the soil, the seeds, and the crops. Throughout winter and early spring, students can prepare for planting their garden by attending classes and workshops that might be sponsored by local nurseries, garden centers, and community volunteers. Plans should be made for the layout of the garden, and organizations should be approached for donations. Field trips to public parks, gardens, greenhouses, and arboreta could be used to stimulate students' interest.

A bountiful garden is also a means to restore faith in God. Out of the suffering of those who experienced the Holocaust first-hand, a bountiful harvest of nutritious vegetables or beautiful flowers that are dedicated in memory of the victims of the Holocaust can bring new hope for peace and tranquility for all humanity.

Conclusion

Through the units on the Holocaust and Anne Frank, student learning is enchanced by Dr. Howard Gardner's theory of multiple intelligences in many important ways. Engagement in the various activities translates into powerful reminders for students that the Holocaust did occur and was the result of moral choices made by real individuals and groups. Through these enrichment experiences and post-activity discussions in my language arts classes, students learn to make important connections between what occurred in history and the moral choices that they face in their own lives. These learning experiences convey a strong message that prejudice and intolerance are unacceptable in today's society and that it is up to the youth of today to promote and build multicultural and multiethnic understanding.

Studying the Holocaust need not be a dismal experience. Yes, the topic itself is horrific and the events are inhumane, but it is not necessary to focus on the dehumanization and destruction alone. Students should be taught how to apply the lessons of the Holocaust to their own lives. Let the past teach us the harmful side effects of intolerance and discrimination. Racial and religious bigotry must be replaced by cultural understanding and the promotion of personal differences.

Holocaust Selected Reading List

Key: NF = Non–Fiction M = Memoir /Diary F = Historical Fiction

NF   Bachrach, Susan D. (1994). *Tell Them We Remember: The Story of the Holocaust*. Boston: Little, Brown.

NF   Berenbaum, Michael. (1993). *The World Must Know: The History of the Holocaust as Told in the United States Holocaust Memorial Museum*. Boston: Little, Brown.

M   Frank, Anne. (1967). *The Diary of a Young Girl*. New York: Doubleday.

M   Klein, Gerda Weissmann. (1995). *All But My Life*. New York: Hill and Wang.

M   Koehn, Ilse. (1990). *Mischling, Second Degree: My Childhood in Nazi Germany*. New York: Puffin Books.

F   Lasky, Kathryn. (1986). *The Night Journey*. New York: Puffin Books.

M   Leitner, Isabella. (1992). *The Big Lie: A True Story*. New York: Scholastic.

F   Matas, Carol. (1996). *After the War*. New York: Simon & Schuster.

F   Matas, Carol. (1993). *Daniel's Story*. New York: Scholastic.

M   Nolan, Han. (1994). *If I Should Die Before I Wake*. New York, NY: Harcourt Brace.

F   Orgel, Doris. (1988). *The Devil in Vienna*. New York: Puffin.

M   Reiss, Johanna. (1990). *The Upstairs Room*. New York, HarperCollins.

F   Richter, Hans P. (1987). *Friedrich*. New York, Puffin Books.

NF   Rogasky, Barbara (1988). *Smoke and Ashes: The Story of the Holocaust*. New York, Holiday House.

NF   Rossell, Seymour (1990). *The Holocaust: The Fire that Raged*. New York, Franklin Watts.

M   Sender, Ruth M. (1986) *The Cage*. New York, Macmillan.

M   Siegal, Aranka (1994). *Upon the Head of the Goat*. New York, Puffin Books.

F   Spiegelman, Art (1997). *Maus; A Survivor's Tale*. New York, Pantheon Books.

M   TenBoom, Corrie (1971). *The Hiding Place*. New York, Bantam Books.

NF   United States Holocaust Memorial Museum (1996). *Historical Atlas of the Holocaust*. New York, Macmillan.

M   Volavkova, Hana, ed. (1993) *I Never Saw Another Butterfly: Children's Drawings and Poems from Terezin Concentration Camp 1942-1944*. New York, Schocken.

M   Wiesel, Elie (1986). *Night*. New York, Bantam Books.

F   Yolen, Jane (1988). *The Devil's Arithmetic*. New York, Viking.

References

Abernethy, H. S. (1994). The home front: 1941–1945. In *Literature and Language* (pp. 258–266). Evanston, IL: McDougal, Littell & Company.

America goes to war: The home front—WWII (1989). [Videotape]. PBS Video. New York: Anthony Potter Productions.

Teacher's Educational Poster Set. (1993). Washington, DC: United States Holocaust Memorial Council.

Beallor, J., & Moll, J. (1996). *Survivors of the Holocaust*. [Videotape]. Turner Original Productions.

Burns, M. (1981). *The Hanukkah book*. New York: Macmillan.

Chaikin, M. (1981). *Light another candle: The story and meaning of Hanukkah*. New York: Clarion Books.

Cusenza, D. P., & Davenport, M. (1997). *Holocaust*. Grand Rapids, MI: Instructional Fair.

Frank, A. (1967). *The diary of a young girl*. New York: Doubleday.

Haggerty, B. A. (1995). *Nurturing intelligences: A guide to multiple intelligences theory and teaching*. New York: Addison-Wesley Publishing Company.

Gertz, Cantor G. (1989). *A journey through Hanukkah: The Festival of Lights*. Audio Pathways.

Glatzer, S., et al. (1982). *Hanukkah resource manual: A resource book for teaching Hanukkah for ages 7–15*. New York: Board of Jewish Education of Greater New York, Inc.

Innocenti, R. (1985). *Rose Blanche*. Mankato, MN: Creative Education, Inc.

Isaacman, C. (1988). *Pathways through the Holocaust: An oral history by eyewitnesses*. Hoboken, NJ: KTAV Publishing House.

Kassenoff, M. K., & and Meinbach, A. M. (1994). *Memories of the night: A study of the Holocaust*. Torrance, CA: Frank Schaffer Publications.

Klein, G. W. (1998). *All But my Life*. New York: Hill and Wang.

Lowry, L. (1990). *Number the stars*. New York: Yearling Books.

Matas, C. (1993). *Daniel's story*. New York: Scholastic.

Matas, C. (1996). *After the war*. New York: Simon & Schuster .

Ogle, D. M. (1986). K-W-L: A teaching model that develops active reading of expository text. *The Reading Teacher, 38* (6), 54–570.

One survivor remembers: Gerta Klein. Home Box Office and U.S. Holocaust Memorial Museum.

Rockland, M. S. (1975). *The Hanukkah book*. New York: Schocken Books.

Survivors of the Shoah visual history foundation website, http://www.vhf.org.

Survivors of the Holocaust 4 (1996)

Wiesel, E. (1986). *Night*. New York: Bantam Books.

Wikler, M., & and Groner, J. (1987). *Miracle meals: Eight nights of food 'n fun for Chanukah*. Rockville, MF: Kar-Ben Copies, Inc.

Wikler, M., & and Saypol, J. R. (1977). *My very own Chanukah*. Rockville, MD: Kar-Ben Copies, Inc.

CHAPTER 3

Surviving the Civil War in Cambodia Through Immigration with Crew's *Children of the River*

Lin Robinson with Jackie Glasgow

Introduction

Can you imagine leaving the United States of America and living in a foreign country? Can you fathom a life without the subtle comforts of clean water, clean clothes and a cozy shelter? What if you lost your loved ones, your home, and everything you own in a twelve-hour period? In Crew's *Children of the River*, thirteen-year-old, Sundara, finds herself rudely uprooted from her Cambodian homeland, herded into a death-trap freighter to fight for her life, and transported into a new and confusing lifestyle in the United States. This is a story revealing Cambodian family ties, values, and traditions—all of which are challenged by the American influence. Leaving the past Cambodian memories and horrors, with the guilt of leaving loved ones behind, and trying to enter into a life of confusion, excitement, and love are the challenges for this young Cambodian girl, Sundara, and her extended family. Crew presents family traditions and lifestyles in a way that exposes coming-of-age issues that transcend cultural conflicts and differences.

In this unit, students will utilize their multiple intelligences by responding to Crew's *Children of the River*, which describes Sundara's journey from Cambodia to the United States. Using Lazear's (1991) developmental stages to teach with multiple intelligences, activities will be included for each of the four stages: 1) *Awaken Intelligence* by activating the senses and communication with others, activating also "inner senses" such as intuition, metacognition, and spiritual insight; 2) *Amplify Intelligence* through exercise and strengthen awakened capacities through regular application; 3) *Teach for/with Intelligence* through structured lessons for each intelligence; 4) *Transfer Intelligence* using multiple ways of knowing and problem solving beyond the classroom (p. xix). Through one-minute vocabulary reports, students will use verbal/linguistic and visual/spatial intelligence to represent their learning about the Cambodian geography, language, and the civil strife that provides a context for the novel. Students will create a multi-genre Family Heritage Portfolio for Sundara which includes her immigration experiences, family foods and rituals, values and beliefs, cultural clashes, and school experiences. The culminating activity for this unit will be an Asian Culture Fair. At the Culture Fair, students will share current events, folklore, art, music, food, holidays, and family rituals taken from the young adult novels they have read. See the Annotated Bibliography at the end of the chapter for related books for this unit. The following activities listed in Table 3.1 provide an overview of ways to nurture and develop the students' multiple intelligences at Lazear's (1991) four stages.

Verbal/Linguistic, Visual/Spatial Intelligences

One-Minute Vocabulary Reports

After reading selected passages of *Children of the River* (1989) to awaken the students' verbal/linguistic intelligence and peak their interest in the story, ask them to prepare one-minute vocabulary reports. This will provide background knowledge of the time period, phrases, places, and names that they will find in the story. During this activity, students should become acquainted with Cambodian geography, civil war, politics, and customs in order to understand Sundara's experience in leaving her country, people, and family behind. Ask students, in pairs, to choose a topic for research from the list in Table 3.2. Ask students to represent their information on note cards and on posterboard. Students should create a visual aid or an artifact before sharing their information with the rest of the class. Use the following guidelines for the one-minute report: who or what the topic is; when it was important; why it was important; and what its impact was on society or the world. Students should take notes during the reports for a possible quiz over the terms.

An excellent website for information about Cambodia is: http://www.Cambodia-web.net/index.htm.

TABLE 3.1: FOUR STAGES TO DEVELOP AND NURTURE STUDENTS' MULTIPLE INTELLIGENCES FOR "SURVIVING THE CIVIL WAR IN CAMBODIA THROUGH IMMIGRATION"

Intelligence	Stage 1 Awaken Intelligence (Activate the Senses)	Stage 2 Amplify Intelligence (Exercise and Strengthen Awakened Capacities)	Stage 3 Teach for/with Intelligence (Structure lessons for Multiple Intelligences)	Stage 4 Transfer Intelligence (Multiple Ways of Knowing Beyond the Classroom)
Verbal/Linguistic "The capacity to use words effectively, whether orally or in writing."	Reading aloud portions of the novel. Storytelling Reading Haiku	One-minute vocabulary report News headlines Death notices Elegy	Write a narrative on school experiences French lesson	Interview someone learning English as a second language Letters to support refugees
Logical/Mathematical "The capacity to use numbers effectively and reason well."	Brainstorming what you know about Cambodia	Timeline of Cambodia Family tree Crossword Puzzle of famous people	Origami Immigration map	Grandma's recipe Lifeline
Visual/Spatial "The ability to perceive the visual-spatial world accurately and to perform transformations upon those perceptions."	Identify themes in Chinese brush painting Khmer Art and Sculpture	Chinese brush painting Haiku illustration using brush painting	Origami Family photos Heraldry Family flag Travel brochure for Cambodia	Ideal girl collage
Musical/Rhythmic "The capacity to perceive, discriminate, transform, and express musical forms."	Listen to Cambodian tunes Video of classical dance	Mourning songs Patriotic songs Identify tonal patterns of music	Music video Set a poem to music	Collect family songs and perform them
Bodily/Kinesthetic "Expertise in using one's whole body to express ideas and feelings and facility in using one's hands to produce or transform things."	Sit cross-legged on the floor to meditate or discuss a chapter of the book Play charades for people and events	Asian cooking Khmer Cuisine Tableau of events	Classical dance Music videos Create a cultural artifact	Immigration skits Cooking Khmer recipes Learning centers for culture fair
Interpersonal "The ability to perceive and make distinctions in the moods, intentions, motivations, and feelings of other people."	Discussion of American Values and Customs Identify Cultural Conflicts for Sundara at school	Satchel simulation Family photos and emblems Split-open mind Conflicts at home	Letters to support Cambodian Refugees Refugee interviews	CNN news show
Intrapersonal "Self-knowledge and the ability to act adaptively on the basis of that knowledge." (Armstrong, 1994, p. 2-3)	What shall I pack? What do I value most?	Diary entries My body image Lifeline Family Heraldry Conflicts at Home	Dealing with death Dealing with guilt Cultural identity Letters to support Cambodian Refugees	Elegy Monk monologue Self-reflection paper

TABLE 3.2: ONE-MINUTE VOCABULARY TOPICS

Ankor Wat (p. 111)	Lamthon (p. 64)
Buddha (p. 19)	Lycée (p. 43)
Cambodia (p. 1)	Mekong (p. 99)
Camp Pendleton (p. 60)	Phnom Pehn (p. 2)
Communist (p. 2)	Pol Pot (p. 143)
Evacuation of Cambodia in 1975 (p. 51)	Réam (p. 1)
Genocide (p. 138)	Refugee camp (p. 60)
Kamprea (p. 48)	Riel—basic unit of currency
Kampuchea (p. 18)	Sampots (p. 56)
Kaob (p. 185)	Sarong (p. 8)
karup kanow (p. 56)	Sihanouk (p. 61)
Katha (p. 125)	Tonie Sap (p. 189)
Khao-I-Dang (p. 13)	Vietnamese invasion (p. 61)
Khmer (p. 13)	Water Festival (Bon Om Tuk) (p. 188)
Khmer Rouge (p. 3)	Willamette Grove (p. 24)
Killing Fields of Choeung Ek Krama (p. 4)	

Multi-genre and Multiple Intelligences

Family Heritage Portfolio

According to a Chinese proverb, "To forget one's ancestors is to be a brook without a source, a tree without root." The Family Heritage Portfolio will be used here to capture Sundara's family experiences, but can also be used to capture the heritage of the students if they create a portfolio for their own families. The Family Heritage Portfolio includes immigration experiences, family foods and rituals, values and beliefs, cultural clashes, and school experiences. This multi-genre project requires students to make meaning of Sundara's life and represent their knowledge in a variety of ways as they amplify their multiple intelligences to complete the projects.

Intrapersonal, Interpersonal, Visual/Spatial Intelligences

Satchel Simulation

Naro jumped off his motorcycle, hauled out a two-wheeled cart from under the house, and yelled, "Throw our things in this. Now." (p. 3). Sundara dashed into the house and tossed her clothes into a satchel. On the way out of the door she grabbed a basket of dried fish, a small gas stove, dishes, mats and food. She also grabbed her most valued possession—the parasol—a gift from her father. Off they staggered toward the wharf, hoping to board a freighter that would take them away from the destruction. Because Naro knew the right people, they were able to board (p. 4–5).

In this simulation, students will be grouped into families similar to Sundara's that must run for their lives from the Khmer Rouge invasion. *They* must evacuate their home immediately. Each family member must decide what objects will fit in their satchel and what objects they will, as a family, throw into the cart. As a group, they must produce a brainstorming/prewriting and final paragraph explaining both their choices and reasoning.

Visual/Spatial and Logical/Mathematical Intelligences

Immigration Map

Give each student a world map and colored markers. Ask students to trace Sundara's immigration experience from Phnom Pehn, her native city, to a small village of Réam in Cambodia, to her present home in Oregon. Sundara's journey begins when Phnom Pehn was being destroyed in the Khmer Rouge takeover (p. 48). Her father put her on a plane headed for the small coastal village of Réam to live in safety with her aunt and uncle. Then, when the Communists advanced into this area, the family boarded a refugee boat to escape the destruction. According to Sundara, once she boarded the ship they floated around for six or seven weeks: to Thailand, to Malaysia, to Indonesia. Later, they sailed to an American camp in the Philippines, to California, and finally to Oregon (1989, p. 51). When the maps are completed, students should write a narrative of Sundara's immigration story.

Family Tree

From the information provided in *Children of the River* (1989), ask students to construct a three generational family tree. Begin with Grandmother (Tep Naro's mother) who immigrates with Naro's family. The next level would include Tep Naro and his wife, Kem Soka (p. 77). Soka has two sisters, Valinn (p. 13) and Sundara's mother. The next level of the family tree should include the children. Tep and Soka have three children: Ravy, Pon, and the baby. Sundara Sovann has an older brother, Samet (p. 27) and a younger sister, Mayoury (p. 50). Ask students to color-code the emotional connections between family members. For instance, green might represent Sundara's guilt toward Soka for not saving her baby; blue might represent the responsibility that Soka feels toward Sundara in raising her for her sister. Students should provide a key and a rationale for their decisions. This logical/mathematical activity will serve as a graphic organizer for understanding the relationships and structure of this particular family.

Visual/Spatial Intelligence

Photographs

Every Family Heritage Portfolio should contain photographs of historical value. Ask students to include at least three photos (real or created) that capture important events in the lives of Sundara's family. They could be portraits of family members, pictures of the family picking fruits and vegetables, football pictures from Ravvy's games, Sundara's high school graduation, Valinn's arrival at the airport, or Mayoury's picture from the refugee camp. Students can take photographs with instant cameras, digital cameras, or download photographs from the internet.

Visual/Spatial, Interpersonal, and Intrapersonal Intelligences

Heraldry—Family Shield

Although the original purpose of heraldic devices was as identification on fields of battle, heraldry is an art form that uses a system of symbols to understand family history and values. While students may want to create their own original family crest, shield, mantle, or coat of arms for Sundara, the following template provides a structure for more personal information about her character and personality. Students draw the shape of a shield on posterboard and divide it into six parts. Then, they either draw, find magazine pictures, or use clip art images to depict the following information:

- Draw something Sundara does well.
- Draw the place where she feels most at home.
- Draw something she is striving to become.
- Draw an emotion that she finds most difficult to express.
- What is the personal motto by which she lives?
- What would she do if she knew she had only three years to live?

Students can place a replica or smaller version of their shield in the portfolio. Shields should be saved for display at the Culture Fair at the end of the unit. This six-part shield is also meaningful for the students to complete about their own lives to build self-esteem and share with the class as an ice-breaker or community-builder.

Verbal/Linguistic and Visual/Spatial Intelligences

Flag

Ask students to include a flag (real or created) for Sundara and her family in their Family Heritage Portfolios. Students should create or replicate the design and then explain the history, colors and symbolism. Students should choose the media and size of the project whether it be presented on posterboard, fabric, or paper. They can learn about the Cambodian or other ASEAN (Association of South East Asian Nations) flags or design an original flag appropriate for Sundara's family. Flags should be discussed at this point and then displayed later at the Culture Fair.

Logical/Mathematical and Bodily/Kinethetic Intelligences

Grandmother's Recipe

When immigrants come to America, they bring with them many customs, memories and traditions. For most families, the dinner table is the best way to understand the place where those traditions were practiced. The Jews have an old saying, "Only from your own table can you go away full." (Smith, 1992, p. 517). In other words, if you are eating fast foods and not dining with your "ancestors," you really do not have a table, and you will never be full or satisfied. For this activity, students might compare their grandmothers' recipes with Sundara's grandmother. The Cambodian immigrants disliked American food and customs of eating while working (p. 17). Grandmother complains about the poor quality of rice she can buy here in the United States. Students can research the difference in foods and collect recipes for Cambodian dishes. Students might also attend to table manners such as squatting to eat and asking others before taking seconds (p. 82). At this point, students might take a field trip to a Cambodian, Vietnamese or Chinese/American restaurant or invite a chef to visit the class and to prepare food.

Visual/Spatial and Logical/Mathematical Intelligences

Lifeline: The River of Life

Perhaps because the Mekong River is such a predominant geographical feature in the lives of the Cambodians, Sundara talks about life as a river rather than a road. The river of life is different from a road in that on a river one never has to choose which way to go. "On a river we try to steer a good course, but all the time we getting swept along by a force greater than ourselves . . . a river never stop. All the river flow together and become one" (p. 146). Considering Sundara's philosophy, create a lifeline for her journey down the river of life on posterboard, complete with graphic images. Include the major dates and places mentioned in the book beginning with her life in Phnom Pehn, Réam, aboard ship, Camp Pendleton, Kennedy High School, and Willamette Grove High School. Include influential people in her life, such as family members, friends, peers, and teachers, as well as the Khmer Rouge. Include major events that occurred along the way, such as leaving Cambodia, arriving in the United States, the poem read in English class, working for Mr. Bonner, sailing with the McKinnon family, receiving news of Chamroeun's death and Mayoury's life, and reconciliation with Jonathon. Share the results with the class and include copies or drafts in the portfolio.

Verbal/Linguistic and Interpersonal Intelligences

School Experiences

One of the culture clashes facing Sundara in high school is the difference between the educational values and customs of Asians and Americans. Butterfield reports that among the children of 6,800 Indochinese who have arrived in the United States since 1978, "one-quarter . . . earned straight A's and 44 percent got an A average in math, though two-thirds of them arrived in the United States knowing no English" (1986, p. 18–19). These successes are attributed to a belief in the efficacy of hard work and the malleability of human nature, part of the Confucian ethic. "The belief that people can always be improved by proper effort and instruction is a basic tenet of Confucianism. This philosophy, propounded by the Chinese sage in the fifth century B.C., in time became a dynamic force not only in China, but throughout Asia, sanctifying the family and glorifying education" (Butterfield, p. 21). A top priority among Southeast Asians is acquisition of the English language. Ask students to find examples in *Children of the River* of Sundara's ways of learning English. Here are some examples:

- Sundara's serious poem, after studying English only 4 years (p. 10)
- Useful phrases to obtain work (i.e., "Those other people not pick clean. We pick clean." Or, "We happy to start more early in the morning if you want.) (pp. 19–20)
- Sundara learned English by listening and watching TV (p. 32)
- Sundara brings home straight "A's" (p. 173).

Throughout the novel, Sundara contrasts her experiences at Willamette Grove High School with expectations of her culture. She was constantly shocked by the students' behavior in class and their lack of respect for the teachers. Ask students to compare and contrast these values and customs by preparing a chart of these cultural conflicts at school as a pre-writing or pre-discussion activity.

Verbal/Linguistic Intelligence

Language

Language is inextricably linked to culture. It is the primary means by which people express their cultural values and the lens through which they view the world. However, because of the lack of bilingual programs, many immigrant students learn that culture is unimportant in the school environment. According to Nieto's (1996) research, "the more students are involved in resisting assimilation while maintaining their culture and language, the more successful they will be in school" (p. 291). Perhaps this is why Sundara performed so well in school. She maintained her Khmer language at home and remembers her French from school in Phnom Pehn (p. 32). Sundara knew the importance of learning English "Cannot talk is like prison. Cannot make new life" (p. 32). To affirm Sundara's native language and empower all students, bring in examples of Khmer words or symbols, such as "peba" for "crazy," "Yekabon" for "I want to go home," and "muk" for "like." Have students silk screen a letter, symbol, or word and display their work. Or, ask a native speaker to make a tape for the class to listen to—like the one that Sundara made for Doctor McKinnon before his trip to Cambodia (p. 195). Have students learn basic greetings in Khmer. This might also be a good opportunity for students to practice their French with each other in a classroom activity.

Visual/Spatial, and Interpersonal Intelligences

Characteristics of the Ideal All-American Girl

As Sundara becomes interested in Jonathan, she recognizes how very different she is from Jonathan's current girlfriend, Cathy Gates. Cathy seems to epitomize the ideal characteristics of the all-American girl, while Sundara remains the "outsider." Ask students to transfer their visual/spatial intelligence from the novel to modern America by making a collage of images from current magazines that compares and contrasts Sundara and Cathy. The images for Cathy should reflect images that represent the "ideal" body, personality, achievements, school activities, social class, race, and religion. For internet sites that discuss cultural expectations of women portrayed by the media, study the following resources:

- *How Seventeen Undermines Young Women:* <http://www.fair.org/extra/best-of-extra/seventeen.html>
- *Reflections of Girls in the Media:* <http://www.childrennow.org/media/mc97/mcopenletter.html>
- *About Face Facts on Body Image, Appearance, SES, Ethnicity, and the Thin Ideal:* <http://www.about-face.org/resources/facts/>
- *Killing Us Softly: Advertising's Image of Women:* www.mediaed.org/catalog/media/softly.html
- Or, go to search engine at <www.dogpile.com> and do phrase searches like these:

    "How seventeen undermines young women"

    "Reflections of girls in the media"

    "Killing us softly: advertising's images of women"

The images for Sundara should focus on issues that students face when they fail to meet the American ideals. After students complete their projects, they should talk about discriminatory practices that may occur in their high schools as well as discuss other aspects of dating relationships. Since Cathy meets the ideal stereotype, why would Jonathan even consider a relationship with Sundara? What does Sundara have to offer Jonathan? Does race matter? Sundara wonders if Jonathon's parents mind that she's not White (p. 103). She admits her family prejudice, "they don't even pretend that race doesn't matter. And they don't like the American way about marriage" (p. 104). What do students think about biracial marriages? What are some of the obstacles they must confront to make one work? What problems do they expect Sundara and Jonathon will have to solve?

Verbal/Linguistic and Intrapersonal Intelligences

Cultural Clash at Home

In addition to glorifying education, Sundara's family attempted to resist assimilation and to keep the Khmer way. Sundara explained the order of priorities when she said, "Family must come first. Bloodlines must not be broken. Destroy the order and it will destroy you" (p. 71–72). Family loyalty is best explained in the proverb, "A bundle of chopsticks cannot be broken like one alone" (p. 23). Put another way, Sundara would not be permitted to work alone at a job which took her from the family. As the novel progresses and Sundara is drawn into Jonathon's world and family, Sundara experiences more and more discontinuity with her family. She finds it harder and harder to resist Jonathan and to respect her family's wishes (p. 130). Even though the family has spent four years in a new country, they manage to preserve many of their traditions and customs from Cambodia. Ask students to identify the Asian customs observed by Sundara's family and compare them with their own family rituals.

Logical/Mathematical and Visual/Spatial Intelligences

Origami Projects.

Origami comes from the Japanese words for folding, "ori," and the Japanese word for paper," ka," which when combined, "kami" becomes "gami" and the word is "origami." According to Cranksaw (1997), the origins of origami are in dispute since the Chinese, Koreans, and Japanese all claim its development. A Chinese eunuch by the name of Ts'ai Lun invented a material that we call paper today replacing cloth as a writing surface in 250 B.C. The Japanese learned about paper-making in the early seventh century from a Buddist monk who came to Japan from China through Korea in 538 A.D. Then the Japanese began making paper of their own. With the invention of paper and the development of written language, folding paper in artistic ways became part of the ceremonial tradition of the nobility. The samurai in Japan exchanged gifts in a form known as "noshi." A noshi was paper folded with a strip of dried abalone or meat, considered a good luck token. Shinto Noblemen celebrated weddings by wrapping glasses of sake in butterfly form, representing the bride and groom. What began as elaborate paper-folding has evolved into a sophisticated art form that blends philosophies, art styles and passion. It takes the shape of books, greeting cards and traditional crafts. It generally adheres to strict rules of form. Most people agree that each model is created from a single piece of paper. There is no tearing of the paper, no gluing, no decorating. Origami models require students to create, memorize sequences, follow directions, and concentrate on the final product.

To enhance students' awareness for eastern culture paper arts and teach a concept through visual/spatial intelligence, ask students to create an origami model to represent an idea or theme from the novel, *Children of the River* (1989). They might consider making symbols for abstract ideas such as peace, war, love, friendship, family, and/or patriotism. They could also choose symbols directly from the book such as Sundara's parasol or Jonathan's sailboat. For paper-folding ideas and instructions, there are many interesting internet web pages, as well as library books that explain the process. Robert Lang's *The Complete Book of Origami: Step-by-Step Instructions in Over 1000 Diagrams,* John Montroll's (1985) *Animal Origami for the Enthusiast,* and Samuel Randlett's (1961) *The Art of Origami, Paper Folding, Traditional and Modern* are excellent resources. Instructions for their models should be included in their portfolios, but the models could be used as decorations for the culture fair held at the end of the unit.

Verbal/Linguistic and Visual/Spatial Intelligences

Haiku Poetry

While many of the master poets associated with Haiku (meaning "beginning phrase") are Japanese, this and other forms of poetry have traveled widely and have been adapted to many languages. Traditionally and ideally, this oriental art form presents a pair of contrasting images: one suggestive of time and place; the other a vivid but fleeting observation. Working together, they evoke mood and emotion. According to Funk and Wagnall's *Microsoft Encarta* (1994), haiku evolved from the earlier linked-verse known as the "renga" and was used extensively by Zen Buddhist monks in the 15th and 16th centuries. In the next 200 years, the verse form achieved its greatest popularity.

Originally, this short poem lived by strict rules. For example, haiku should be seventeen syllables long, should consist of three lines (5-7-5), and should always contain a "season word" or symbol of the season. Many haiku writers go beyond the strict use of the season word to include almost anything in the natural world as fair game for their poetry (Lewis, 1995).

After awakening the students' verbal/linguistic intelligence by reading

Haiku written by the masters, amplify this intelligence by asking students to write Haiku poems that are based on Sundara's memories and longing for her native land, Cambodia. For ideas, consider writing about Sundara's memories of the lighted floats on the Mekong River during the Water Festival (p. 188), the Tonle Sap full of fish (189), and the beautiful temple at Angkor Wat (p. 189). Ask students to copy their poems on large, glossy paper using black felt-tip markers. After students have copied the poems, go around and give them several drops of india ink in a configuration of their choice. Students then take soda straws and blow the ink around in ways that illustrate their poems giving them an abstract, oriental appearance. Set them aside to dry and then display them in prominent places around the classroom. Ask them to include a copy in their portfolios. Here are two Haiku's written by ninth grade students:

Water is life and   Nature in silence
Death. Flowing and rushing the   cries its accolades of peace
memories of then.   To the sounds of war.

Verbal/Linguistic, Intrapersonal and Interpersonal Intelligences

Letters to Support Cambodian Refugees

A Family Heritage Portfolio would not be complete without a collection of important family letters. Sundara's family received "piles of letters from people [she] didn't even know, asking for money for food, for guns—" (p. 123), as well as letters from her friends. Ask students to tap into their verbal/linguistic intelligence and write three to five of the following letters to include in their portfolios:

- Write a letter from Moni to the Red Cross in Thailand asking for news of her little, baby girl (p. 122).
- Write a letter to Soka from The Office of the United Nations High Commissioner for Refugees, Thailand, announcing the arrival of Soka's sister, Valinn, who had scrambled down Khao-I-Dang mountain into a Thai border camp and collapsed in the camp in a malarial stupor (p. 13).
- Write a letter from Sundara to the President of the United States requesting funds, food, and medical supplies for Kampuchea in Thai Refugee Camps.
- Write a letter from Mayoury to Sundara asking her to rescue her from the refugee camp by sponsoring her trip to the United States.
- Write a letter from Sundara to her mother expressing her regret for the last angry moments at the airport (p. 118) and writing a tribute for the sacrifices she made on behalf of the family.

- Write a letter from an unknown resistance fighter for money to buy guns to save the country.
- Write a formal letter on letterhead stationery from the President, Red Cross, United Nations, or World Vision in response to the family member's request.
- Using the Red Cross for delivery, write a letter from Sundara to Chamroeun assuring him of her concern for his safety and willingness to sponsor him to the United States.

These letters should be included in the portfolios and selected ones shared at the Culture Fair at the end of the unit.

Verbal/Linguistic and Intrapersonal Intelligences

Death Notices

Among important family papers are death notices, particularly for those who die in war. Awaken students' thinking about death by reading passages from *Children of the River* (1989). Sundara's family often received death notices of their family and friends. Soka receives notice that her friend, Theary, and her whole family were massacred by the Communists (p. 139). In another letter Soka opened, she learned that Sundara's beloved Chamroeun was killed (p. 140). Later Sundara tells the story to Jonathan of how Chamroem was killed for stealing a potato, such a disgrace for a freedom fighter (p. 143). In the novel, Sundara never does find out about her parents and brother, only that her sister was alive. Amplify the intrapersonal intelligence by asking students to write at least one death notice to include in their portfolios.

Elegy

Sundara suffers deeply both for the death of Soka's baby, for whom she felt so responsible, and for the death of her beloved Chamroeun. Strong emotions such as grief, loss, sadness, anger, and confusion are often best expressed in poetry. To amplify the intrapersonal intelligence that has already been awakened, ask students to write an elegy for one of Sundara's losses using the template provided in Table 3.3 to structure the poem. Also in Table 3.3, is an elegy written by Lin Robinson to Soka's Baby.

Musical/Rhythmic and Verbal/Linguistic Intelligences

Family Songs

Family Heritage Portfolios include songs that are particularly meaningful to various family members. For Cambodian families that suffered separation and loss of family and friends, the music should reflect mourning and sorrow. For those displaced from their homeland, the music should reflect their homesickness and longing for their native land. As news of the destruction became widespread, the music should reflect their prayers for peace and safety. After awakening students' musical intelligence by playing recordings of Cambodian music, amplify the intelligence by asking students to find or create songs that express these themes. Musically talented students should consider composing and performing music for Sundara's poem written for her English class (p. 10–11).

TABLE 3.3: TEMPLATE FOR AN ELEGY AND ELEGY TO SOKA'S BABY

Template for an Elegy	Elegy to Soka's Baby
I would like to show you . . . But I would not want you to see . . . I wish that . . . I wish that . . . You would have . . . (or, It would have reminded you of . . .)	I wish I had the chance to show you how to have freedom in life. But I would not want you to see your war-torn homeland with bloodshed, hatred vengeful men. I wish that my inner love could have saved you from the watery grave. I wish that my body could have sustained your life and held your spirit here on earth. You would have grown strong and compassionate to go back and rescue others from hunger, disease, and despair.

Verbal/Linguistic Intelligence

Headlines and News Articles

Family Heritage Portfolios often contained evidence of historical events that reflect the time period and causes for the family's immigration and assimilation to the American way of life. Sundara's family fled from the Khmer Rouge by ship from a coastal village, but other families escaped over the mountains into Thailand. From the Internet, library, and/or the imagination, ask students to create at least four fictional, but accurate headlines and news articles detailing the activities of the Khmer Rouge or Vietnamese Communist forces that caused the fall of Phnom Penh and the death of an estimated two million Cambodians (especially the educated). Students could also write about events that have occurred since the writing of the novel, such as the United Nations elections in 1993 that reinstated Norodom Sihanouk as king.

All the Multiple Intelligences

Cambodian Culture Fair

The Cambodian Culture Fair will be the culminating activity for this unit, a time to celebrate all that students have learned about Cambodia from their study of *Children of the River* (1989). Students will work collaboratively in groups according to their cultural interests in food, music, games, dances, art, storytelling, and artifacts to produce a learning center with a particular focus on Cambodian culture. In their learning centers, they will display products from their Family Heritage Portfolios such as family trees, immigration maps, lifelines, Haiku, photos, and origami. Students should be encouraged to come dressed in oriental garb prepared for a Khmer day. As record of their preparations, students should also prepare a one-page handout for the rest of the class that explains the focus for their center and describes the multiple intelligences used in creating the center.

Verbal/Linguistic Intelligence

Storytelling

This group will prepare stories, choral readings, and poetry to be presented at the Culture Fair. They could tell survival stories (real or created) of Cambodian Refugee families such as the one told in *Where the River Runs: A Portrait of a Refugee Family* (1993) by Nancy Price Graff. Students could read some of the outstanding letters and/or poetry from other students' Family Heritage Portfolios. They could prepare choral readings from the journal entries students wrote about Sundara's thoughts about the war; her family's struggle to assimilate, and the conflict in departing from the Khmer way to date Jonathan. They could retell folktales from Cambodia or even China which historically influenced Cambodia's heritage. After reading about Cambodia, they could create a crossword puzzle from the basic information they learned. This group could lead the class in a French writing lesson: La Dictée (Dictation method used in France). Choose a passage from a book such as *Dragonwings* (1990) by Laurence Yep to read to the class. While you read the passage sentence by sentence, the class members write what you dictate. You read each sentence only twice: once for listening only and once for writing. Then discuss the ideas in the passage.

Logical/Mathematical Intelligence

Maps and Timelines

Students in this group can make a topographical map of Cambodia to show its boundaries, mountains, rivers, major cities, population, and natural resources. Another idea for this group would be to research and create a timeline for either Cambodia's history or Cambodia's gifts to the western world. These gifts could be broadened to include products from China such as silk, paper, playing cards, porcelain, gunpowder, kites, and certain fruits indigenous to the area. Students in this group might create a game based on Khmer Rouge.

Visual/Spatial Intelligence

Khmer Art and Sculpture

Among the achievements of the Khmer civilization are the magisterial temples of Angkor. The "wats" (temple-monasteries) include: Wat Ounalom, Wat Phnom, and Wat Lang Ka. Khmer culture can be viewed in the National Museum and at the Royal Palace. This group will study the art and sculpture found in this complex. For a slide show of these wonders, go to the following internet site: http://www. lonelyplanet.com.au/road/witness/sld-bod.htm. This group might also specialize in the art of Chinese brush painting. To make the beautiful figures used in classic Chinese writing use white paper, a brush, and black tempera paint to create words and symbols from the Chinese or Khmer language. For more information, read a book such as *You Can Write Chinese* (1945) by Kurt Wiese. Another idea for this group would be to make a class book of Haiku. Copy, illustrate, and bind the poems created earlier by classmates. This group might also be interested in creating more elaborate origami projects after searching the internet sites that show the color and forms of this art.

Bodily/Kinesthetic Intelligence

Khmer Cuisine

This group will collect recipes and prepare them to eat and enjoy at the Culture Fair. They can begin with the Grandmothers' Recipes students collected for their portfolios and then develop a typical meal menu and decide which foods to prepare for the class. For more information go to the following website: http://www. lonelyplanet.com.au/dest/sea/camb.htm. There are many more websites if students search "Khmer cuisine". To learn more about cooking, students can video cooking shows that demonstrate Chinese cooking methods. In addition to preparing food, this group could present immigration skits that show the cultural shock and changes people make in assimilating into the American way of life. This group might also create a series of tableaux (still life statue formations) of critical scenes from the novel. For instance, they could do a tableau of migrant works, football game, family squatting to eat, Sundara's fight with Cathy in the restroom, sailing with the McKinnon's, or other memorable scenes.

Musical/Rhythmic Intelligence

Classical Dance and Music

Cambodia's classical dance is highly stylized and usually accompanied by an orchestra or choral narration. After researching classical dance, students may choose to imitate the basic ideas or create their own form. Dances should be based on the themes of the novel, *Children of the River*, and reflect the culture or cultural conflicts studied in the unit. Students should select appropriate oriental music as background for the dance which should be performed at the Culture Fair. Other musically inclined students could perform the songs they wrote for Sundara's poem. Students could demonstrate melodies on oriental instruments or make a music video. Using musical software, students can write an original score and words to a song relating to the story, then either give a video or "live" presentation at the Culture Fair.

Interpersonal and Verbal/Linguistic Intelligences

CNN News

Students in this group should use the Internet to research current events, headlines, weather, sports, and cultural events. Using this information they should create a news show, complete with commercials, to give at the Culture Fair. Another idea for this group should be to simulate a travel agency and organize a trip to Cambodia. They should give facts and warnings, passport information, money and costs for their travelers. They should set a date (preferably not during the monsoon season) and determine a safe itinerary. This group should consider attending a prominent event such as Bon Om Tuk (Water Festival) or Chaul Chnam (Khmer New Year) to provide travelers with a cultural experience. For another newsworthy topic, students could report on labor laws and disputes for migrant workers or changes in immigration patterns and laws for Asians.

Intrapersonal and Verbal/Linguistic Intelligences

Monologue of a Buddhist Monk

Students in this group will prepare monologues containing the basic tenets of Theravade Buddhism and the life of the Buddhist monk. They can find a creative way to present the noble truths, the eightfold path, the boundless states, and the fetters of existence. An ambitious group might wear costumes, impersonate a monk, or describe the daily life of a monk. This group could create a powerpoint or hyper studio slide show of the temples, statues of Buddha, and venerated monks which they use as part of the presentation.

After the Culture Fair, students should engage in self-reflection both about their Family Heritage Portfolios and their contributions to the Culture Fair. They should discuss their successes and their difficulties in completing the projects. They should discuss the adequacy of the time allotted to the projects and the quality of the instructions. They should describe their effort and interest in this type of unit and offer advice to next year's students in order to assist them in successful completion of the projects. Finally, they should evaluate their development and utilization of the multiple intelligences. Did they develop further their strongest intelligences and/or did they take risks to nurture less preferred intelligences? Were they proud of their projects and performance? Why or why not? What goals will they set for the future? See Table 3.4 for Assessing Exhibitions of Products and Skills at the Culture Fair.

TABLE 3.4: ASSESSING EXHIBITIONS OF PRODUCTS AND SKILLS AT THE CULTURE FAIR

Exhibiting Products and Skills at the Culture Fair						
Student's Name:			Teacher's Name:			
	Skilled			Needs Work		

The Product was Well-Prepared
    Well-Planned
    Prepared with care and effort
    Complete On time
	5	4	3	2	1	

Exhibition of Product was Well-Prepared
    Display was organized (had a good plan)
    Used artifacts
    Used multiple intelligences (music, visuals,
      movement, taste, posters, etc.)
    Presentation was rehearsed
	5	4	3	2	1	

Presentation of the Product was Skillful
    Made eye contact with audience
    Presentation was well-organized
    Entertained questions and interaction
      with audience
	5	4	3	2	1	

Exhibition of Product Showed Knowledge
    Showed evidence of research
    Showed depth of knowledge
    Gave concrete examples to support research
	5	4	3	2	1	

Self-Reflection Paper
    Described successes/difficulties in
      completing projects
    Described their time and effort
    Described their relationship to their peers
    Described use of their multiple intelligences
    Set goals for next projects
	5	4	3	2	1	

The Rating for the Whole Exhibition and Performance	5	4	3	2	1	0

Annotated Bibliography of Young Adult Literature of Asian-American Immigration and Assimilation

Books

Haemi Balgassi

Haemi Balgassi was inspired by the real-life experiences of her own mother and grandparents who escaped Seoul during the Korean War and moved to the United States. In addition to an informative picture book, *Peacebound Trains*, (1996) she wrote:

- *Tae's Sonata* (1997)

Sook Nyul Choi

Sook Nyul Choi immigrated from Korea to the United States to pursue her college education. She now resides in Cambridge, Massachusetts as a full-time writer. She is author of a picture book, *Halmoni and the Picnic* (1993), as well as the following:

- *Year of the Impossible Goodbyes* (1991)
- *Echoes of the White Giraffe* (1993)
- *Gathering of Pearls* (1994)
- *The Best Older Sister* (1997)

Nancy Price Graff

Nancy Price Graff writes a story about a family of immigrants from Cambodia struggling to make a better life for themselves in Boston as they embrace American culture while still treasuring much of their Cambodian heritage in:

- *Where the River Runs: A Portrait of a Refugee Family* (1993)

Jeanne Wakatsuki Houston and James D. Houston

Jeanne Wakatsuki was seven years old in 1942 when her family was uprooted from their home and sent to live at Manzanar internment camp. She tells of a Japanese-American family's experiences in her book:

- *Farewell to Manzanar: A True Story of Japanese American Experience During and After World War II Internment* (1983)

Marie G. Lee

Marie G. Lee is a second-generation Korean-American who was born and raised in Hibbing, Minnesota. Her books show the struggle of Korean American adolescents who face racism and assimilation issues:

- *Finding My Voice* (1994)
- *Saying Goodbye* (1994)
- *If It Hadn't Been for Yoon Jun* (1995)
- *Necessary Roughness* (1996)
- *Night of the Chupacabras* (1998)
- *F is for Fabuloso* (1999)

Kyoko Mori

Kyoko Mori was born in Japan and came to the United States when she was sixteen. She has won numerous awards for her novels, poetry, and short stories. Her story is told in:

- *Shizuko's Daughter* (1995)

Yoshiko Uchida

Yoshiko Uchida vividly tells about growing up as a Japanese-American in California and being sent to a concentration camp during World War II. In addition to her picture book, *The Bracelet* (1996), she has written the following books that pertain to the theme:

- *Desert Exile: The Uprooting of a Japanese-American Family* (1984)
- *Jar of Dreams* (1993)
- *The Invisible Thread: An Autobiography* (1995)

Laurence Yep

Two-time Newbery Honor author Laurence Yep has written many books about the Chinese-American experience as he interweaves fantasy, humor, and celebration of family values into his stories. The following pertain to the theme of this unit:

- *Dragonwings* (1990)
- *Child of the Owl* (1997)
- *Dragon's Gate* (1993)
- *The Serpent's Children* (1996)
- *Mountain Light* (1995)
- *The Cook's Family* (1999)
- *The Imp that Ate My Homework* (1998)

Film

Christine Keyser produced a film about Southeast Asian immigrants. This film explores the cultural heritage of the Vietnamese, Laotian, and Khmer people, and conveys the pain and frustration of resettlement in the United States.

- *The Price You Pay*. (1988). Online catalogue: http://www.aems.uiuc.edu/html/results.las

Folk Stories

Norma J. Livo and Dia Cha compiled folklore, tales, and social life and custom of Southeast Asian people. Since the Hmong language did not acquire a written form until the 1950s, the Hmong people have had to depend primarily on an oral and artistic tradition to pass on their history, legends, beliefs, and culture from one generation to the next. This book is an effort to collect and make available folk stories of the Hmong people to Americans seeking to understand the culture and to Hmong children who might not otherwise have access to the stories and traditions of their people.

- *Folk Stories of the Hmong: Peoples of Laos, Thailand, and Vietnam* (1991)

References

About face: Facts on body image, appearance, SES, ethnicity, and the thin ideal. http://www.about-face.org/resources/facts/

Armstrong, T. (1994). *Multiple intelligences in the classroom.* Alexandria, VA: Association for Supervision and Curriculum Development.

Butterfield, F. (1986, August 3). Why Asians are going to the head of the class. *New York Times,* Education Section, pp. 18–19.

Cambodia. http://www. Cambodia-web.net/index.htm.

Crew, L. (1989). *Children of the river.* New York: Laurel-Leaf Books.

Crankshaw, E. (1997, November). The east and west of Origami. http://fly.hiway. net/~ejcranks/arth193b.html.

Graff, N. P. (1993). *Where the river runs: A portrait of a refugee family.* New York: Little Brown and Company.

Haiku (1994). Microsoft Encarta. Funk & Wagnalls Corporation. Microsoft Company.

How *Seventeen* undermines young women. http://www.fair.org/extra/best-of-extra/seventeen.html

Keyser, C. (1988). *The price you pay* [film]. http://www.aems.uiuc.edu/html/results.las

Khmer art and sculpture. http://www.lonelyplanet.com.au/dest/sea/camb.htm

Khmer cuisine. http://www.lonelyplanet.com.au/dest/sea/camb.htm

Killing us softly: Advertising's image of women. http://www.mediaed.org/catalog/media/softly.html

Lang, R. (1988). *The complete book of origami: Step-by-step instructions in over 1000 diagrams.* New York: Dover.

Lazear, D. (1991). *Seven ways of teaching.* Palatine, IL: IRI/Skylight Publishing, Inc.

Lewis, J. P. (1995). *Black swan white crow.* New York: Atheneum Books for Young Readers.

Montroll, J. (1985). *Animal origami for the enthusiast.* New York: Dover Publications.

Nieto, S. (1996). *Affirming diversity: The sociopolitical context of multicultural education.* New York: Longman.

Olson, C. B., & Schiesl, S. (1996, Spring). A multiple intelligences approach to teaching multicultural literature. *Language Arts Journal of Michigan, 12*(1), pp. 21–28.

Randlett, S. (1961). *The art of origami: Paper folding, traditional and modern.* New York: Dutton.

Reflections on gender studies in the media. http://www.childrennow.org/media/.

Smith, J. (1992). *The Frugal Gourmet on our immigrant ancestors: Recipes you should have gotten from your grandmother.* New York: Avon.

Wiese, K. (1945). *You can write Chinese.* New York: Viking Press.

Yep, L. (1990). *Dragonwings.* New York: Cornerstone Books.

CHAPTER 4

Heroes, Heartbreak, and Healing: What was it like in Vietnam?

Joyce Rowland with Jackie Glasgow

Introduction

"It still boils down to suffering, and the thing about Vietnam that most bothers me is that it is treated as a political experience, a sociological experience, and the human element of what a soldier goes through—and what the Vietnamese went through—is not only neglected: it is almost cast aside as superfluous." Tim O'Brien, U.S. Army (Deneberg, 1995, p. x)

With due respect to the more than two and a half million American men and women who served in Vietnam, this unit will focus on the human element of the Vietnam experience through young adult literature. Even though Americans are divided politically and morally about the war in Vietnam, they must move beyond the darkness of pain, error, and ignorance in order to hear truth in the stories told by those who found a way to tell it. After all, the stories in *Voices from Vietnam* (1995) and *Dear America: Letters Home from Vietnam* (1985) are stories from adolescents. The average age of the American combatant in Vietnam was 19 years as compared with 26 years for the soldier in World War II (Wittman, 1998). Much of the literature of Vietnam, including Walter Dean Myer's *Fallen Angels* (1988), focuses on the adolescent experience— written about naive teenagers far away from home who are transformed by the war experience. Although life in Vietnam was quite different from the American one, youth today struggle with many similar issues—survival, invincibility, family relationships, friends, coded language, identity, independence, and tough decisions. Young adults today can find themselves and identify with characters in the literature narrated by those who were about the same age and who lived in Vietnam. In addition to the literature presented in this unit, resources for teaching about the Vietnam conflict are readily available. Larry Johannessen's *Illumination Rounds: Teaching the Literature of the Vietnam War* (1992) provides a wealth of teaching activities drawn from his experiences as a marine in Vietnam. Vietnam: Yesterday and Today at (http://www. oakton.edu/ ~wittman/ or search the keywords Vietnam Yesterday and Today under Yahoo; these sites offer teachers a rich selection of bibliographies for teaching more about various aspects of the Vietnam War.

In this unit, students will utilize their multiple intelligences to examine the human element of the Vietnam experience by responding to young adult literature that gives voice to those who sacrificed and served in the war. In order to motivate students and prepare them for this study, the unit is devised with multiple entry points as Howard Gardner suggests in his book, *The Unschooled Mind: How Children Think & How Schools Should Teach* (1991). Gardner states his belief that "any rich, nourishing topic—any concept worth teaching— can be approached in at least five different ways that, roughly speaking, map onto the multiple intelligences" (p. 245). He believes that awareness of these entry points can help teachers introduce new materials in ways by which they can be easily grasped by a range of students. Then as students explore other entry points, they have the chance to develop those multiple perspectives that are the best antidote to stereotypical thinking. The five entry points or doors to new material are as follows:

- Narrative entry point, one presents a story or narrative about the concept in questions;
- Logical-quantitative entry point, one approaches the concept by invoking numerical considerations or deductive reasoning processes;
- Foundational entry point examines the philosophical and terminological facets of the concept;
- Esthetic approach focuses on an appeal to students who favor an artistic stance to the experiences of living;
- Experiential approach is hands-on, dealing directly with the materials that embody or convey the concept (245–246).

See Table 4.1 for MI Activities for Entry and Development of Multiple Perspectives Of the Heroes, Heartbreak, and Healing in Vietnam.

TABLE 4.1: MI ACTIVITIES FOR ENTRY AND DEVELOPMENT OF MULTIPLE PERSPECTIVES
OF THE HEROES, HEARTBREAK, AND HEALING IN VIETNAM

Entry Points	Entry Approaches	Development of Multiple Perspectives
Narrational	Reader's Theater of Voices from Vietnam (1995) and Dear America: letters Home from Vietnam (1985).	Read *Fallen Angels* Read or listen to speeches by LBJ, Nixon, Kennedy Read *Things They Carried* and other books of the women's experience in Vietman Image Freewrite Write letters from Vietnam Write death notices, warning letter of desertion, news articles, letter to congress and poems for Vietnam Scrapbook Write letter to school board censoring *Fallen Angels*
Logical-Quantitative	Examine statistics from the Vietnam Conflict: how many dead, missing in action, prisoners of war?	Compare the 18 stages of a hero's journey for Beowulf and Rich Perry Mapping the Story Structure, figure out rations for platoon for food, clothing, ammunition, and figure attack plans Create a timeline for Vietnam Conflict Create a town map and description for Vietnam Scrapbook
Foundational	Historical and Political roles of US involvement in Vietnam One Minute Vocabulary Presentations of important people, events, and places of the conflict	Create a map study of Vietnam War Zones Research geography, agricultural products, natural resources, manufacturing products, historical sites Study the history for Vietnam War Memorial Character choices, perspectives, family history for Vietnam Scrapbook
Esthetic or Artistic	Play recordings or Rock and Roll tunes about Vietnam and/or Visit website for Vietnam Veterans Art Museum	Analyse messages in Rock and Roll tunes Analyse songs from Vietnam Create ABC Book for *Fallen Angels* Create Who Am I? Poster for characters in *Fallen Angels* Create pictures and artwork for Vietnam Scrapbook Write song lyrics for your character Create a soundtrack for H.S. Class Reunion
Experiential	Interview men of draft age Compare contents of their backpacks with items carried on patrol in Vietnam	Interview Vietnam Veterans Simulate a minefield Create a Vietnam Memorial for your location Create Vietnam Scrapbook Role-play Class Reunion 1969 Simulation

Narrational Entry Point

Vietnam Readers' Theater

In this rendition of readers' theater, students give voice to those who suffered and sacrificed their lives in Vietnam. McCaslin (1990) defines readers' theater as the oral presentation of drama, prose, or poetry by two or more readers. A common format for readers' theater is for participants to perform their excerpt sitting or standing in a line on a stage (or front of the room) with no backdrop, costumes, or special effects. In this case, students will remain in their seats and read an excerpt from either *Voices from Vietnam* (1995) or *Dear America: Letters Home from Vietnam* (1985). Joyce Rowland created the script in advance of the class meeting. She selected the excerpts, noted the name and page number on separate index cards (or just handed them the laminated page), and made a master copy of the performance. See Table 4.2 for Rowland's *Vietnam Readers' Theater.*

Table 4.2: Vietnam Readers' Theater

Introduction (*Letters*, xxix)	Walter Cronkite 1 (*Voices*, 123)
Captain Joseph Bush, Jr. (*Letters*, xxix)	Anne Bramson (*Letters*, xxix)
John Mecklin (*Voices*, 16-17)	John Buchanan 1 (*Voices*, 34-35
Narrator 4 (*Voices*, 17)	John Buchanan 2 (*Voices*, 35)
Ken Moorefield (*Voices*, 162)	John Buchanan 3 (*Voices*, 35)
Brian (*Letters*, 205)	James Hagenzieker (*Voices*, 207-8)
Angel Quintana (*Voices*, 162)	Walter Cronkite 2 (*Writing*, 7)
Tom Pellaton (*Letters*, 206)	Narrator 2 (*Letters*, xxxviii)
Phil (*Letters*, 226)	John Kerry (*Voices*, 209)
Richard Cantale (*Letters*, 207)	Narrator 3 (*Voices*, 209)
Paul Kelly (*Letters*, 95-95)	Donald Hines (*Voices*, 212)
Graham McFarlane (*Letters*, 204-205)	Eleanor Wimbish (*Voices*, 217)
Jack Perkins TET (*Voices*, 115)	Major Michael Davis O'Donnell (*Letters*, xxxix)

When students arrived at the classroom door on the day of the performance, each student received a card indicating the excerpt she/he would read. Students were given a few minutes to locate their piece and practice reading it in their "one-foot" voice (reading aloud quietly to themselves). When everyone was ready, Joyce darkened the room (leaving enough outside light to read), turned on soft music of Vietnam, and began the performance. As she read each name indicated on the master list, the student who had that name read the excerpt. The readings evoked sympathy and compassion for the people who had served their country and sacrificed their lives. By the end of the readers' theater, the room was silent. All present spent several minutes in quiet meditation giving respect for the lives sacrificed in this war. Unlike Tim O'Brien's experience, the human element was not cast aside as superfluous (Deneberg, 1995, p. x).

Logical-Quantitative Entry Point

Vietnam Conflict Statistics

As an entry point for students strong in logical/mathematical intelligence, ask them to gather statistics from the Vietnam Conflict. Find the numbers of veterans, deaths, missing in action, and prisoners of war. Ask students to make a table that compares those numbers to other wars with U.S. involvement.

Foundational Entry Point

One-Minute Vocabulary Presentations

In order to prepare students with background information for reading the literature of Vietnam, give a brief introduction of the historical and political roles of the U.S. involvement in Vietnam. Make a list of people, places, and events that students should know to study the Vietnam conflict. Then, ask students to give one-minute vocabulary presentations. Group students in pairs to research a topic and to present their information to the rest of the class. In a one–two minute presentation, students should give basic background of the time period and the phrases, places and names they will be reading and hearing about during the Vietnam Unit. The pair must share with the rest of the class (with the help of a visual):

- who or what the topic is
- when it was important
- why it was important
- what its impact was on the war or on our society today

Ask students to take notes during the presentations, and then give a quiz based on the information presented.

Esthetic or Artistic Entry Point

Listening to Rock and Roll Songs about Vietnam

To engage students who are musically oriented, collect recordings of music so that students can identify and appreciate various perspectives or views of the war. Begin by playing "Ballad of the Green Berets." This is a pro-fighting point of view written by Sergeant Barry Sadler. Next consider "The Great Mandella" performed by Peter, Paul and Mary and "Blowin' in the Wind" by Bob Dylan. These are songs about conscientious objectors. The "Fortunate Son," performed by Creedence Clearwater Revival, tells of men receiving "special" consideration because of their wealth or political connections. Finally, "Alice's Restaurant Massacre" performed by Arlo Guthrie, presents a humorous view of dodging the draft. Discuss what the artists express in their works.

If time allows and music is available, continue this listening and analysing of music from the Vietnam War. Divide students into small groups and give each group a recording of a song along with written lyrics. For a bibliography of selected recordings, go to Lesson 36 at the Rock and Roll Hall of Fame Website: http://www.rockhall.com/programs/institute.asp and click on lesson plans or contact the RRHFM Educational Dept. at 216-515-1234. Have students present an analysis of their song to the class. They should play the song, present the lyrics, and explain the meaning and point of view of the song.

Experiential Entry Point

Interview Men of Draft Age

Every male, upon reaching age eighteen, was required to register with the selective service. Men found themselves either willingly enlisting, trying for deferments as full-time students or for other acceptable reasons, or leaving the country for Canada. Conscientious Objectors, including a young boxer named Muhammad Ali, became a part of the war's picture. Some men allegedly received "special treatment" from their local draft boards. America developed a lottery to decide who would be called upon first.

The purpose of this lesson is to have students empathize with the decisions young men had to make when they reached the age of eighteen. In order to accomplish this goal, students will interview men of draft age. This lesson was contributed by Joe Knap, Bay High School, Bay Village, Ohio, and can be found at the Rock and Roll Hall of Fame website: http://www.rockhall.com/programs/institute.asp and click on lesson plans.

Assign students to interview three people who were of draft age during the Vietnam War. Specifically, they should find out how these people dealt with the dilemma of the draft and how they spent the war years. Ask students to write a one-page paper for each of the interviews. They should introduce the person and report the questions and answers from the interview. After the interviewing process, students participate in a role-play based upon the people they interviewed. Make color-coded nametags using fictitious names to represent the characters' views of the war (draft dodger, conscientious objector, or veteran). Divide the students into small groups. Try to mix up the groups so that all views are represented. Allow about fifteen minutes for the role-play. At the conclusion of the activity, hold a class discussion to share information and evaluate the exercise.

Esthetic Entry Point or Development of Multiple Perspectives

"Vietnam: Reflexes and Reflections"

"Vietnam: Reflexes and Reflections" is the title of the exhibit at the

National Vietnam Veterans Art Museum which opened in August, 1996, and is located in Chicago's Historic Prairie Avenue District. The Museum houses over 600 works of art created by artists who served as soldiers in the Vietnam conflict. All of the artwork depicts their individual experiences in the war. Currently, the Museum includes works from 115 artists from the United States, Australia, Cambodia, and Thailand, as well as North and South Vietnam. In addition to paintings, drawings, photography and sculpture, the Museum houses a comprehensive collection of artifacts such as medals, uniforms, weapons and a Huey helicopter. This collection of art, along with biographies of the artists, are available to you and your students at the Museum website: http://www.NVVAM.org. Encourage students to spend time reflecting on the themes they find expressed in the artwork. Ask them to make connections between the art and the literature they have been reading. This experience can be part of the healing process for everyone.

Verbal/Linguistic and Visual/Spatial Intelligences

Development of Multiple Perspectives: Vietnam ABC Book

In *Fallen Angels*, Walter Dean Myers uses language that was unique to the Vietnam War. According to Johannessen (1992), it consists of "a combination of Americanized foreign words and phrases, military jargon, rock music lyrics, and a unique in-country vocabulary derived from various sources" (p. 163). To become acquainted with this language, students will make a Vietnam ABC Book. Assign each student a letter of the alphabet and ask them to find a word beginning with that letter unique to the Vietnam experience, noting the page of *Fallen Angels* (1988) from which they got it. They are to define the word and create an illustration for it. The illustrations can be drawings, paintings, clip art, internet images, photos, or magazine pictures. After students have completed their pages, collate and bind them into a class book. Make copies for each class member to use as a reference for reading *Fallen Angels*.

Development of Multiple Perspectives: Image Freewrite

The purpose of this activity is to encourage students to infer meaning from a given statement and create a visual expression of the idea. Ask students to choose a quotation from their readings on Vietnam that particularly moved them. Then, ask them to create a picture that in some way represents the words. For this project, their artwork may use only up to three colors and three symbols. After they create their pictures, ask them to freewrite about their thoughts about the images and symbols they created. This activity was adapted from a lesson by Carol Olson and Sharon Schiesl (1996).

For example, Katelyn Pemberton, a student in Rowland's 11th grade class, chose a quote from *Fallen Angels* (1988) at the place when Lieutenant Carroll, Richie's platoon leader, had just been shot. As the soldiers carried him back to the village, somebody shot off another flare. Johnson put Carroll down and set up the M-60. "The sixty—the pig—was hungry, angry that they had hit our man, our leader" (p. 126). Katelyn describes her picture in the following excerpt from her freewrite:

> The visualization I have created from my mind is a grotesque one. It was hard just using three symbols and three colors. First, I drew the sixty, huge and dominating, its cold, hard blackness glinting in the light. Then beneath it I showed the bubbling, bloody-red entrails of a Vietcong. The third and most important symbol is the pigs: tiny pigs, pink and bug-like, eating away the insides of the soldier, just as the war was eating away the souls of the soldiers, perhaps on both sides.

Verbal/Linguistic, Intrapersonal Intelligences

Development of Multiple Perspectives: Writing an Elegy

War is about death and dying. To the young men fighting in Vietnam, death was shocking, horrifying, and traumatic. In *Fallen Angels*, Richie first encountered death when a platoon member, Jenkins, stepped on a mine. Even though Richie had just met the man, he was deeply moved by his death: "the only dead person I had ever seen before [was] my grandmother . . . Jenkins had been walking with me and talking with me only hours before" (p. 43). This was a moving and tragic moment for Richie as well as the readers of this passage. Richie mentions Jenkins many times in the story, as if struggling to cope with this harsh reality. One way to deal with these tough emotions is to write an elegy. See Table 4.3 for a Template for an Elegy and Wayne Potash's *Elegy to Angel Warrior Jenkins*. The template works well for students who have difficulty "getting started" with a poem. It can serve as a "jumping off" point for others.

TABLE 4.3: ELEGY TEMPLATE AND AN ELEGY TO ANGEL WARRIOR JENKINS

Elegy Template	Elegy To Angel Warrior Jenkins
Elegy To Angel Warrior Jenkins	I would like to show you your own gentleness blowing like a breeze.
I would like to show you...	But I would not want you to see how you wore fear in the jungle like a heavy overcoat
But I would not want you to see...	I wish that you could have foretold life for yourself, instead of death.
I wish that...	I wish that your ability to imitate could have grown up and made people laugh, as well as yourself.
I wish that...	You would have been like Eddie Murphy, making fun of hell, while you ran for your life.
You would have...	
(or, It would have reminded you of...)	

Students can also write elegies for veterans listed on the wall at the Vietnam War Memorial in Washington, D.C. Begin this lesson by reading Eve Bunting's (1990) picture book, *The Wall*. This moving story about a grandfather and his grandson's pilgrimage to the Wall in search of the boy's father will inspire creative thoughts for writing. Judy Donnelly's (1991) *A Wall of Names* is also an excellent picture book telling the story of mixed sentiments toward the war and the cathartic effect of building the Memorial. As an activity to personalize this experience for students, ask them to research veterans who lived in their local area, city or town. Check to see when the Moveable Wall will be in your area. Through Friends of Vietnam Veterans, students can research a local veteran, find his/her name on the wall, make a "rubbing" of the name (either real or simulated), and write an elegy, biopoem or other message under it.

Verbal/Linguistic, Logical/Math, and Intrapersonal Intelligences

Development of Multiple Perspectives: The Life of the Hero

The Hero's Journey is similar to the primitive Rite of Passage, which initiates a child into adulthood. In a rite of passage, a child first faces separation, when she/he is taken from the mother to confront some fearful monster or danger. The child faces the monster and goes through an initiation, giving up the role of the dependent child. Then the child/adult must return to the village as an adult, ready to take on adult responsibilities. This pattern is not simply the invention of the ancient storytellers. It is part of the human process of growth and discovery. Myths are metaphors for this process. While the journey is more obvious in classical myths, it is repeated in literature, movies, and even in our personal lives.

According to Thompson and Harris (1992), the journey can be divided into eight different stages. Each of these must be passed successfully if the initiate is to become a hero. To turn back at any point would mean our initiate is rejecting his own need to grow and mature. The separation phase includes *the call* inviting the initiate into the adventure, the threshold or *jumping off point* into the unknown, and *the descent* into uncharted territory. The initiation phase includes first, *the tests and ordeals* which challenge her/him to the utmost; second, *the abyss* when the initiate faces the greatest danger and challenge of the journey; third, *the transformation* when the initiate overcomes her/his fear and rebirth emerges through revelation; and last, *the atonement* when the hero receives a "boon" or gift based on the new level of skill and awareness. After the transformation and atonement, the hero faces one of the most difficult stages of the journey: she/he must return to everyday life to begin *the labor of bringing the boon back to humanity*. The hero and boon may renew the community, found a nation, or create a great order. However, if things don't go smoothly, the hero(ine) may find frustration with the state of the world and have difficulty maintaining the new-found cosmic viewpoint in a fragmented world.

To stimulate a discussion of a hero, distribute the words to "Holding Out for a Hero" (Steinman and Prichard, 1984) from the movie, *Footloose*, and sing it with the class or play the soundtrack, if you feel more inclined. Have students brainstorm to develop a list of words to characterize a hero in the song (strong, fast, sure, street-wise, white knight, superman, etc). Then, ask students to find passages in their reading of *Fallen Angels* (1988), *Voices from Vietnam* (1995) or *Dear America: Letters Home from Vietnam* (1985) that they consider heroic acts. Discuss and define characteristics of heroes in the context of the Vietnam experience. Then ask students to compare heroes in a familiar myth such as Beowulf with a Vietnam veteran using the stages of the hero's journey based on Thompson and Harris (1992), but developed by Whorsham and Garrard (1996). See Table 4.4 for a class generated sample of a completed chart comparing Beowulf to Richard Perry from Rowland's 11th-Grade English Class.

Visual/Spatial, Interpersonal, Intrapersonal Intelligences

Development of Multiple Perspectives: Who Am I? Poster

In *Fallen Angels* (1988), Walter Dean Myers paints a vivid picture of each character in Richard Perry's squadron. Each of these young men struggles to define both himself and his mission in a foreign land. As they walked through the boonies, past rice paddies, and through the mine traps, each character had to answer the "Who am I?", "Why am I here?", and "Where am I going?" questions. They defined themselves in relation to one another and to their circumstances. For this activity, ask students to select a character from *Fallen Angels* (1988), or other young adult novels and make a "Who am I?" poster. Students should find pictures from magazines, clip art, internet graphics or photographs to show images of their character's personality. Each image should be labeled with a quote from the text that explains the picture. For example, a quote to begin a poster on Richie would be the one made by his High School English teacher, Mrs. Liebow: "You're too young to be just an observer in life" (p. 35). Richie was painfully aware that he was "just an observer in life" (p. 35). But Richie knew he was somebody when he played basketball in high school: "I was somebody else there: Mr. In-Your-Face, jiving and driving, looping and hooping, staying clean and being mean, the inside rover till the game was over" (1988, p. 35). In the war, Richie becomes aware that survival might mean becoming "somebody else," somebody other than the "Mr. In-Your-Face" he has been. He starts to realize that he must kill the Congs before

TABLE 4.4: STAGES OF A HERO'S JOURNEY: BEOWULF AND VIETNAM VETERANS

Stages	Beowulf	Richard Perry
	The Separation	
The Call	Called by the Storm-Geats to save Hrothgar and the Spear-Danes from Grendel	Perry volunteered to join the army when his plans for college fell through
The Separation	Left southern coast of Sweden to go help the Spear-Danes	Left his mother and little brother for a tour of duty in Vietnam
The Threshold	Fight with Grendel in the Hall of Heorot, tearing his arm off the rest of his body	Fight the Viet Cong; Perry defaced an enemy; no return to innocence
The Descent	Beowulf goes into the misty moor to fight the She-Wolf	Soldiers are forced to fight and kill in a war that was never declared by Congress; goals for the war were uncertain
	The Initiation	
Tests and Ordeals	Tests of physical strength and endurance due to the spell cast on swords.	No clear combat zones; no front; no rear; unfamiliar culture and language; drug abuse; financial corruption; racism; low moral , suicide, theft, murder
Into the Abyss	Battles with Grendel's mother in the sea cave all by himself	Soldiers in the jungle and rice fields; territory taken, lost, and taken repeatedly
The Transformation or Revelation	Beowulf saves the people and their countryside Beowulf realizes the greatness of his deeds; so do the people	Soldiers are hardened and made into killers The soldiers realize the cruelty of war and the corruption of the military
The Atonement and "boon"	Hrothgar gave Beowulf twelve treasures and Hygelac awarded him a golden sword	Soldiers received medals of honor; Myers writes the book to exonerate and heal his heart.
	The Return (Fulfillment)	
Returning to society	Beowulf was the most highly honored of men and ruled over Geatland for 50 years.	Soldiers return without parades suffering from Agent Orange or post-traumatic stress disorder. Patriots make the pilgrimage to the Vietnam Memorial in Washington DC

they kill him, and he knows that this means "being some other person" from whom he was on arrival to Vietnam: "Maybe that was what I had to be. Somebody else." (1988, p. 216). The posters should capture the character's reasons for joining the military, their fears, their values, their hopes for the future, their thoughts about the war, and their experience of critical events in Vietnam. Allow students to explain their completed posters to the class.

Verbal/Linguistic and Interpersonal Intelligences

Development of Multiple Perspectives: Letters From Vietnam

In *Fallen Angels* (1988), Richard Perry was chosen to write letters of notification to the families of the dead because of his skill with words. Throughout the novel, he also writes letters to his mother and brother and sometimes writes letters for others, such as for Peewee. These two kinds of letters organize Richie's experiences in Vietnam. Ask students to compare and contrast the letters at the beginning of the novel with those near the end. For instance, in the first polite letter that he wrote about Lieutenant Carroll's death, he describes his bravery and courage (p. 131). But near the end of the novel, Richie imagines a very bitter letter that he would write to the mothers of the men who lost their lives in a devastating carnage, the bodies of fallen comrades burned so that the enemy cannot mutilate them (p. 256). What other changes in Richie do students notice from reading his letters? Following this discussion, ask students to write one of the following letters:

- Write the letter that Richie wrote home, and later tore up, to his mother after Jenkins died (p. 46).
- Write a letter from one of the other characters to their parents, siblings, or girlfriends.
- Write a letter from Richie to his mother informing her that he'd received his second Purple Heart and that he would soon be home (p. 305).

Richie's bitterness seems to heal in the final scene: he hallucinates while soaring upward on the wings of a silver plane, the Freedom Bird, as Richie and Peewee "are headed back to the World" (p. 309).

Logical/Mathematical, Visual/Spatial Intelligences

Development of Multiple Perspectives: Making Maps and Timelines

In *Fallen Angels* (1988), the protagonist, Richard Perry, makes a quest. Ask them to trace Richie's journey through Vietnam two ways: follow his journey on a map and make a timeline of major events in the story. During his journey or quest, Richie traveled far from home, encountered obstacles, traipsed through rice paddies and jungle, and responded to danger and to challenge. Think about Richie's quest and draw a map or timeline that depicts it. Consider the following questions (Smagorinsky, 1991):

- Over what sort of terrain does he travel?
- What are the major events of the journey?
- What is the sequence of events?
- What direction does the hero travel?

Students should make preliminary notes and/or sketches of Richie's quest and choose the materials they will need for the project. They should be encouraged to add whatever creative touches they desire. They may include any sort of artwork they wish in order to illustrate Richie's quest. Be sure to share and explain projects with the class.

Bodily/Kinesthetic and Logical/Mathematical Intelligences

Development of Multiple Perspectives: The Minefield: A Simulation

This simulation of traveling with a platoon through a mined jungle was adapted by Rowland from Larry *Johannessen's Illumination Rounds: Teaching the Literature of the Vietnam War* (1992) on pages 35–38. Although he suggests using it prior to the reading, Rowland feels that the students react better to the activity if done following the reading of *Fallen Angels*. Although it takes some preparation, it is well worth it.

First, find a cooperative colleague with a prep period during your class and arrange to "park" students with him/her during this activity (1-2 periods depending on class size). Prepare seatwork assignment for students. Then, choose a squad of 3-4 students to prepare the classroom for the minefield simulation. This could also have been prepared previously by study hall students if the room were available. You will need beige or black thread, about 20 coffee or other tin cans, packing tape, and paper or visquine to cover the windows. You may even want to bring in some mats from the gymnasium if available.

In the empty classroom, cover windows with visquine and darken the room. Arrange the desks and furniture to create two trails through the room. Connect thread strung coffee cans at various levels across the pathways, using thread the color of the floor for best effects. Background noise of crickets helps set the tone, and a small space heater to warm up the room makes it the proper jungle temperature.

When the room is ready, bring in students in "squads" of three or four. Have each squad member put on a heavy backpack and carry a simulated weapon, such as a stick. Then allow them to decide who will be the captain, the point man, and the rear man with the M-60. The objective is to make it through a trail and back to the door of the room without tripping a wire and thereby "killing" the squad. Students may not go on desk tops; however, they may (and often do) crawl. Squads may want to take turns setting up the room, depending on how much time there is for this activity. To debrief the simulation, elicit student response in writing and discussion after the activity. Johannessen offers some questions to stimulate their thinking:

- Was teamwork important in your squad? Why or why not?
- What makes a good leader in this situation? A good point man? A good machine gunner?
- How did you feel as you went through the simulation?
- What have you learned about the conditions of war in Vietnam from this activity?

Verbal/Linguistic Intelligence

Development of Multiple Perspectives: Vietnam Literature By and About Women In Vietnam

Fallen Angels (1988) gives a detailed, realistic portrayal of the experiences of the young male soldiers in Vietnam; however, it only touches briefly upon the role that women played in the war. To introduce this topic, read Deborah Kent's *The Vietnam Women's Memorial* (1993). The memorial was dedicated in 1993 to honor the more than 13,000 women who served in the war. Most served as nurses, but others served as traffic controllers, intelligence officers, mapmakers, clerks, journalists and volunteers with other organizations aiding the Vietnam conflict. Young adult literature addresses the woman's experience for those left in Vietnam, those who fled to the United States, and those who suffered at home. For a touching love story of a girl who was shunned and mistreated because of her mixed heritage, read Garland's (1992) *Song of the Buffalo Boy*. Cao's (1997) *Monkey Bridge* is a story of a young Vietnamese woman who comes of age in America after fleeing Saigon. Rebecca Phillips, in White's *The Road Home* (1995), was a nurse in Vietnam who has difficulties in adjusting to American life when she returns home, until she finds her way to her soldier's home. In Hahn's (1991) *December Stillness*, fourteen-year-old Kelly tries to befriend Mr. Weems, a disturbed, homeless Vietnam War veteran who spends his days in her suburban library. A book most often included in high school curricula is Mason's (1985) *In Country*. This is a story of Sam who just graduated from high school and lives with her Uncle Emmet, a Vietnam veteran who suffers from Post Traumatic Stress Disorder. Sam is obsessed with finding out what took her father's life, and what really happened in Vietnam. For a more complete discussion of women's involvement in the war, read Kazemek's (1998) *The Things They Carried: Vietnam War Literature By and About Women in the Secondary Classroom*.

Letter to Local School Board

At the end of the unit, students write letters to their local school board recommending or censoring the book, *Fallen Angels*, for future classes. Last year's class of 28 students voted 3 against and 25 for continuing to teach the book. Those students opposed to the book objected to either the harsh language or the historical content of the book. Most students agreed the language was graphic in places, but felt they heard and used most of that language themselves outside of school. See Table 4.5 for excerpts from the students' letters.

TABLE 4.5: STUDENTS' AGAINST CENSORSHIP OF *FALLEN ANGELS*

"Maybe the language isn't appropriate, but the truth is."
"I had no idea how the veteran's of Vietnam felt. I now know they suffered greatly."
"This book provided a window to the past that all people should look through."
"You cannot always shield your child from the ugly, but truthful lives that men have lived."
" I have learned more about human nature in the past four weeks than ever before."
"*Fallen Angels* made me care about what happened 20 years ago and understand the unbearable times that Vietnam soldiers went through."
"I never really thought about Vietnam before we read this book in English."
"I don't like to read, but once I got started, I couldn't put the book down."
"*Fallen Angels* makes you feel like you are in the war, fighting with the soldiers around you."
"This book has a lot of heart . . . there are worse books with less meaning."

All the Multiple Intelligences

High School Class Reunion of 1969

As the culminating activity for this unit, students will create and then become fictitious members of the class of 1969. Students select a persona from their reading, interviews, or scrapbook family. In order to participate in this role-play, students need to wear a nametag that is color-coded to represent their view of the war (veteran, draft dodger, or conscientious objector). Some students should be ghosts of those killed in the war, who come as silent participants. When classmates ask about them, they can tell their stories. In any case, students should plan for the role-play by writing a character sketch of their persona so that they will be able to stay in character.

- Will they refer to classmates who are not present at the reunion?
- Will they talk about their character's friends who are no longer alive or have moved away?
- What have they done with their lives since leaving high school?
- What are the effects of the Vietnam War in today's world?

Divide students into groups to plan the Class Reunion Simulation. One group is responsible for planning, collecting, recording and playing the music for the big event. For instance, as an ice-breaker, the Class Reunion could begin by playing Jimi Hendrix's version of "The Star Spangled Banner." Another group will collect news headlines that occurred during their four years of high school (1965-1969) and read them at some point in the schedule of events. Another group will collect television news clips from the time period to be shown at the reunion. Other groups can plan the food, costumes, and entertainment for the event. One group needs to make the name tags which could include pictures taken from an old yearbook, and needs to organize the discussion groups so that each person has time to share their views. Each group should have all of the points of view represented, if possible. After meeting with one group, students rotate to another group. When students have had a chance to mingle with their old friends and share scrapbooks, they should take a group photograph for the archives. End the Reunion with a sharing of experiences as a whole class.

Young Adult Literature for Teaching Vietnam

Butler, Robert Olen (1992). _A Good Scent from a Strange Mountain: Stories._ New York: Henry Holt.
> In a collection of bittersweet stories about Vietnamese expatriates living in the American South, Pulitzer Prize-winning author Butler, blends Vietnamese folklore and American realities, lyric, dreamlike passages and comic turn, to create a panoramic tapestry of a people struggling to find a balance between their hearts and their hopes.

Cao, Lan (1997). _Monkey Bridge._ New York: Viking.
> Mai Nguyen, a young Vietnamese woman, comes of age in America after leaving Saigon in 1975, while her mother has difficulty adjusting to life in their new country. It is a moving novel filled with Vietnamese lore.

Deneberg, Barry (1995). _Voices from Vietnam._ New York: Scholastic, Inc.
> Tracing the history of the Vietnam War in chronological sequence, the volume contains personal narratives of those who were involved—from presidents and generals to soldiers, nurses, and Vietnamese citizens.

Edelman, Bernard (ed.) (1985). _Dear America: Letters Home From Vietnam._ New York, NY: Pocketbooks, a division of Simon & Schuster, Inc.
> Edelman has gathered over 100 letters from Vietnam Veterans that represent various attitudes about the war. Nothing, with the exception of his rifle, was more important to an American in Vietnam than mail. Soldiers could mail their letters free of charge; their reprieve from the war was writing and receiving mail.

Garland, Sherry (1992). _Song of the Buffalo Boy._ New York: Harcourt Brace & Company.
> Shunned and mistreated because of her mixed heritage and determined to avoid an arranged marriage, 17-year-old Loi runs away to Ho Chi

Minh City with the hope that she and the boy she loves will be able to go to the United States to find her American father.

Hahn, Mary Downing (1991). *December Stillness*. New York: Clarion. Fourteen-year-old Kelly tries to befriend Mr. Weems, a disturbed, homeless Vietnam War veteran who spends his days in her suburban library, though the man makes it clear he wants to be left alone.

Mason, Bobbie Ann (1985). *In Country*. New York: Harper & Row. Everyone Sam knows and cares about was heavily involved in the Vietnam War. She is obsessed with finding out what really happened over there and what it was really like. A trip to the Vietnam Memorial helped them cope with life when they returned.

Myers, Walter Dean (1988). *Fallen Angels*. New York: Scholastic, Inc. Perry, a Harlem teenager, volunteers for the service when his dream of attending college falls through. Sent to the front lines, Perry and his platoon came face-to-face with the Vietcong and the real horror of warfare. But violence and death weren't the only hardships: As Perry struggled to find virtue in himself and his comrades, he questioned why the United States was there at all.

O'Brien, Tim (1990). *The Things They Carried*. New York: Houghton Mifflin. They carried all the emotional baggage of men who might die. They carried grief, terror, love, and longing. They carried shameful memoirs, cowardice, and fear. It takes place in the adolescence of its characters, in the jungles of Vietnam and back home in America two decades later.

White, Ellen Emerson (1995). *The Road Home*. New York: Scholastic, Inc. Rebecca Phillips, 22, was a nurse in Vietnam who had seen endless bloodshed, horror, and suffering. When her helicopter crashed in the jungle, she faced a brutal showdown for survival that changed her forever. Unable to deal with life home in Boston, she searched for and found her way to her soldier's home and heart.

Children's Literature for Teaching Vietnam

Boyd, Candy Dawson (1987). *Charlie Pippin*. New York: Macmillan. A story in which a sixth-grade African-American girl embarks on a search for the truth about the Vietnam War and her father's part in it.

Bunting, Eve (1990). *The Wall*. Illustrated by Ronald Himler. New York: Clarion. A picture book that describes a grandfather who takes his grandson to visit the Vietnam Veterans Memorial to find his father's name.

Donnelly, Judy (1991). *A Wall of Names: The Story of the Vietnam Veterans Memorial.* New York: Random House.
Full-color and black and white photos portray the wall carved with names of all the United States soldiers who died in Vietnam. The Memorial was built to honor these men and women and to heal the deep wounds left by the longest and most hated one ever fought.

Gilson, Jamie (1992). *Hello, My Name Is Scrambled Eggs.* Illustrated by John Wallner. New York: A Minstrel Book, published by Pocket Books, a division of Simon and Schuster, Inc.
When his folks host a Vietnamese family that has come to settle in their town, Harvey enjoys Americanizing twelve-year-old Tuan.

Kent, Deborah (1995). *The Vietnam Women's Memorial.* Children's Press.
A book written in tribute to the over 13,000 women who served in Vietnam. The Memorial was dedicated in 1993. Most served as nurses, but others served as traffic controllers, intelligence officers, map makers, clerks, journalists and volunteers with other organizations.

Nhuong, Huynh Quang (1982). *The Land I Lost: Adventures of a Boy in Vietnam.* New York: HarperCollins Publishers.
A collection of personal reminiscences of the author's youth in a hamlet on the central highlands of Vietnam.

Paterson, Katherine (1988). *Park's Quest.* New York: Puffin Books.
Eleven-year-old Park makes some startling discoveries when he travels to his grandfather's farm in Virginia to learn about his father who died in the Vietnam War.

Tran, Khanh Tuyet Tran (1987). *The Little Weaver of Thai-Yen Village.* Illustrator Nancy Horn. San Francisco: Children's Book Press.

References

Anderson, C. (1996, March 23). *Vietnam scrapbook.* Presentation at NCTE Spring Conference, Boston. (Bethel High School, Spanaway, WA)

Beck, I. L., McKeown, M. G., McCaslin, E., & Burket, A. (1979). *Instructional dimensions that may affect reading comprehension: Examples of two commercial reading programs.* Pittsburgh, PA: University of Pittsburgh Language Research and Development Center.

Cronkite, W. (1997, April/May). The war on the evening news. In *Writing.* Curriculum Innovations Group (900 Skokie Boulevard, Suite 200, Northbrook, IL 60062-4028

Dylan, B. (1988) "Blowin' in the Wind" in *The Freewheelin' Bob Dylan,* Sony/Columbia ASIN: B0000024RQ.

Gardner, H. (1991). *The unschooled mind: How children think and how schools should teach.* New York: Basic Books.

Hendrix, J. (1970). "The Star Spangled Banner." Atlantic 82618-2.

Johannessen, L. (1992). *Illumination rounds: Teaching the literature of the Vietnam war.* Urbana, IL: NCTE.

Kazemek, F. E. (1998, November). The things they carried: Vietnam war literature by and about women in the secondary classroom. *Journal of Adolescent & Adult Literacy, 42* (3), 156–165.

Knap, J. (1998). Empathy and the Vietnam war. *Rock and Roll Hall of Fame Website*: Lesson Plan 36. http://www.rockhall.com/programs/institute.asp

McCaslin, N. (1990). *Creative drama in the classroom* (5th ed.). White Plains, NY: Longman.

Olson, C., & Schiesl, S. (1996). A multiple intelligences approach to teaching multicultural literature. *Language Arts Journal of Michigan, 12* (1), 21-28.

Rock and Roll Hall of Fame website: http://www.rockhall.com/programs/institute.asp

Shinner, T. (1997, April/May). *Writing.* Teacher's Edition. Curriculum Innovations Group, 19:7, p. 4. (900 Skokie Boulevard, Suite 200, Northbrook, IL 60062-4028)

Smagorinsky, P. (1991). *Expressions: Multiple intelligences for the English class.* Urbana, IL: NCTE.

Steinman, J., & Pritchard, D. (1984). "Holding out for a hero." Sung by Bonnie Tyler from *Footloose.*

Thompson, S., & Harris, R. (1992). The hero(ine)'s journey in life and literature. CATE.

Vacca, J. A., Vacca, R., & Gove, M. K. (1995). *Reading and learning to read.* New York: HarperCollins College Publisher.

"Vietnam reflexes and reflections" (1998). National Vietnam Veterans Art Museum. http://www.NVVAM.org.

Wittman, S. (1998). *Vietnam: Yesterday and today* (http://www.oakton.edu/~wittman/

Worsham, P and Garrard, B. (1996, March). *Of heroes and healing: Teaching the literature of the Vietnam war.* Presentation at NCTE Spring Conference, Boston, Massachusetts. (E.C. Glass High School, Lynchburg, VA).

CHAPTER 5

Children at Work: From Paterson's Textile Mills to Modern Sweatshops

Jackie Glasgow

Introduction

No one wants to purchase products made by children, teenage girls—or any other workers—stripped of their rights and forced to work long hours in harsh sweatshop conditions under armed guards for wages of twenty to thirty cents an hour. The people of the United States deserve to know the truth and have the chance to raise their voices to affirm the dignity of life and human rights over corporate indifference and greed. This unit is designed to explore and highlight employment practices in the Global Market, especially concerning children's labor and working conditions. The unit begins by asking students to search their homes for toys, games, and clothing and then to note the country where the product was made. Then they make a collage of drawings, magazine advertisements, or computer clip art of the objects they find and place the collage objects on a world map drawing lines to connect products with the country where they are produced. From this initial awareness of the Global Community, students will research the lives behind the labels through Global Sweatshop Resources included in the unit materials. Current videos produced by UNICEF and the National Labor Committee create a meaningful context for studying this theme. While Katherine Paterson's *Lyddie* (1991) is the primary novel for this unit, students may examine historical influences and modern perspectives of child labor laws in this country by also reading Susan Terris' *Nell's Quilt* (1987) and Virginia Euwer Wolff's *Make Lemonade* (1993). To gain further understanding of children's labor, the following picture books are recommended:

- Russell Freedman's *Kids at Work: Lewis Hine and the Crusade Against Child Labor* (1994)
- Stephen Currie's *We Have Marched Together: The Working Children's Crusade* (1997)
- Penny Colman's *Strike! The Bitter Struggle of American Workers From Colonial Times to the Present* (1995)
- Penny Colman's *Mother Jones and the March of the Mill Children* (1994)
- Susan Campbell Bartoletti's *Growing Up in Coal Country* (1996)
- Diane Hoyt-Goldsmith's *Migrant Worker, A Boy from the Rio Grande Valley* (1996).

Students utilize multiple intelligences to express their responses to past and present day sweatshop abuses. They write work poems, design awareness posters, and craft editorials on common themes found in their research. Students collect and present information about current child labor laws in places where they are employed. They study the "Race to the Bottom" occurring right here in the United States. Near the end of the unit, students draft a Bill of Human Rights expressing their beliefs about children at work. The culminating activity for this unit is the "Child Labor/Global Sweatshop: Making a Difference Project." Students choose both the topic and the form of the project, adhering to only one requirement: they must take their project outside the walls of the classroom into the real world. See Table 5.1 for MI Activities and Bloom's Taxonomy for Children at Work. The activities for this unit incorporate the six levels of complexity based on Benjamin Bloom's (1956) famous "taxonomy of educational objectives." The six levels are:

- *Knowledge*: recalling facts, terms, concepts, or procedures
- *Comprehension*: understanding, translating, paraphrasing, or interpreting material
- *Application*: solving problems or transferring knowledge from one setting to another
- *Analysis*: discovering and differentiating the component part of a larger whole
- *Synthesis*: weaving together component parts into a coherent whole
- *Evaluation*: judging the value or utility of information using a set of standards.

This taxonomy provides a kind of lens through which one can judge how deeply students' minds have been engaged by a multiple-intelligence curriculum. While it is not necessary to engage students in every activity, Table 5.1 shows how a teacher can articulate competencies that address all eight intelligences as well as Bloom's six levels of cognitive complexity.

TABLE 5.1: MI ACTIVITIES AND BLOOM'S TAXONOMY FOR CHILDREN AT WORK

	Bloom's Six Levels of Educational Objectives					
	Knowledge	**Comprehension**	**Application**	**Analysis**	**Synthesis**	**Evaluation**
Verbal/ Linguistic	Define Vocabulary words	Present one-minute vocabulary report to class	Write poems for two voices	Write letters to CEO's with recommendations	Create Bill of Children's Rights	Write an editorial on Child Labor
Logical/ Mathematical	Label a map of manufacturing sites for toys and clothing	Compare cost of living in various countries; determine manufacturing patterns	Make pie chart of daily schedule	Determine lunch menus for sixty cents a day	Design productivity charts; work safety charts	What is the cost for boycotting foreign made products?
Visual/ Spatial	Make vocabulary visuals	Make work safety posters	"Perfect Body" Collage	Construct a photo essay of children at work in your neighborhood	Design a political cartoon for a sweatshop product	Illustrate a book about children's work, health, literacy or other theme
Bodily/ Kinesthetic	Toy and clothes hunt	Impersonation of a main character	Weave cloth or rugs; Make maple syrup or candy	Collect items for school kits and/or health kits	Dramatic performance portraying a sweatshop issue	March for Children's Rights
Musical/ Rhythmic	Listen to songs about work	Compare songs from different periods and occupations	Write a work song of your own or do a copy change song	Write a rap on a child labor issue	Create a music video	Create and perform a Sweatshop ballet or modern dance
Interpersonal	Discuss the "bears" in Lyddie's life in a journal entry	Compare the gender issues in Lyddie's work place with your own	Interview children about working conditions	What are the cultural expectations for women and children at work?	Prepare a testimony for your local school board to keep children in school	Design a presentation to give at an elementary school for sweatshop awareness
Intrapersonal	Identify the "bears" in your own life	Compare Lyddie's "bears" to your own in a journal entry	Have you ever been dissatisfied with your gender? Explain	Discuss the advantages and disadvantages of your gender in the workplace	Think of solutions for gender equity in workplace	Self-reflection paper on "Making a Difference" project
Naturalist	Keep a journal of the changes in the environment near a workplace or new business	Collect objects from the natural world near a workplace	Categorize the objects collected	Compare natural observations with others	Complete a wildlife protection project	Evaluate the balance of nature near a workplace or new business

Verbal/Linguistic and Intrapersonal Intelligences

Bear Journal

In the opening paragraph of *Lyddie* (1991), the Worthens had to ward off a hungry bear that entered their wood cabin. They scrambled to safety high up in the loft and watched the bear explore the cabin. Eventually the bear discovered the oatmeal cooking over the fire, stuck his head in, burned his nose, raised up and ran out the door with the kettle still smoldering on his head. While this was a physical bear, Lyddie and her family faced many other "bears" or challenges throughout the story. Ask students to identify the bears in Lyddie's life. Hunger and starvation were the bears after her mother took the two younger girls and left she and Charlie to survive on their own the winter after the bear. Bears at the Tavern took the shape of loneliness, hard work, and indentured service. Leaving the Tavern and acquiring a job at the mill presented bears in the travel and boarding house experiences. At the mill, she faced down bears with the looms, overseer, roommates, friends, hard work, low pay, and the farm debt. And in the end, she felt the bear had won: The beast in her flew out at Mr. Marsden leading to her dismissal. As the bear stole her dreams, she grieved the loss of family and farm, and eventually the loss of her job.

In a journal, ask students to keep track of the bears—challenges, not complaints—in their lives. What are the bears in their personal life? What are the bears at school? If students work outside the home, do they find bears in the workplace? Discuss strategies for dealing with bears. Lyddie talks about staring them down. What other tactics does she employ? Ask students what works for them. How do they cope with tough situations? What gives them strength to go on when they are depressed? How do they help others through their down times?

Balance the negative focus of this journal with gratitude. Ask students to list aspects of Lyddie's life for which she was grateful, such as friends like Tiphenia at Cutler's and Diana at the mill. At the end of each journal entry, ask students to list five things they are thankful for that have occurred in the same time period. They might be thankful for small things such as a word of encouragement from a teacher or a friend. They might be thankful for global issues such as health, nutritious meals, a warm home, good friends, a loving family, or well-paying job. Have students reflect on the positive aspects of life and notice the difference between real bear challenges and complaints about less significant issues.

Verbal/Linguistic, Visual/Spatial, Interpersonal Intelligences

Literacy Issues

At the farm, Lyddie was reluctant to leave her unstable mother and the young children to attend school. Neither the Tavern Mistress nor the Concord Corporation assumed responsibility for Lyddie's education. But, as Lyddie's roommate and coworker at the mill, Betsy, read to her from Dicken's *Oliver Twist*, she connected strongly with Oliver's poorhouse, reminding her of the hunger she and her siblings suffered in the winter of the bear. Through the anticipation of the story's ending, Lyddie managed to escape the atrocities at the mill. Her desire to read was quickened as she learned of Betsy's aspirations to attend a female college in Ohio. Lyddie taught herself by pasting pages of text on the looms to puzzle out passages as she worked and by studying in all her free time at home. She sacrificed her hard-earned money to buy the book rather than continuing to pay the library fees for borrowing it. She secured her dream world and continued to learn the text. Notice how she used *Oliver* to check her spelling and grammar when writing to her mother. She certainly wished her sister, Rachel, could attend school rather than enter the workforce as a doffer. Her prized possession was the *American Notes for General Circulation* by Charles Dickens, given to her as a gift from Diana. When she had lost her home, family, and friend Diana, she took solace in the books she purchased—the *Bible* and the *Narrative of the Life of Frederick Douglass: an American Slave Written by Himself.* The joy of words and letters spewed from her mouth as she taught Brigid to read and their friendship grew as they discussed books together. Then after she was dismissed from the mill, she bought a dictionary to understand the charges of moral turpitude filed against her.

One of the strategies Lyddie used for teaching Brigid the alphabet was to illustrate the letters with an image to represent the letter (Chapter 20, *B is for Brigid*). Students should make a class ABC Book for weaving terms as Lyddie was doing or make one for a different occupation. Students could work collaboratively and independently describing the terms of their chosen career; or they could choose one that parallels with their study of global sweatshops such as athletic shoes, garment factories, or rug weavers. The books can be illustrated by hand, with photos or pictures, or generated with computer clip art.

Verbal/Linguistic, Intrapersonal Intelligences

Children Past and Present (1800-1990s): Asset or Liability?

The role of children in our society has changed from the time Lyddie lived in 1843 to our time in the new millenium. In the past, children were considered to be economic assets, or units of production as they worked on the farm, on the hunt, and in the factories. On farms, children were often raised in an extended family situation where there were several responsible adults to care for them. Home and work were fused as children's chores included both domestic and field responsibilities in a communal or social context. Children were raised to work until all the work was done before quitting for the day. They fulfilled obligations to kin before they considered pleasures of their own. By contrast, modern children are considered emotional assets but economic liabilities, because of the high cost of raising children. In some families, children are considered to be more liability than asset, especially if they become involved in social problems like violence, crime, drugs, pregnancy.

Today, American children usually live in a single-family, sometimes single parent setting where home and work are separate and private. Individual needs and desires of the children are often placed above family plans, especially when children play sports, take music lessons, or want to take a trip to the mall. In order to get students thinking about these changes, ask them to compare and contrast their lives with Lyddie's. How have times changed since 1843 when Lyddie went to work. What are the survival issues today? This discussion should prepare students to examine the cultural expections of girls and boys in the work place. Use this activity as prewriting for a verbal/linguistic activity such as composing a poem for two voices.

The poem for two voices has been popularized by Paul Fleischman in his poetry books *I Am Phoenix* (1985), and *Joyful Noise* (1988). There is more than one way to compose a poem for two voices as a way of responding to fiction; for instance, two characters from the same book or story can speak to each other about a critical event or situation they have in common thus giving two points of view. In this case, though, students are to compare either their personal or work life with Lyddie's. Sometimes Lyddie will speak, other times the student's voice will speak, and at times they will both speak together. Two people or two groups of people are needed to read the poem; each person or group reads one column. See Table 5.2 for Andrew's Poem in Two Voices comparing his life to Lyddie's.

TABLE 5.2: POEM FOR TWO VOICES FOR LYDDIE

A Poem for Two Voices	
Lyddie	

My name is
  Andrew
	My name is
	  Lyddie

We are so different.	We are so different

I work at
  McDonald's.
	I work at
	  a cotton mill.

I breathe
  grease.
	I breathe
	  lint.

I joined
  the union.
	I joined
	  the resistance.

I have benefits.	I am sick.

I dream for
  a car.
	I dream for
	  my family to be together.

I live
  with my family.
	I live
	  in a boarding house.

I make
  minimum wage.
	I make
	  a pittance.

I am
  frustrated.
	I am
	  lonely.

My boss harasses me
  verbally.
	My boss harasses me
	  sexually.

But we are alike	But we are alike
WE WORK LONG HOURS!	WE WORK LONG HOURS!
WE HATE OUR JOBS!	WE HATE OUR JOBS!

Intrapersonal, Interpersonal, Visual/Spatial Intelligences

Images of a Perfect Body

After Lyddie's mother deserted the farm and left two of her children behind for the winter, she eventually required Lyddie to work at the Cutler's Tavern to help pay off family debts. When Lyddie arrived at the tavern to begin her servitude, she was painfully aware of her sorry appearance. Her four-year-old dress was ragged and her boots no longer fit on her feet. She was also aware of her body changing to womanhood. She wondered "why she couldn't be as thin and straight as a boy? Why couldn't she have been a boy? Perhaps, then, her father would not have had to leave. With an older son to help, maybe he could have made a living for them on the hill farm" (Paterson, 1991, p. 22). In their journals, ask students to explore their own feelings about their gender, whether male or female. Have they ever been dissatisfied with it? If they had a choice, what gender would they choose to be? Why? What would be the advantages and disadvantages, specifically, in the context of the work place?

In *Lyddie* (1991), Mrs. Bedlow had the difficult job of preparing the urchin, Lyddie, who arrived on her doorstep, for her interview with the Concord Corporation. Mrs. Bedlow knew that girls are hired on the basis of their dress and shoes, "The Almighty may look at the heart, but 'man looketh on the outward appearance' as the Good Book says, and that goes for women, too, I fear" (Paterson, 1991, p. 54). Lyddie must spend everything she has plus take a loan from Mrs. Bedlow to buy the proper attire. There were other expectations of factory girls, as well. Regardless of their beliefs, they were expected to attend church in order "to look respectable" (p. 57). To work the looms in the mill, girls had to be physically fit, strong enough to run the shuttles, and physically dexterous enough to tie the weaver's knots. After working at the mill and becoming quite proficient, Lyddie also had to ward off the advances of her overseer, Mr. Marsden. While she was not fired for stomping on his toe, she was blacklisted for helping her friend resist him. Though she grieved the loss of her job and her dream of reuniting her family on the farm, she still considered Luke's invitation to marry as more than a compromise. She would not be bought or rescued from her vulnerable position of homeless fugitive.

Because of Lyddie's savings account, she had the power to decline Luke's offer for marriage; not many girls were so fortunate. In *Nell's Quilt* (1987), eighteen-year-old Nell struggled with her family and herself by taking a stand against an unwanted marriage that would get her family out of debt. Nell delayed the event by working on a quilt, slowly starving herself, while observing the unhappy lot of many women in turn-of-the-century Massachusetts; she finally arrived at a decision to rescue herself from the brink of death and take charge of her life.

In *Make Lemonade* (1993), Jolly, like Lyddie, was fired from her job for spurning a harassing boss. Jolly is a near-illiterate, seventeen-year-old unmarried mother of two young children working at low paying jobs to support her children. Fourteen-year-old LaVaughn, whose goal is to escape poverty by earning money to go to college, babysits for Jolly's children. The girls struggle with the care and nurturing of the young children while trying to earn a living. Jolly is too proud to ask for welfare and fears losing her children, but, with difficulty, LaVaughn persuades Jolly to enter a high-school program for young mothers. Jolly begins to "take hold" of her life and LaVaughn's grades go back up. Both girls take steps toward putting their lives on track.

The episodes from these three books provide an opportunity to discuss the cultural expectations of girls' appearance, health, earning power, and behavior in our society. Ask students to make a collage that portrays cultural expectations of young women. For the collage, students should collect and mount on construction paper images taken from current teen magazines that reflect a focus: fashion, perfect bodies, sports, cars, family, cigarettes, alcohol, or beauty products. Then, ask students to determine the messages sent by the advertisements. What are the needs and appeals used by the advertisement industry? What comprises the perfect female? What are the physical, emotional, and social attributes? What are the costs that girls pay to attain the ideal? What are the health issues? What happens if girls don't fit in? Are expectations for employment different for girls in other parts of the world? See Chapter 3, Characteristics of the Ideal All-American Girl, p. 80, for internet sites that discuss cultural expectations of women portrayed by the media.

Gender Discrimination in Global Sweatshops

In countries where girls are considered to be burdens to both their parents and to society, they either marry young or are sold to employers in much the same way Lyddie was sold to the Tavern. In Nepal, forty-percent of the girls are married by age fourteen and suffer the highest maternal mortality rate in the world as shown in the video *Ujeli: Child Bride in Nepal*, 1992. If not married, the girls are bought from their parents for a mere fifteen dollars and prepared for prostitution. They are adorned with expensive gowns, ornate jewelry, sandals, and then locked in their rooms to perform their service. In another video, *Tomorrow We Will Finish* (1994), we learn that more than 150,000 girls between the ages of seven and sixteen work in the 2,000 carpet factories of Nepal. With no adult to defend them, they work sixteen-hour days and receive punishments for not meeting high-production quotas. The video, *The World Through Kids' Eyes* (1997) documents the lives of six children from six countries. In India, twelve-year-old Yasmin is a burden to her family who must provide a dowry before she can marry. Orphaned and abandoned children in Brazil are often brutalized and even murdered at the behest of drug lords, merchants, and others who find them undesirable. Children in Peru struggle to continue their education as they work to support their families. A fourteen-year-old boy from South Africa recounts how he was shot during violent conflicts between members of the African National Congress and the Zulu Inkatha movement. In *Zoned for Slavery: The Child Behind the Label* (1995), the girls of Central America are treated like slaves in the garment factories. These girls work in harsh environments, called global sweatshops, where they are often punished or harassed. According to Pharis Harvey, Executive Director, International Labor Rights Fund, a sweatshop is "any workplace where the wages are inadequate, the hours too long, and the working conditions endanger safety or health, whether or not any laws are violated" (Rethinking Schools, 1997, p. 16). For additional global sweatshop readers, articles, videos, organizations and web pages, read, "The Human Lives Behind the Labels" by Bill Bigelow in *Phi Delta Kappan*, October 1997. He supplies an annotated bibliography with names, costs, and addresses for acquiring materials.

Sweatshops in Third World countries exploit workers in order to attain extreme profits for Western industries. Nike and other transnational companies make very conscious decisions to employ young, "passive, obedient, quiet" and poor Asian women in order to justify the maintenance of their companies. This stereotyping is clearly being used to perpetuate a horrific system of inequality. See information on-line at www.saigon.com/~nike/ or do a search on boycott Nike. Are there alternatives for these young women?

Logical/Mathematical, Interpersonal, Intrapersonal Intelligences

Working Conditions—You decide: Is this humane?

Ask students to compare Lyddie's working and living conditions to other children mentioned in their study of the global sweatshops. For Lyddie, they should mention the deafening noise, thirteen-hour-days in the hot summer, swirling dust and lint, low wages, working by the bell behind locked gates, meeting quotas, speeded-up looms, slowed- down clocks, no bathhouses, and inhumane treatment including sexual harassment from employers. If the girls left without permission they would be blacklisted from all the mills in Lowell; if they got sick or pregnant, they were dismissed and expected to pay their own medical bills. The girls lived apart from their families and only visited during the summer break; those girls with no families worked through the heat of the summer. They were expected to train others, even the lower-class Irish Catholics, without compensation for the time lost from their loom. They feared causing a fire by using oil lamps for light. Many girls became ill from the lint and dust they breathed on the job. In a journal entry or class discussion, respond to Lyddie's quote as she laments Betsy's ill health, "It ain't right for this place to suck the strength of their youth, then cast them off like dry husks to the wind" (Paterson, 1991, p. 113). No wonder Diana and her friends began laying groundwork for the Female Labor Reform Association and publishing *The Voice of Industry*. But if they dared a "turnout" or strike, they were blacklisted and dismissed. Students should compare their "job" with Lyddie's. What are grounds for dismissal? What benefits do they have? What kind of jobs support medical and dental benefits, paid holiday and personal leave days? What would the consequences be for speaking out against injustice?

Intrapersonal and Logical/Mathematical Intelligences

Wages: Is Time More Precious Than Money?

To introduce this lesson, ask students to make a pie chart of their use of a day's time. How much time each day do they spend studying, working, sleeping, eating, playing sports, watching T.V., talking on the phone, doing chores, and other activities. Ask students to rank items from most to least valuable and determine the underlying value for the ranking. If the students are working, what conflicts do they experience between home, school, and work? What would they do if they had more time? They should write a journal entry that reflects their attitudes and values concerning the demands of their time. Then ask students to compare their lives to the demands and lifestyle created in Lyddie's life after she went to work at the Tavern. Ask them to consider her salary, her expenses, her work time, and her leisure time.

Discuss Betsy's quote, "Time is more precious than money, Lyddie girl. If only I had two more free hours of an evening—what I couldn't do" (Paterson, 1991, p. 91). Why was it that Lyddie agreed with Betsy? How might Lyddie's life have been different had she taken some time for herself? While Lyddie may not have been able to take responsibility for her parents' debt, she did earn enough to provide for her basic needs. In other parts of the world today, this would not be true.

Lunch on Sixty Cents—The most basic, simple meal in Vietnam rice, vegetables, and tofu—costs sixty cents. So, three meals would cost $2.10, yet many of the young women at the Keyhinge factory making McDonald's/Disney toys earn just sixty cents after a ten-hour shift. Just to eat and get back and forth to work, the women estimate they would need to earn, after deductions, at least thirty-two cents an hour. So, the wages at the Keyhinge factory do not even cover twenty-percent of the daily food and travel costs for a single worker, let alone her family—not to mention rent, which averages

$6.00 a month for a single room, and other basic expenses. In order to make this wage real to students, sponsor a contest to see which student can make sixty cents go the farthest. On a given day, ask students to bring in the food and the grocery receipts showing what sixty cents can buy. Students might prepare the sixty cent foods and eat them for lunch in memory of the Vietnamese surviving on that amount of money.

Portfolio on Cost of Living/Minimum Standards—In addition to experiencing the limitations of living on sixty cents worth of food, students might do a project in which they discover what it takes to sustain a family's life in their geographical area. Where is the most inexpensive housing? What does it cost to live there? What clothes do they need, and how much do they cost? What food does a person need as a minimum for survival? How much would that cost? What about transportation? How much money do you need for a car, insurance, and gasoline to get to work? Is public transportation available? What is the minimum wage in the United States? Does that wage provide for subsistance living? What kind of life style does minimum wage accommodate? How much money would the students need to earn to sustain their present or dream lifestyle? What career choices would provide that lifestyle?

Productivity Issues—How productive can a human be? Lyddie worked fourteen-hour days. Girls working at carpet factories spent days and many nights weaving to achieve their quotas. Girls in toy and garment factories continue to work long hours just to afford dinner for their families. In order to test your productivity, keep track of your ability to concentrate on a particular activity—such as studying, working, reading, listening to music— keep a chart of the length of time you can engage in the activity before you need a break. Research the human factors that employers consider in the frequency and length of breaks at various workplaces. Examine the length of your class periods for productivity. What would be the perfect length for classes—forty-five minutes, fifty-five minutes or a block schedule that permits an hour and a half?

Verbal/Linguistic and Intrapersonal Intelligences

Work Poems

Ask students to write poems that capture some aspect of the human lives connected to the products we use every day. They can draw on any situation, product, individual, or relationship connected with this unit. As prompts, have students read work poems collected from *Saturday's Children: Poems of Work* by Helen Plotz (1982). In this book, there is a section of poems that date back to the nineteenth century when hundreds of young women were working in the factories of Lowell, Massachusetts (pp. 58–65). Students can also collect children's poems about work from internet sites such as http://www.oneworld.org/ni/issue292/simply.html and student poems in *Rethinking Schools* (Summer 1997, p 17). Ask students to brainstorm ways they might complete the assignment. For instance, they might write poems from the point of view of products, workers, or consumers. They might consider writing a dialogue poem from the point of view of worker and owner, or worker and consumer. They might write a poem in the form of a letter to one of the products or to one of the owners. See Table 5.3 for an "I Am Poem" suggested by Suzi Me (1987) which Natalia Ljahovic wrote capturing the intent of this assignment.

TABLE 5.3: "I AM" POEM ON CHILD LABOR

Template for "I Am" Poem Suzi Me	Child Labor Natalia Ljahovic
I am (two special characteristics you have)	I am only a child, a social outcast
I wonder (something you are curious about)	I wonder who enjoys the rugs I weave
I hear (an imaginary sound)	I hear doors lock behind me
I see (an imaginary sight)	I see young girls tending babies at their looms
I want (an actual desire)	I want to be free of the sex trade
I am (the first line of the poem repeated)	I am only a child, a social outcast
I pretend (something you pretend to do)	I pretend that the master dies
I feel (a feeling about something imaginary)	I feel my fingers bleed
I touch (an imaginary touch)	I touch the girls with AIDS
I worry (something that really bothers you)	I worry about my sister's future
I cry (something that makes you very sad)	I cry for my childhood
I am (the first line of the poem repeated)	I am only a child, a social outcast
I understand (something you know is true)	I understand that I must search for food
I say (something you believe in)	I say to hell with my family who sold me
I dream (something you dream about)	I dream of an unshackled life
I try (something you make an effort about)	I try to meet my quotas
I hope (something you hope for)	I hope my life will change
I am (the first line of the poem repeated)	I am only a child, a social outcast

As students read their poems aloud, ask them to record lines or images that they find particularly striking and note themes that recur. They should also give positive feedback to one another after each person reads. The ensuing discussion should focus on their observations, emotional reactions, and awareness of the problems inherent in child labor around the world. As a result of this discussion, students should be ready to consider solutions or activities that would mitigate against the exploitation of children. One idea would be to consider limiting their purchases to products made in the United States.

Intrapersonal, Interpersonal, Logical/Mathematical Intelligences

Made in the U.S.A.

Why do many people buy Nike and Reebok shoes? Are they better made or just better sold than their competitors? Do people buy athletic shoes for quality or for status? After understanding the lives behind the labels, are students more likely to buy sneakers made in this country? Students should take a poll in their school or community and determine what percentages of people are inclined to do so. They should make a graph of the survey reports compiled by the class members who participated in the project.

If students were to boycott foreign-made products, what costs would be incurred socially and economically? Students should study the prices of athletic shoes, soccer balls, T-shirts or toys comparing those prices, advertising appeals, appeals to social class, and lifestyles as well as quality/durability of the products. This project could be completed individually or collaboratively, with each group choosing a different product. The research should be presented in a portfolio that includes: advertisements mounted on construction paper and laminated, a discussion of advertising appeals, a cost comparison chart, data collection on quality as to whether generic products last as long as namebrands, and a self-reflection paper on the consequences of wearing certain labels to assure conformity.

Anthony Crotti, telling his story to ESPN Sportszone, believes we have the power—one dollar at a time—to decide who we will and who we won't support. He says that the main reason we don't buy generic brands is because we lack the courage of our convictions. Crotti bought a pair of New Balance running shoes, which weren't as "cool" as Nikes, but were very comfortable and made in the United States. They were eighty-five dollars, similar to the cost of Nike. "I'm sure that the labor costs were higher, but because NB doesn't have to support (an expensive) marketing and advertising budget, the cost equals out." He feels that sometimes we just have to say, "I don't have to have the latest and greatest, or the most expensive." You can make a moral choice with your dollars—JUST DO IT!

Verbal/Linguistic and Interpersonal Intelligences

Bill of Human Rights for Children

Freedman's *Kids at Work* (1994), a photo essay of Lewis Hine's Crusade Against Child Labor, shows children at work in mines, factories, streets and fields of the United States at the turn of the century. Some states had child-labor laws at that time, but most did not. Lewis Hine took his earliest photos for the National Child Labor Committee established in 1912 to investigate the working conditions of children and to mobilize public opinion against child labor. Child labor began to disappear only during the Great Depression of the 1930s when adults competed for even the lowest-paying jobs held by children. Federal legislation did not succeed until 1938 when President Franklin Delano Roosevelt signed the Fair Labor Standards Act which set minimum wage and maximum hour standards for everyone and placed limitations on child labor. Today federal laws prohibit children under sixteen from working during school hours and limit the number of hours they can work after school and on weekends. Yet, there are still children of recent immigrants who work beside their mothers in sweatshops; children of migrant farm workers who work to overcome poverty; and thousands of youngsters who either hold jobs prohibited by law or work excessive hours while attending school (Freedman, 1994, pp. 96–97).

Ask students to compose a Bill of Human Rights for the children of the world today. For more ideas, they can review the Declaration of Dependence written by the National Child Labor Committee, 1913 (Freedman, 1994, p. 91). Other resources are available at internet sites such as http://www.oneworld.org giving voice to children in third world countries. Working children are starting to organize all over the world to protect themselves not only from exploitation, but also from international action which they fear might deprive them of their livelihood. Although these children may never attain power over their circumstances this way, it is still important to listen to the perspective of this burgeoning activist movement. Students can read a document produced at an international conference with child delegates from thirty-three countries called, "We, the working children of the Third World, propose . . . Online at http://www.oneworld.org/ni/issue292/simply.html. In this document, issues of education, leisure, poverty, health care, security, and working with dignity are addressed. In creating a Bill of Human Rights, students should discuss and voice their priorities for equity and survival based on their research and understanding of the human condition.

All the Intelligences

Making a Difference Project

As a culminating experience for this unit on child labor and global sweatshops, students are asked to take their learning outside the walls of the classroom and into the real world. Students may choose from the following list of suggested activities or devise their own. Students may work collaboratively or independently and must submit a plan, rough drafts, and final renditions of the project to the class before moving into the larger school and community. If students work as a group, they must provide evidence that everyone has participated. The projects should show evidence of their research or raise important questions. Students must use at least five sources for collecting information for their projects, so even their questions should indicate their accumulated knowledge. Projects must be presented, revised and approved before leaving the classroom. See Table 5.4 for Eight Steps for Doing Projects.

TABLE 5.4: EIGHT STEPS FOR DOING PROJECTS

Eight Steps for Doing Projects
1. State your goal.
2. Put your goal into the form of a question.
3. List at least five sources of information you will use.
4. Describe the steps you will use to achieve your goal.
5. List at least three main concepts or ideas you want to research.
6. List at least three methods you will use to present your project.
7. Organize the project into a timeline.
8. Decide how to evaluate your project.

The following began with Bill Bigelow's list of projects mentioned in "The Human Lives Behind the Labels," *Rethinking Schools*, Summer 1997, and has been revised and adapted by local teachers who contributed to this project. From this list students may find ideas for their own projects or create a new one. In Bigelow's words, "Remember to go deep with this. Point out specific conditions that need changing, but also remember to talk about the deeper causes of these problems" (1997, p. 14).

- Write a detailed letter of opinion or inquiry to someone connected with children's labor or sweatshop issues—for example, Philip Knight; Michael Jordan; President Bush; U.S. labor unions; the Disney Company; the governments of China, Vietnam, or Indonesia.
- Prepare a testimony for your local school board or some other agency or office that could make a difference in liberating children at home or somewhere in the world.
- Design a presentation for other high school, middle school, or elementary classes in your district to teach others about these sweatshop issues. This dramatic performance might take the form of a skit, debate, monologue, impersonation, dialogue, interview, reader's theater, or puppet show.
- Write and illustrate a children's book about children's work, health,

literacy, or other related theme that you have read and then discuss it with an appropriate group of elementary children.

- Study the safety issues at the job where you work or a particular sweatshop. Make safety posters for your job and/or safety posters for a particular sweatshop.

- Become involved with a group that is trying to make a difference on these issues. Write up your reasons for choosing this group and what you hope to accomplish. For instance one group might become involved in Craig Kielburger's projects for *Free the Children* described on his web page at http://freethechildren.org. This group suggests many ways to become involved in helping children get to school by sending School Kits and/or Health Kits.

- Produce a rap, audiotape, video, or visual display on these issues. You should include an essay explaining and defending your point of view.)

- Videotape a one-minute T.V. commercial on a product from the point of view of the children working in sweatshops.

- Design a political cartoon for a sweatshop product and write an explication of the images and slogans utilized.

- Write a research paper or compile a scrapbook of important people who have campaigned against child labor. Read books such as Currie's (1997) *We Have Marched Together*, Colman's (1994) *Mother Jones and the March of the Mill Children*, and Colman's (1995) *Strike! The Bitter Struggle of American Workers From Colonial Times to the Present*.

- Visit a homeless shelter, YWCA, YMCA or other latchkey program and make arrangements to help children with their homework, read stories, or play games. Keep a journal of your activities and the children's responses.

- Read Russell Freedman's (1994) *Kids at Work: Lewis Hine and the Crusade Against Child Labor*. Construct a photo essay of children at work in your neighborhood, suburb, or community. Write an explanation of your choices or contrast your images with children in other countries.

- Make a collage of groups of children working in sweatshops in the United States. Read such books as Hoyt-Goldsmith's (1996) *Migrant Worker: A Boy from the Rio Grande Valley* and Bartoletti's (1996) *Growing Up in Coal Country*. Write a paper explaining the wages and working conditions of those groups of children.

- Write a Sweatshop Ballet, Mime, or Modern Dance. In the dance, portray the physical demands of the job—weaving textiles or rugs, sewing at machines or by hand; illustrate reactions to working conditions, hunger, thirst, and exhaustion. Find or write music that expresses the difficulty of the work. You may portray a particular sweatshop or design a medley.

- Write a research paper on the "Race to the Bottom" that is occurring here in the United States. Either publish the paper as an editorial in a local newspaper or place it on an appropriate website for others to read.
- Sponsor a "Right to Read Week." Collect materials about child labor or global sweatshops and distribute to teachers and/or parents willing to spend ten minutes a day reading the resources.
- Design your own project that demonstrates your understanding of these issues that can be taken beyond the classroom.

The point in asking students to engage in the "Making a Difference Project" is to move them beyond the anger of awareness of the problems toward projects that provide them an opportunity to use their knowledge for making a positive difference. The idea is not to promote particular organizations or forms of social action, but rather to convey the notion that no matter how overwhelming the problem of inequity and injustice is, there is always something positive that can be done, however small the step may be. See Table 5.5 for Assessment Rubric for "Making a Difference Project."

TABLE 5.5. ASSESSMENT RUBRIC FOR "MAKING A DIFFERENCE PROJECT"

"Making a Difference Project" Student's Name:				
Project:	Superior (8)	Effective (6)	Competent (4)	Not Yet (2)
Research Skills				
Information and Facts				
Product Development				
Organization				
Responsibility and Effort				
Presentation				
Making a Difference				
Peer Evaluation				
Self-Reflection				
Self-Evaluation				

Verbal/Linguistic, Intrapersonal Intelligences

Self-Reflection Papers

At the end of the unit, ask students to write about their experiences throughout the unit and especially about their "Making a Difference Project." This paper should serve to debrief students from such an emotionally charged topic. They should include aspects of the unit that they found to be especially beneficial, as well as aspects that could be improved. They might discuss which, if any, of their attitudes changed about work and about child labor issues. Students might also reflect on their attitudes about social action. Do they feel they made a difference, even though a small one, in affecting a change in the way people feel about child labor/sweatshop issues? In this paper, students might assess the multiple intelligences they utilized in the unit. Which intelligences do they prefer? Which ones did they nurture in this unit? Which ones would they like to strengthen in the next unit? Students might suggest topics of interest that emerged during the unit which they would like to pursue at a later time.

References

Bartoletti, S. C. (1996). *Growing up in coal country*. New York: Houghton Mifflin Company.

Bigelow, B. (1997, October). The human lives behind the labels. *Phi Delta Kappan, 79* (2), 112–119.

Colman, P. (1994). *Mother Jones and the march of the mill children*. Brookfield, CT: The Millbrook Press.

Colman, P. (1995). *Strike! The bitter struggle of American workers from colonial times to the present*. Brookfield, CT: The Millbrook Press.

Currie, S. (1997). *We have marched together: The working children's crusade*. Minneapolis: Lerner Publications Company.

ESPN SportsZone. (1998, October). Labor abuses must be addressed. http://espn.sportszone.com/gen/features/sneakers/wednesday.html

Fleischman, P. (1985). *I am Phoenix: Poems for two voices*. New York: Harper & Row.

Fleischman, P. (1988). *Joyful noise: Poems for two voices*. New York: Harper & Row.

Freedman, R. (1994). *Kids at work: Lewis Hine and the crusade against child labor*. New York: Clarion Books.

Harvey, P. (1997, Summer). Sweatshop definition. *Rethinking Schools, 11* (4), 16.

Hoyt-Goldsmith, D. (1996). *Migrant worker: A boy from the Rio Grande valley*. Photographs by Lawrence Migdale. New York: Holiday House.

Kielburger, C. (1998, October). *Free the children*. http://freethechildren.org.

McDonald's/Disney linked to sweatshops. (1998, October). http://www.nlcnet.org/resources.htm.

Me, S. (1987). "I am poem." In R. Padgett (Ed.). *The teachers & writers handbook of poetic forms*. New York: Teachers and Writers Collaborative.

Paterson, K. (1991). *Lyddie.* New York: Puffin Books.

Plotz, H. (Ed.). (1982). *Saturday's children: Poems of work.* New York: Greenwillow Books.

Terris, S. (1987). *Nell's quilt.* Canada: HarperCollins Canada Ltd.

Tomorrow we will finish. (1994). A UNICEF Production Video (26 minutes), distributed by Maryknoll World Productions, PO Box 308, Maryknoll, NY 10545-0308. Tel: 800-227- 8523.

Ujeli: Child bride in Nepal. (1992). Video (60 minutes) produced by Maryknoll World Productions, PO Box 308, Maryknoll, NY 10545-0308. Tel: 800-227-8523.

We, the working children of the Third World, propose . . . http://www.oneworld. org/ni/issue292/simply.html.

Wolff, V. E. (1993). *Make lemonade.* New York: Henry Holt and Company.

The world through kids' eyes. (1997). Video (67 minutes) produced by Maryknoll World Productions, PO Box 308, Maryknoll, NY 10545-0308. Tel: 800, 227, 8523.

Zoned for slavery: The child behind the label. (1995). Crowing Rooster Arts. Distributed by the National Labor Committee, 275 Seventh Avenue, 15th Floor, New York, New York 10001. Phone: 212-242-3002.

Preservation of People, Places, and Planet

Part II includes literature based on the theme of *Preservation of People, Places, and Planet*. The thematic units in this section focus on developing strong interpersonal relationships that overcome racial prejudice, poverty, and persecution. Preservation of family and friends can be difficult when one is challenged by gangs, unconventional relationships, and unpopular opinions. Preservation of places is important when the environment is threatened by poachers, greed, or even natural phenomena. Confronting our fears about nuclear war moves us to consider the options and preserve the planet.

Chapter 6: The importance of preserving family and peer relationships is presented in a unit, "Living in an Outsider Society," built on the *Outsiders* by S.E. Hinton. The culminating activity for this unit is a Sock Hop with 1960s music, costumes, and decorations.

Chapter 7: Preservation of people is introduced by the unit: "Building Tolerance and Empathy Toward Others" which pairs Trudy Krisher's *Spite Fences* with Harper Lee's *To Kill a Mockingbird*. To develop empathy for others, students bring in an old pair of shoes, write a story about the person's life who wore them, and then contribute the shoes to a local charity.

Chapter 8: "New Ties, Unconventional Relationships" is a unit based on works by M. E. Kerr: *Deliver Us from Evie*, *Night Kites*, and *'Hello,' I Lied*. This unit deals primarily with the personal intelligences as young adults explore serious issues of sexual identity in unconventional relationships. The culminating activity is writing and performing Reader's Theater from one of the books.

Chapter 9: Issues of "Conformity vs Individuality" are explored in Cormier's *Chocolate War*. Students either create a video tape of a favorite scene or a music video that summarizes the novel.

Chapter 10: "Preservation of Self and the Environment" through reading Will Hobbs' *Beardance, Bearsong* and *Big Wander*. After researchig the Ute history and culture, students simulate the Annual Ute Bear Dance as the culminating activity for the unit.

Chapter 11: "Confronting the Nuclear Threat" to preserve the planet with Robert O'Brien's *Z for Zacharia*. The culminating activity for this unit is a field trip to a local bomb shelter where students survive a twenty-four hour visit with students from a rival school.

Chapter 6

Living in an Outsider Society
with S.E. Hinton

Allison L. Baer

Introduction

Drive-in movies and roller skates, car hops, Elvis, Poodle skirts and bobby socks, blue jean jackets, blue mustangs and switchblades. Ah . . . the Fifties . . . the Sixties. Nostalgia kicks in and the mind wanders back to wistful thoughts of Sock Hops and *Happy Days*. These, however, were not happy times for Ponyboy, Johnny, Sodapop, and the rest of the gang. They are *The Outsiders*. The reality, however, for kids like Ponyboy and Johnny was sleeping in a park on cold nights and seeing blood-covered switchblades flashing in the streetlights.

By immersing students in the music and images of the Fifties and Sixties, Hinton's (1967) *The Outsiders* took on new life and students found themselves reflecting on such questions as what rules dictate who is on the inside and who is on the outside? Who wrote those rules? What are the rules for my group? How do I know if I fit in? The goals for this unit are for students to search out the answers to these questions and to develop a better understanding of not only the society of the Fifties and Sixties, but also the society in which they find themselves on a daily basis: home, community, and school. The culminating activity for *The Outsiders* was a 60s Sock Hop for which the students planned food, researched the music, learned dances, made poodle skirts, drew posters, and wrote invitations. Although the *The Outsiders* served as the focal book for the unit, students also explored other young adult novels with protagonists who live in an outsider society. In literature circles (Daniels, 1994), students chose contemporary books about adolescents who live in outsider situations, such as:

- Shusterman's (1996) *Scorpion Shards*
- Bennett's (1998) *Life in the Fat Lane*
- Carter's (1998) *Up Country*
- Philbrick's (1993) *Freak the Mighty*
- Spinelli's (1990) *Maniac Magee,* or
- Klass's (1996) *California Blue.*

See the annotated bibliography at the end of the chapter for other young adult literature related to this theme. In the end, students were encouraged to reflect on their own lives and to examine ways they live inside or outside of society's norms.

During this unit, students strengthened their personal intelligences by participating in both group and individual activities. Visual/spatial and logical/mathematical learners excelled in creating flow charts based on character's lives and forming Individual Learning Plan Posters to help Ponyboy (and themselves) succeed in school. Students utilized their musical/rhythmic intelligence while making music videos, writing song lyrics, and creating sound tracks. Students developed bodily/kinesthetic intelligence by constructing freeze frames from movies such as *West Side Story* and *The Outsiders*, and preparing dances for the Sock Hop. Students utilized their verbal/linguistic intelligence to write the script for a reader's theater and to compose found poems and copy-change poems. See Table 6.1 for unit activities to nurture and develop the students' multiple intelligences for the thematic unit, "Living in an Outsider Society."

Working with Your Weakest Link

One of the goals for this unit was to help students identify their strengths and strengthen their weakest links. "My motto is to find out what you cannot do and discard it. Find another way," says Dr. Florence Haseltine, director of the Center for Population Research of the National Institute of Child Health and Human Development. Dr. Haseltine has difficulty with writing tasks and frequently uses the telephone instead of writing notes to communicate with others on the job (Armstrong, 1993, p. 177). Many of the students participating in this study also had difficulty with reading and writing activities in the English classroom. They were urban youth experiencing both difficult home situations and low self-esteem. Multiple Intelligences theory provides for our weakest links through cognitive bypassing. As Armstrong admonishes, "don't

TABLE 6.1: MI ACTIVITIES FOR "LIVING IN AN OUTSIDER SOCIETY"

Intelligence	Activities
Verbal/Linguistic	Reflective journals
	Character journals
	Found poems
	Copy-change poems
	Flow charts
	Reader's theater
	Book report
Logical/Mathematical	Flow charts
	Analogies
	Venn diagrams
	Compare/contrast characters and themes
	Neighborhood maps
Visual/Spatial	Graphics for flow charts
	Backdrop for music video
	Story board
	Individual Learning Plan Posters
	"Me and My Groups" collage
Bodily/Kinesthetic	Choreography for music video
	Sock hop dances
	Simulations
	Scavenger hunt
	Freeze frames
Musical/Rhythmic	Music video
	Sock hop songs
	Writing song lyrics
	Compare/contrast period music
	Create sound tracks
Interpersonal	Group projects for sock hop, music video, flow chart
	Group discussions
	Community service
Intrapersonal	Response journals
	Reflective essays
	Feelings inventory

let your learning difficulties get in the way of being a successful human being" (p. 175). He says the chances are great that there are tests available to detect something wrong with the way just about anybody in our society learns. To help students identify their weak links and see them as learning opportunities, ask them to complete the Learning Difficulties Checklist in Appendix B developed by Armstrong (p. 255–257). Use the results of the Checklist to guide students through the unit activities. Help them learn to *bypass* their difficulties and find alternative ways to get the job done.

Interpersonal, Intrapersonal, Bodily/Kinesthetic Intelligences

Ice-Breaker

As students walk into class the first day of *The Outsiders* unit, give them either a red badge or a blue badge. Unknown to them, red stands for greasers and blue stands for Soc's. Proceed with the daily activities making sure that the Soc's are favored over the Greasers. In this manner, students will experience bias based on nothing but the color of a little scrap of paper. Listen politely to the students wearing the blue badges; ignore the students wearing red badges. While a few of the students may realize what is going on, the majority often do not. At some point, engage them in a discussion about how they are feeling about the class today. After letting them in on the "secret," discuss their feelings regarding the prejudice and injustice they have just witnessed. Other questions to raise are: "Who was on the inside and who was on the outside? How did you know? Who decided who was on the inside? How did it feel?" As a follow-up activity, ask students to make a "Me and My Groups" collage. Ask them to collect photographs, computer graphics, and/or magazine images to represent the various groups they belong to, such as family, relatives, church, friends at school, team members of sports they play, girl/boy scouts, and other groups to which they may belong. Then, as they present their posters to the class, ask them to explain how they felt about their affiliation with those groups.

If time permits, show the film, "The Eye of the Storm" by ABC News. This documentary explores the nature of prejudice in a dramatic third-grade experiment, much like the one described above, conducted in a small Midwestern town without ghettos, blacks, or campus unrest. It demonstrates how quickly wholesome, friendly school children can be infected with the ugly virus of discrimination that leads to frustration, broken friendships, and vicious behavior. Follow-up the film viewing by making a list of examples of prejudice or outsider experiences that students have encountered themselves or that they have learned about on the radio, TV, or reading.

Verbal/Lingustic, Visual/Spatial, Bodily/Kinestic and Logical/Mathematical Intelligences

Reading and Responding to **The Outsiders**

Students read and responded to the text in a variety of ways. Sometimes the reading will be oral; other times round-robin, or independent readings. Students respond to the text through a variety of reader response activities. See Table 6.2 for Reader Response Activities.

TABLE 6.2: READER RESPONSE ACTIVITIES

Reader Response Questions:
- Draw one character and write a few lines about why you chose that character.
- Choose any passage you have read so far. How did it make you feel and why?
- Response to your project: How did you come up with your plan? What was easy? Hard? What do you like best? What have you learned about yourself in doing this project?
- What does this section of the book remind you of? Describe the section and the memory.
- As you read, write down interesting or unknown words. Why did you choose these words?

Mnemonic Exercise:
- List the main characters of the story. How can you remember these characters?
- Picture a house in your mind. Place one character in each room. Why did you place them in these rooms? For example: Dally in the kitchen because he likes to eat and Darry in the garage because he works on cars.
- After you mentally place each character in the house, draw the house and where each character is placed.
- Reflect on the process (see Reader Response above).

Freeze Frame:
- In groups, choose one moment in time from the book.
- Choose who will become which character and how the group will portray a picture of the chosen scene.
- Each group will place themselves into that picture and create a life-size, 3 dimensional picture of the chosen scene.
- Reflect on the process (see Reader Response above).

Individual Learning Plan Poster:
- Discuss Pony's problems in school and brainstorm ways to help him study.
- Ask students to work either collaboratively or individually to create a poster containing study strategies to help Pony (and themselves) become more successful in school.

Visual/Spatial and Logical/Mathematical Intelligences

Creating a Flow Chart

When students work in cooperative learning groups it is like creating a huge multi-faceted MI brain with many different mouths, feelings, and personalities. Bringing together the individual MI strengths and weaknesses allows showcasing those strengths and enhancing the weaknesses. The creation of a flow chart, described in Linda Campbell's (1996) *Teaching & Learning Through Multiple Intelligences*, requires strong visual/spatial and logical/mathematical skills. Students strong in visual/spatial intelligence prefer showing their understanding through the process of charting, drawing, and manipulating their environment. The logical/mathematical students have a keen ability to discern patterns and relationships as well as to problem solve. The flow chart draws on both of these intelligences as well as verbal/linguistic (taking

notes), bodily/kinesthetic (cutting out construction paper shapes), and working in a group requires strong interpersonal skills (if the students want to get
anything accomplished). As well as accomplishing the above MI goals, the
flow chart shows the consequences of the actions and decisions of each character and how they contributed to their lives on the outside of society. The
main idea of the flow chart is to chart the "flow" of a given character's life
throughout the book. Students select one of the five lead characters, Ponyboy,
Sodapop, Darry, Johnny, and Dallas, and form groups based on their selection.
Through a discussion, students decide that the main events in a character's life
should be what is included in the flow chart: little things, like what they ate
for dinner or when they put the grease in their hair were not as important as
situations like Johnny and Ponyboy meeting Marcia and Cherry at the Nightly
Double Movie. Each group selects the media and form they will use to create
the flow chart. They select supplies available in the room such as perforated
computer paper, construction paper, markers, crayons, scissors, and glue sticks.
It could be mounted horizontally on a chalkboard or vertically on the wall.
Using perforated computer paper for dot matrix printers allows them to un-
fold pages as they progress through the novel. The students should revisit the
beginning of the book and trace the main activities of their character. By
focusing on the big events, they can easily create a list of eight or ten items to
construct their flow chart. At the end of each class period, students should
complete a self-evaluation form. See Table 6.3 How Well Are We Doing?

Another type of assessment used while students worked in their groups is
the Teacher Observation Sheet. This assessment provides a way to discuss the
student's progress in interpersonal relationships. It also provides a way for
students to set goals for future group sessions. See Table 6.4 for the Teacher
Observation Sheet.

TABLE 6.3: HOW WELL ARE WE DOING?

How Well Are We Doing? Self-Evaluation for: _____
- I worked hard in my group:
  All of   Some of   Not much of   the time
- I listened to others when they were sharing ideas:
  All of   Some of   Not much of   the time
- I thought my group listened to me when I shared ideas:
  All of   Some of   Not much of   the time
- I thought my group had good ideas:
  All of   Some of   Not much of   the time
- I enjoyed working with this group
  All of   Some of   Not much of   the time
- List one thing your group did well today.
- List one thing you will improve tomorrow.

TABLE 6.4: TEACHER OBSERVATION SHEET

Teacher Observation Sheet			
Student Name:			Date:
	Always	Most of Time	Not Enough
Active Participation 1. Stays on task 2. Allows others to remain on task 3. Comes prepared with materials 4. Respects property			
Interaction with Others 1. Uses appropriate voice and language 2. Respects opinion of others 3. Interacts appropriately with others 4. Refrains from harassment			
Level of Enthusiasm 1. Displays positive character 2. Displays productive character 3. Displays a concern for learning			
Making Progress			
Student's Comments and/or Reactions: **Future Goals (designated by student)**			
Student's Signature:		Teacher's Signature:	

Adapted from Meinbach, Rothlein, and Fredericks, 1995, p. 69. Reprinted by permission of Christopher-Gordon Publishers, Inc.

Following the flow of each character's life proves to be an invaluable tool in that students become experts on their chosen character. While they focus on one particular character, they also see the strong relationships between the other characters. There is no easy way to separate each character, and many times the students will have to decide if a certain event is a "main event" in their person's life. All in all, this proved to be a satisfying cooperative activity that not only required strong MI skills, but also links the entire reading of the book, shows the consequences of each character's decisions and actions, strengthens the students understanding of life on the outside of society; it also provides for some creative decorations as the flow charts "grow" around the room. See Table 6.5 for excerpts from student flow charts.

TABLE 6.5: STUDENT FLOW CHARTS

Ponyboy Flow Chart—This portion is from the events revolving around Ponyboy and Johnny's time spent in the country church. Students might choose to use church shapes for events happening in the church and bubbles for decisions and thoughts.

Ponyboy and Johnny started off on the trip to the church. When they finally got there it was a stone floor and was very creepy.	Ponyboy was remembering how he would always go to church after his parents' death. He even asked Johnny and Soda to come.	Ponyboy woke up in the church thinking he would still be at home and Darry would wake him for breakfast. Then he quit pretending and finally woke up.	Ponyboy woke up finding out that he was alone. Johnny had left for the store.

Dally Flow Chart—This portion is from the events at the beginning of the book. The students may choose to draw simple pictures on each square to display the written events.

Ponyboy got jumped by Soc's and Dally and the rest of the gang chased them off.	Dally went to the theater with Johnny and Ponyboy.	Dally talked dirty to Cherry and Marcia.	Dally went to get drinks for Ponyboy, Johnny, Marcia, and Cherry.

Verbal/Linguistic, Logical/Mathematical and Interpersonal Intelligences

Character Resumé

With the good understanding that students gain in completing flow charts, they will be ready for another kind of divergent thinking: the character resumé. As a group activity, students will learn even more about their characters by preparing a resumé for them. See Table 6.6 for Resumé Information developed by Colleen Ruggieri, teacher at Boardman High School in Youngstown, Ohio. Students may not prefer to use all this information, and they may want to add categories of their own, but a resumé certainly can help make a character come alive. The resumé can also give students helpful ideas on everything from explaining the character's motivation to conceiving dramatic incidents demonstrating the character's personal traits.

TABLE 6.6: CHARACTER RESUMÉ

Character Resumé
Name: Address: Phone Number: Date & Place of Birth: Height/Weight/Physical Description: Citizenship/Ethnic Origin: Parents' Names & Occupation

cont.

TABLE 6.8: *GREASER'S PARADISE*

As we walk through the alley of the shadow of fear
We take a look at our lives and realize there's something here.
Cause we've been running and chased so long that
People don't even care if we were gone.
But we ain't never crossed a Soc that didn't deserve it
Cause they treat us like nothing, you know that's heard of.
They better watch out for what they do and say
Or they may be gone someday.
We really hate to say it but that's the way things are
Cause we never know when their gonna pull up in their car.
We're the kind of people no one wants to be like
But we're on our knees and praying all night.

Chorus:
 We've been spending most our lives living in a greaser's paradise.
We've been running most our lives living in a greaser's paradise.
We keep living most our lives living in a greaser's's paradise.
We keep running most our lives living in a greaser's paradise.

Look at the way they got us living
We don't live a normal life cause we were raised like this.
So we gotta stick together like a family.
If we don't stick together we won't be a team.
We're uneducated fools with switchblades in our hands
We're ready to go no need to plan.
We're a low down pack together forever that's the way things go.
We're all just a heartbeat away.
ving life do or die, what can we say?
We're together now but will it stay that way?
The way things are going, we don't know.
Tell me why are we so blind to see,
That the ones we hurt are you and me?

Chorus

Soc after Greaser, Greaser after Soc,
Minute after minute, hour after hour.
Everybody's running but half of them ain't watching
All they wanna do is keep on talking.
They say we got to learn but nobody's here to teach us
If they can't understand us, how can they reach us?
We guess they can't , we guess they won't, we guess they want to
That's why we know our lives are out of luck, Fool.

Chorus

time to rock around the clock. As a culminating celebration of *The Outsiders*, students will organize a Sock Hop that showcases all of the students' MI strengths. They also will decide which society members they will choose to be at the sock hop—the insiders or the outsiders. Most students choose to attend dressed as "outsiders". Students are actively involved because they choose what piece of the celebration belongs to them.

After some discussion of just what a Sock Hop is—try using clips of American Bandstand for this—students brainstorm the necessary components of the *Outsiders Sock Hop*. They usually create a list that includes music, food, dances, decorations, costumes, and invitations. Most classes choose to invite other school personnel and their parents to attend this gala event. Then, students sign up for the committee of their choice and the planning begins to bring the Sock Hop into a reality.

Literature Circle Project

Students are now ready to broaden their thinking and reading to other stories and protagonists living in an outsider society. Daniel's (1994) literature circles provide an excellent structure to accomplish these goals. Students convene into groups according to the books they have chosen to read from the reading list. See annotated bibliography at the end of the chapter. The circles have regular meetings with discussion roles rotating each session. Since these students may be new to literature circles, they need to learn the roles that Daniels' (1994) suggests: discussion director, literary luminary, illustrator, connector, summarizer, vocabulary enricher, travel tracer, investigator, and passage picker. Students choose the role they will assume each day, and when they finish reading the book, each circle plans a way to share highlights of their reading with the rest of the class. The *Holes* (1998) group might use their visual/spatial intelligence by first taking pictures of their circle projects with the digital camera and then putting them into a PowerPoint presentation. The *Up Country* (1998) group, perhaps strong in bodily/kinesthetic intelligence, might make a video of key events in the story that students acted out and taped. Another group with strong visual/ spatial intelligence might make a photo essay for Klass's *California Blue* (1996): taking photographs of the wildlife surrounding a new highway construction project; taking pictures of the caterpillars, shovels, plows, and tar trucks that would cut the new road. They might capture John's dilemma: should they take the insider view by supporting the highway project or the outsider view by starting a campaign to save the land? The group that reads Bennett's (1998) *Life in the Fat Lane* may produce a dramatic Reader's Theater production. Each member may write a part that reflects Lara's conscience as she changes from perfect model to fat girl. By portraying voices in Lara's head, they captured all of her losses: her parent's "perfect" marriage, her friends, her boyfriend, her doctors, and then the lessons she learned. The group that read *Ender's Shadow* (1999) by Orson Scott Card, might make a PowerPoint presentation of the ways Bean survives in the ghettos of

Rotterdam. These projects are evidence of what happens when students have opportunities to learn through their strengths: unexpected and positive cognitive, emotional, social, and even physical changes appear.

Young Adult Literature for Teaching Life on the Outside of Society

Bennett, Cherie (1998). *Life in the Fat Lane*. Bantam Doubleday Dell Publishers.

A teenager who has it all—perfect body, personality, grades, boyfriend—loses it all and becomes part of an outsider society when she gains a hundred pounds.

Card, Orson Scott (1999). *Ender's Shadow*. New York: Tor.

Ender Wiggin is a very bright young boy with a powerful skill. One of a group of children bred to be military geniuses and save Earth from an inevitable attack by aliens, known here as "buggers," Ender becomes unbeatable in war games and seems poised to lead Earth to triumph over the buggers. Meanwhile, his brother and sister plot to wrest power from Ender.

Carter, Alden R. (1998). *Up Country*. New York: Scholastic Point Signature.

After his alcoholic mom was arrested, Carl had to give up his stolen car radio operation and move up in the country to live with his straight-laced relatives. He wanted to run away, but how can you run away from people who really care?

Christopher, J. (1967). *The White Mountains*. New York: Simon & Schuster.

After seeing the extreme change in his favorite cousin after being "capped" by the Tripods, Will Parker decides that he would rather face the risks in seeking freedom in the White Mountains than go along with the accepted fate of all thirteen-year-olds in his society.

Cushman, K. (1995). *The Midwife's Apprentice*. New York: Clarion.

Beetle gets her name from the time she was found sleeping in a dung heap. Set in Medieval England, the homeless and orphaned Beetle becomes the midwife's apprentice in her search to belong.

Hesse, K. (1997). *Out of the Dust*. New York: Scholastic.

This tale of the Dust Bowl, tells of a young girl tragically burned in a freak accident and her journey to find where she belongs.

Hobbs, W. (1989). *Bearstone*. New York: Atheneum.

Cloyd Atcitty does not fit in with the other Native Americans on the reservation. A rebel and trouble-maker, Cloyd is sent to live with Walter Landis in the Colorado mountains. While there, Cloyd learns how to be a part of a small, caring community.

Klass, David (1996). *California Blue*. New York: Scholastic.
Discovering a beautiful blue butterfly, John is forced to choose between an important cause and his own townspeople when he learns that the butterfly is unique in all the world and that the local mill must be closed in order to save it.

Lowry, L. (1993). *The Giver*. Coldwater, MI: Houghton Mifflin.
A young boy experiences the ultimate in life outside of the accepted norm when he inherits an unwanted position of extreme responsibility from the Giver.

Philbrick, R. (1993). *Freak the Mighty*. New York: Scholastic.
When the two outcasts of the preschool—the intelligent, dwarfed, handicapped Freak, and his oversized, tough, slow-witted friend—team up, they find that even outcasts can do great things.

Rapp, Adam. (1997). *The Buffalo Tree*. New York: HarperCollins Publishers.
While serving a six-month sentence at a juvenile detention center, thirteen-year-old Sura and his friend, Coly Jo, struggle to survive the stocks' sadistic games with their bodies and spirits in tact. Will they be tough and cool, or real and true?

Sachar, Louis (1998). *Holes*. New York: Farrar, Straus and Giroux.
Through a miscarriage of justice, Stanley Yelnats ends up at a boys' juvenile detention center, Camp Green Lake. Through digging holes in the desert, he finds his first real friend and a new sense of himself.

Shusterman, Neal (1996). *Scorpion Shards*. New York: Tor Books.
Five archetype outsiders—the fat kid, the pimply kid, the sex symbol, the scaredy-cat, and the destructive kid—come to terms with the inner demons in a journey of self-discovery and redemption.

Spinelli, J. (1997). *The Library Card*. New York: Scholastic.
Four short stories tell the tales of four adolescents living outside of their societies and how the magic of an illusive library card helped them fit in.

Spinelli, J. (1990). *Maniac Magee*. New York: HarperCollins Publishers.
Homeless, Jeffrey Magee finds himself in the middle of a long-standing racial dispute between the East Side blacks and the West Side whites. Through a process of legendary "miracles", Maniac is able to not only

bridge the gap between the two races, but also to find himself a place within society.

References

Armstrong, T. (1993). *7 kinds of smart: Identifying and developing your many intelligences.* New York: Penguin Books.

Campbell, L. (1996) *Teaching and learning through multiple intelligences.* Needham Heights, MA: Allyn & Bacon.

Coolio, (Performer). (1995). *Gangsta' paradise.* (Compact Disc Recording). New York: Tommy Boy Records.

Daniels, H. (1994). *Literature circles: Voice and choice in the student-centered classroom.* York, ME: Stenhouse Publishers.

Dunning, S., & Stafford, W. (1992). *Getting the knack.* Urbana, IL: NCTE.

"Eye of the storm." ABC News Documentary. The Center for Humanities, Inc., Box 1000, Mount Kisco, New York 10549.

Hinton, S. E. (1967) *The outsiders.* New York: Dell.

Kagan, S. (1994). *Cooperative learning.* San Juan Capistrano, CA: Kagan Cooperative Learning.

Lazear, D. (1991) *Seven ways of teaching.* Palantine, IL: IRI/Sky Light Publishing, Inc.

Meinbach, A. M., Rothlein, L., & Fredericks, A. D. (1995). *The complete guide to thematic units: Creating the integrated curriculum.* Norwood, MA: Christopher-Gordon Publisher, Inc.

Puff Daddy. (Performer). (1997). *Victory.* (Compact Disc Recording). New York: Bad Boy Records.

Smith, W. (Performer). (1997). *Men in black* (Compact Disc Recording). New York: Columbia.

Shangri-Las. (Performers). (1988). *Leader of the pack.* (Compact Disc Recording). Venice, CA: Dominion Records.

Steam. (Performers). (1989). *Na na hey hey kiss him goodbye.* (Compact Disc Recording). Santa Monica, CA: Rhino Records.

Yankovich, A. (Performer). (1996). *Amish paradise* (Cassette Recording). Santa Monica, CA: Scotti Brother.

CHAPTER 7

Building Tolerance and Empathy Toward Others with Harper Lee

Joyce Rowland

Introduction

tol-er-ance n. the capacity for or the practice of recognizing and respecting the beliefs or practices of others —*The American Heritage Dictionary*

When Gardner's theory of multiple intelligences was first introduced to the public, the idea of "personal intelligences" proved especially controversial. Those believing in traditional models for intelligence were relatively more accepting of spatial intelligence and could contemplate the idea of musical or bodily-kinesthetic intelligences, but the thought that an individual's relation to others or to himself could be construed in a cognitive way was even more difficult to embrace. Perhaps in 1996 when Daniel Goleman's book, *Emotional Intelligence*, became a best-seller, people began to grasp the importance of the personal intelligences. In his book, Goleman says:

> Much evidence testifies that people who are emotionally adept—who know and manage their own feelings well, and who read and deal effectively with other people's feelings—are at an advantage in any domain of life, whether romance and intimate relationships or picking up the unspoken rules that govern success in organizational politics" (p. 36).

Goleman goes on to say that people with well-developed emotional skills are more likely to lead effective, productive lives. People who have difficulty controlling their emotions tend to sabotage their ability to think clearly and to focus on their work. Goleman reports the results of a study done at Bell Laboratories that examined the lives of their most valued and productive electrical engineers who worked in teams of up to 150 people. They found that the best engineers were not those with the highest IQ, the highest academic credentials, or the best scores on achievement tests, but rather those whose social skills included "effectively coordinating their efforts in teamwork; being leaders in building consensus; being able to see things from the perspective of others; persuasiveness, and promoting cooperation while avoiding conflict . . . taking initiative . . . and self-management in the sense of regulating their time and work commitments well" (p. 163). All such skills are aspects of the personal intelligences.

If we want our students to succeed, regardless of how we define that success, we must consciously work to help them develop their Interpersonal and Intrapersonal intelligences. Howard Gardner says, "I find the personal intelligences the most intriguing and challenging ones; they tell us the most about other cultures; and, of course, they tell us the most about ourselves" (In Boggeman, Hoerr and Wallach, 1996, p. viii). This unit, *Building Tolerance and Empathy for Others*, is designed to help teachers in that quest.

The types of intolerance shown by humans toward each other is often a theme in literature, but nowhere is it more dramatically and humanistically portrayed than in Harper Lee's *To Kill a Mockingbird* (1960). With the great depression as a backdrop, the story of a town's blatant display of prejudice against one Negro, Tom Robinson, touches the innermost places in all men's hearts and makes us ponder the questions asked by generations of children: How can one human being treat another so inhumanely just because his skin is a different color? The parallel plot of Boo Radley takes the idea of prejudice past the color issue to a whole new level of perception concerning human cruelty to those who are different from the cultural norm.

This idea of intolerance becomes an exceptionally poignant theme to present to high school students; where better to open the eyes and hearts of people to one another than in the young. Just as Howard Gardner suggests we understand the different intelligences of students, so this unit suggests that students understand the many differences in their peers and to show empathy for their plights by putting themselves in other people's shoes. Although Americans come from a variety of different cultural backgrounds, the tie that binds us together is our humanity.

Perhaps Houston Roberson (1995), who worked on the Teaching Tolerance Project of the Southern Poverty Law Center, summarized the objectives of this unit best in the following words:

> Students will recognize and respect the beliefs or practices of others by understanding that:
> - in the course of American history, some individuals and groups have been feared and discriminated against simply because of who they are.
> - some groups who are victimized in one instance become perpetrators

in other instances.

- certain psychological and historical pressures can cause people to exclude and victimize others.
- such discriminatory behavior violates the basic principles that bind us as a nation—equality, liberty and justice for all. (Roberson, 1995, p. 3)

Although the unit is centered around the novel *To Kill a Mockingbird* (1960), one book is simply not enough to encompass the range of intolerance in America. Other readings must be incorporated to gain the full impact of realization and, thus, understanding. In order to provide students with background knowledge about the history of intolerance in America as a backdrop for all the other readings, begin the unit with Carnes' (1995) *Us and Them: A History of Intolerance in America*. The format of this text allows teachers the ease of choosing which chapters to cover if time prevents a close look at all of them. This magazine-style text with very readable chapters contains stories of intolerance throughout American history. Students can read about such topics as the religious intolerance of the Salem witch trials in the 1600s, the abusive treatment of the Chinese railroad and mine workers of the late 1800s, the heinous actions of the white Floridians who wiped out an African-American community, the abhorrent treatment of the Japanese-Americans in the World War II Internment Camps, and the modern day intolerance against homosexuals. From these readings, students should identify the psychological and historical pressures that cause people to exclude and victimize others.

As an important follow-up to the unfair jury afforded to Tom in *To Kill a Mockingbird* (1960), other important readings will help students learn to recognize and to respect the beliefs of others before and after the Civil Rights Movement. In Meyer's *White Lilacs* (1993) set in 1921, twelve-year-old Rose Lee sees trouble threatening her Black community when the Whites decide to take the land there for a park and forcibly relocate the Black families to an ugly stretch of territory outside the town. In Taylor's *Roll of Thunder Hear My Cry* (1976), students read about Cassie's struggle to overcome intimidation and degradation at school and at home while maintaining pride and respect for her family. In *Freedom's Children* (1993) by Levine, students read the stories of 30 African-Americans who were children fighting segregation in the South during the 1960s. In Krisher's *Spite Fences* (1994) set in the 1960s, thirteen-year-old Maggie Pugh is drawn into violence, hatred, and racial tension in her small Georgia town. For other selections to teach tolerance, see the bibliography provided at the end of this chapter. Through reading these novels and responding to them utilizing their multiple intelligences, students will develop and strengthen their many intelligences. Given the unit focus on the personal intelligences to help students recognize and respect the beliefs of others, lessons are categorized in the other five intelligences: Bodily/Kinesthetic, Verbal/

Linguistic, Logical/Mathematical, Musical and Visual/Spatial. See Table 7.1 for Activities Using the Multiple Intelligences to Build Tolerance and Empathy for Others.

TABLE 7.1: ACTIVITIES USING THE MULTIPLE INTELLIGENCES TO
BUILD TOLERANCE AND EMPATHY FOR OTHERS

Multiple Intelligences	Interpersonal Intelligence	Intrapersonal Intelligence
Verbal/Linguistic	Discuss in literature circles Debate laws Write script for puppet show Create a radio endorsement supporting Atticus for president Write newspaper articles Set up a poetry coffee house Teach a lesson Write a classroom "Bill of Rights"	Write reader response logs Write diary entries Create a poem Carry out the shoes project Write skits
Logical/Mathematical	Create southern meal Make a map of neighborhood Make a chart of social classes Flow chart the action of story Create a "Moody Timeline" Do an internet project	Create a family tree Research and share southern recipes Graph the violence in the story
Visual/Spatial	Put together a museum display Make a photo story Create a collage of themes Draw a storyboard	Make puppets Design a computer generated map Draw an important moment in story Critique film
Bodily/Kinesthetic	Make a human map of neighborhood Produce a puppet show Create a scavenger hunt Do a tableau/frieze Plant a flower garden	Role play a juror Demonstrate target shooting Demonstrate whittling
Musical/Rhythmic	Perform freedom songs Perform Civil Rights Movement music Perform ballad Create sound effects for a scene Make audio tape representing scenes from the book	Collect freedom songs Collect songs from Civil Rights Movement Compose "Ballad of Tom Robinson" Compose a rap for social justice

Historical Perspectives of Intolerance in America

Verbal/Linguistic, Bodily/Kinesthetic, Visual/Spatial, Musical/Rhythmic to Build the Personal Intelligences

Us and Them: A History of Intolerance in America (1995)

The magazine-like book, *Us and Them: A History of Intolerance in America* (1995), distributed as a student text in the *Shadow of Hate* (1995) teaching kit, is an excellent text to introduce the concept of intolerance in America to students. Kits with 25 copies of *Us and Them* are available free to any school upon request. It also includes a teacher's guide by Houston Roberson and an excellent videocassette entitled *The Shadow of Hate: A History of Intolerance in America* (1995). For more information, check out the Southern Poverty Law Association website at www.splcenter.org/ and click on "Teaching Tolerance" and then on "Classroom Resources."

Distribute copies of *Us and Them* (1995) to the students. Discuss the title and read the introduction aloud. Next, divide the students into the number of groups equal to the number of chapters you wish to cover. Five or six chapters gives a solid representation. Selection of the chapters is at the teacher's discretion, but possible suggestions are included here. Assign each group one of the following chapters:

- "The Silencing of Mary Dyer" (religious intolerance)
- "A Rumbling in the Mines" (Chinese intolerance)
- "Ghost Dance at Wounded Knee" (Native American intolerance)
- "Untamed Border" (Mexican intolerance)
- "A Town Called Rosewood" (African-American intolerance)
- "Home Was a Horse Stall" (Japanese-American intolerance during World War II)

Explain that each group will be given one day to "teach" its chapter to the class. Group members must abide by the guidelines provided in Table 7.2 *Us and Them* Project Rules. Encourage them to be as creative as possible. Students will need 3-4 days of in-class preparation.

TABLE 7.2: *Us and Them* PROJECT RULES FOR TEACHING A CHAPTER

Us and them Project Rules for Teaching a Chapter

1. You have 20-35 minutes to teach your chapter. (20 is the minimum, 35 is the maximum)
2. Your lesson must include the following (several may be combined):
    • some historical background
    • a summary of your chapter
    • a reading of an excerpt

cont.

- a piece of music, with or without words, relating to your lesson
- a handout for the class
- a frieze
- a student centered activity
- a poster depicting the stereotyped image of the group that your lesson is about vs. a real person of this group
- modern follow-up on this intolerance
- titles and authors of at least three books for further reading (bring these to class to put on display table)

3. You must turn in the following:
   - Lesson Plan including: Objectives, Procedures, Materials
   - a copy of your Handout
4. If you need a pass to the library, see me.
5. If you will need TV and VCR, or computer with presentation device, or overhead projector, see me at least one day before your project is due.

In order to help students prepare to teach a lesson, ask them to create an assessment rubric or adapt the following one found in Table 7.3 Evaluation Sheet for *Us and Them* Teaching Project.

TABLE 7:3 EVALUATION SHEET FOR US AND THEM TEACHING PROJECT

Evaluation Sheet for Us and Them Teaching Project   Grade_____
Names of Group Members: _____
Chapter: _____   Date: _____

	Great	Good	Adequate	Poor	Missing
1. Historical background	____	____	_____	____	_____
2. A summary of your chapter	____	____	_____	____	_____
3. A reading of an excerpt	____	____	_____	____	_____
4. Music relating to lesson	____	____	_____	____	_____
5. Handout for class	____	____	_____	____	_____
6. A frieze	____	____	_____	____	_____
7. Student-centered activity	____	____	_____	____	_____
8. Poster of stereotypes	____	____	_____	____	_____
9. Modern follow-up	____	____	_____	____	_____
10. Books for further reading	____	____	_____	____	_____
11. Lesson Plans	____	____	_____	____	_____
Objectives	____	____	_____	____	_____
Procedures	____	____	_____	____	_____
Materials	____	____	_____	____	_____
PRESENTATION:					
12. Enthusiasm	____	____	_____	____	_____
13. Showed knowledge of lesson	____	____	_____	____	_____
14. Voices able to be heard	____	____	_____	____	_____
15. Equal participation within group	____	____	_____	____	_____
16. Creativity	____	____	_____	____	_____
Comments:					

As a follow-up to the chapters, show the film *The Shadow of Hate* (1995). Teachers may assign students to describe in writing the segments that interested them the most, and to analyze why those segments were effective.

Recognizing Intolerance in *To Kill A Mockingbird*

Verbal/Linguistic Intelligence to Build Personal Intelligences

Writing Reader Response Logs

After introducing students to the book *To Kill a Mockingbird* (1960), reading should be assigned in five chapter increments. For each reading, students should write a Reader Response Log.

A Reader Response Log is a written response to the reading in which the writer reacts to the reading. It may include answers to the following questions about each scene in the reading, but it should not be written as if it were just answering questions. These are just reminder questions suggested by Nancie Atwell (1990) as prompts for reading response journals to help students respond.

- What did the author have to know about to write this story?
- Finish this sentence: I love the way the author . . .
- Tell about the main character in your story. What kind of person is your character, and why is he or she your favorite?
- How does this book or story make you feel?
- Were you able to guess what was going to happen at the end? How?

Most importantly, the writer should be warned not just to summarize but actually to discuss the actions and moods of the characters in the readings. Reader Response Logs are usually evaluated holistically, with grades of A, B, C, or D assigned (or 1, 2, 3, or 4). Any log that is all summary, no matter how detailed, can receive no higher than a C. Students may be asked to share portions of their logs as discussion starters in class. See Table 7.4 for a Sample Reader Response Log Entry that I wrote from Chapters 6 and 7.

TABLE 7.4: SAMPLE READER RESPONSE LOG ENTRY

What a night for Jem, Dill and Scout! I can imagine sneaking through a neighbor's garden, but I can't imagine looking, or rather peeking, in the windows or being shot at! When the shadow first appeared, I thought it was Mr. Radley, but now I realize it was Boo. What kind of person is this Boo Radley? It must have been Boo who roughly sewed up Jem's pants. (By the way, how could Jem have gone right out in the crowd without his pants?) Now I see a change, a maturity, in Jem as he slowly realizes that Boo sewed up his pants, and Boo has been leaving them the presents in the tree, including the soap-carved figures of themselves. It is Jem who understands the sadness of Boo's plight when Mr. Radley cements up the tree.

Logical/Mathematical, or Bodily/Kinesthetic or Visual/Spatial Intelligences to Build Personal Intelligences

Small Group Activities for Chapters 1-5 of To Kill a Mockingbird

Discussion days for Chapters 1-5 of *To Kill a Mockingbird* may start with these introductory group activities. Divide the class into three groups with each group doing a different activity, or any one activity could be used. Allow only twelve to fifteen minutes for preparation. Presentation of these three projects to the class will ensure that everyone has a good background of characters and locations for a better understanding of the story.

Group 1 (Bodily/Kinesthetic Intelligence)—Make a human map of the neighborhood. Include Atticus, Jem, Dill, Miss Maudie, Scout, Miss Rachel Haverford, Mrs. Dubose, Miss Caroline, and Boo Radley. Each person should stand where his or her character lives on the street. If there are enough people, include the two important trees in the story, the "poisoned" pecan tree and the tree where Scout finds the gum.

Group 2 (Visual/Spatial Intelligence)—Create a visual of Boo Radley as Jem describes him in Chapter 1. The visual should include images that represent the prejudice held by townspeople toward Boo since they haven't seen him for so long. Use any available supplies to make it a 3-D visual, or dress up a member of the group to look like Boo. You will need to provide art supplies.

Group 3 (Logical/Mathematical Intelligence)—Construct Atticus' family tree as far back as possible on a big piece of paper which you have taped to the wall. Page 87, which is from the novel, may be added to the reading to help this group.

Verbal/Linguistic and Visual/Spatial to Build Personal Intelligences

Literature Circles

After experimenting with many different approaches to book discussion groups, I have found Harvey Daniels' *Literature Circles: Voice and Choice in the Student-Centered Classroom* (1994) to be the most effective. Even though Daniels recommends Literature Circles as a technique for generating discussion for groups of students choosing books according to their interest, I have found they work just as well for students reading the same chapter of a book. Divide students into groups of five and ask each group member to select a particular role. The five roles, adapted from Daniels (1994), are as follows:

- Silent Leader—Write 3 or 4 thought provoking questions, to be used only if no one else starts the discussion. These questions will probably start with "how" or "why."

- Excellent Excerpt Elaborator—Pick out three excerpts that were meaningful and merit discussion. Be prepared to tell why the excerpts were chosen.
- Word Wizard—Pick out four or five words that were very important to the reading. Jot down why the words were important.
- Artist with Attitude—Draw an important moment from the reading, either literally or symbolically.
- Thread Thrower—Connect something in the book to the world outside, either personally or generally. Write a brief description of the connection.

When the groups have prepared, they sit knee to knee in order to discuss. Anyone may begin the discussion by starting with what he or she has prepared. The Silent Leader should begin only if no one else will. Allow most of the rest of the period for discussion. Each group should be allowed to share the results of their discussion with the class, if not that day, then the next.

Logical/Mathematical and Visual/Spatial Intelligences to Build Personal Intelligences

Create a "Moody" Time Line

This is a good activity to do either in addition to or in lieu of the reader response log for a five chapter reading assignment, especially in the second half of the reading of *To Kill a Mockingbird* (1960). Simply have students create a 10-sentence time line on these chapters. Their sentences should reflect the ten most important things that happened in the chapters, in the order they happened, and should cover the entire reading assignment. In addition, each sentence of the time line should be color-coded to represent mood or emotion. The student must include a color key to reveal the emotion that each color represents. Students should share these in small groups with their peers, or if time allows, share with the entire class. Adding the mood color representation to the time line creates more stimulated discussion about the action.

Logical/Mathematical and Verbal/Linguistic Intelligences to Build Personal Intelligences

Mockingbird Internet Project

Ask students to choose a topic related to *To Kill a Mockingbird* (1960) to research on the Internet. Topics might include: racial prejudice, Harper Lee, mockingbirds, censorship of books, Southern social classes, jury system of justice, penalties for rape, choosing juries, or other trials similar to Tom Robinson's.

In a computer lab setting, ask students to do an Internet search on their topics using three different search engines. Make a chart, either by hand or on the computer, which includes the name of the site, the address of the site, a summary of the site approximately five sentences long, and a rating for the site: five stars for best, one star for worst. Post these in the classroom for student referral and discussion.

After students have collected their information, ask them to write either a report or a research paper. Other alternatives would be to ask them to share their information orally with the class, present their information on a poster, construct a PowerPoint slide show or hyperstudio presentation.

Visual/Spatial, Logical/Mathematical and Bodily/Kinesthetic Intelligences to Build the Personal Intelligences

Comparison of Tom Robinson to the Boy in 12 **Angry Men**

Twelve Angry Men (1990) is a tension-filled drama of twelve jurors working to reach a verdict in the trial of a teenage boy accused of murdering his father. Although outnumbered eleven to one in the initial vote, juror number eight uses his analytical powers to force each of the other jurors to put aside his own prejudices long enough to realize a reasonable doubt concerning the guilt of the boy. It is a careful, fascinating study in characterizations and social prejudices.

In class, view the film *Twelve Angry Men* (1990). The story and screenplay were written by Reginald Rose; The movie was originally published in 1957 and then renewed in 1984 by Orion-Nova. In 1990, MGM/UP Home Video, Inc. released a video version starring Henry Fonda, Ed Begley and E.G. Marshall. The approximate running time is one hour thirty-three minutes. Any version of the movie will work, or check local community theaters to see if there are currently any live performances.

After viewing the movie, ask students to write a response to the following assignment: Choose one of the jurors who originally voted guilty in *Twelve Angry Men* (1990). Discuss what was in the background of that character which caused him to believe the boy on trial to be guilty. In other words, discuss the juror's hidden prejudices, the causes for those prejudices, and the results of those prejudices. See Table 7.5 for two students' analyses of prejudice for Juror Number 10.

Share the papers in either small group discussion or in full class discussion. Then, select a jury to play the stereotypical roles portrayed in *Twelve Angry Men* (1990), create the jury room setting, and ask that jury to deliberate the case of Tom Robinson. This is an impromptu role-playing exercise following the discussion that would be done with little or no preparation.

TABLE 7.5: STUDENT ANALYSIS OF PREJUDICE FOR JUROR NUMBER 10

"Juror Number 10 was an obnoxious loud mouth who always had something to say. I think that he was just looking at who the person was that was on trial and judging him and not even looking at the facts like some of the other jurors were. He was more or less just stereotyping this boy and saying that he was from the slums, that he's a teenager who doesn't respect his father, and he was obviously very troubled. I think that when he was a kid, he must have had someone that instilled those thoughts into his head, and raised him to think this way because at the beginning he was not going to change his mind for anything. The boy was guilty and that was that." (Excerpt from Sarah Brugler's paper)

"Most of the men had family or home and life problems. The one I chose, Juror Number 10, had all of these. His problems were mostly with his son. He had always tried to teach his son not to walk away from a fight. A 'wimp' was not accepted in his home. Well, after a while, he realized he had taught his son well. This was noticed when the son punched him. Because of that experience, he believed that the sixteen-year-old boy was guilty. All of these years he held a grudge toward kids, and he realized he could pay him back. He was really trying to get back at his son for what happened." (Excerpt from Becky Dyson's paper)

Intolerance Toward African-Americans During the Civil Rights Movement

Verbal/Linguistic, Body/Kinesthetic, Visual/Spatial Intelligences to Build the Personal Intelligences

Show the Video, **The Civil Rights Movement in America.** *Then Have a Puppet Show Based on the Novel* **Freedom's Children** *(1993)*

Another activity that can be done at the same time that students are reading *To Kill A Mockingbird* (1960) centers around other young adult literature from the Civil Rights Movement such as *Freedom's Children* (1993) by Ellen Levine. The teacher should take a copy of the novel and literally tear it apart by chapters. Teachers may even wish to have the pages laminated so that they can be used year after year. Divide students into eight equal groups and assign each group a chapter to present to the class. Chapter 3 is divided into two halves. If there are not enough students to have three or four in a group, then the teacher may choose to assign two chapters per group or may decide to eliminate some of the chapters.

The assignment is that the students, following a careful reading of the chapters, will write a script for a puppet show depicting one or several of the most important scenes from the book. Be sure to tell them to read it aloud to each other first so that they both know the material and so that they can discuss it before choosing the scenes they wish to script. They may even want to do more research on the historical happenings in their chapters before they begin. The students may choose to make their own puppets, or they may use commercially made puppets which they might be able to borrow from a library or other places such as churches. The students may even choose to use animal representations of the people. Using animals promotes the idea that prejudices can be held against anyone; it is not just a Black/White issue. Allow two to three days of class time for small group preparation and at least a week before the actual performances.

A problem teachers often encounter when doing puppet shows is what to use as a theater. I suggest that the teacher go to a builder in the community who has children in the school and ask him if he would build three wooden frames, 6' by 3', with a supporting bar across them a little more than halfway up. If these three frames are then hinged together correctly, they can fold back on themselves for ease in storage and yet can still be opened up with the sides left at a 45 degree angle so that it will stand on its own. The bottom portion of the frames could be covered with bulletin board paper so as not to add any weight onto the frame. Once built, it will last for years to come and many teachers in the school could use it.

Respecting the Beliefs of Others

Verbal/Linguistic Intelligence to Build the Personal Intelligences

Writing a "Bill of Rights" for Our Classroom

Ask students to choose a partner. Discuss the definition of "The Bill of Rights." The teacher might have a poster of "The Bill of Rights" available, or the students may have one in their history books. Explain to the students that they will make a Bill of Rights for their classroom. The format should be as follows:

I have the right to _____

This means that:

(1) _____

(2) _____

(3) _____

Notice that they must write at least three things that this means.

For example:

I have a right to be safe in this room.

This means that no one will hurt me physically,

that no one will speak to me abusively,

and that no one will take from me what is mine.

Allowing students to work with a partner generates better discussion. The teacher might want to screen each first line before students continue to the next line so that ideas are not repeated.

A long piece of paper should be taped to the wall vertically, and students should record their Bill of Rights on the paper for all the classes to see. They should also be given the opportunity to read them aloud.

Musical/Rhythmic and Verbal/Linguistic Intelligences to Build Personal Intelligences

Freedom Songs

Of the myriad of music styles popular in the early 1960s, folk music was the first to become socially relevant and reflected the Civil Rights Movement. Although music had not been a direct organizing force in the Montgomery, Alabama bus boycotts of 1955 and 1956, by the 1960s lunch counter sit-ins and "freedom songs" had become central to the movement. Northern singers such as Bob Dylan, Phil Ochs, Pete Seeger, Joan Baez, and Peter, Paul and Mary traveled south to sing at rallies and churches. Baez's "We Shall Overcome," based on an 18th century hymn, was recorded live at Miles College in Birmingham, Alabama, in 1963. Supplemented by hundreds of amateur singers as well as Black and White college students working as civil rights volunteers, these performers helped make 1964 and 1965 "freedom summers." Most of the groups mentioned above performed during Reverend Martin Luther King, Jr.'s March on Washington in 1963 where he gave his famous "I Have a Dream" speech. Through folk music and later by "soul" music, gospel songs, and the blues, performers spoke out against injustice and discrimination. Collect recordings and lyrics for some of these "freedom songs" for use in the following activities taken from "Keep on Pushing: Popular Music and the Civil Rights Movement," Lesson 2, on The Rock & Roll Hall of Fame website at http://www.rockhall.com/programs/institute.asp.

Compare and contrast "We Shall Overcome" by Joan Baez with "Say It Loud (I'm Black and I'm Proud)" by James Brown, reflecting on the differences in tone and attitude. How do these songs reflect the changing focus of the civil right movement throughout the 1960s as expressed in the following quotes:

- "I'm not fearing any man. Mine eyes have seen the glory of the coming of the Lord."—Martin Luther King Jr.
- "This thing with me will be resolved by death and violence."—Malcolm X.

Use other historical documents, examples from literature, and your knowledge of the history of the 1960s to support your answer.

Divide the class into small groups of three to five students. Assign one freedom song to each group and distribute the lyrics. Instruct each group to listen carefully to the song and relate it to material covered in class, keeping in mind the following questions:

- What emotions are expressed by the song?
- What issues, problems, or events are presented in the song?
- Does the song seem to be written in response to a specific event?
- What points of view or attitudes are revealed?
- What were the circumstances at the time the song was released?
- Does this song suggest any solutions to the issues/problems addressed?
- What, if any, relevance does this song have to American society today?

Have groups report back to the class on their answers to these questions. Have the class compare and contrast the multiple points of view found in the songs.

Verbal/Linguistic Intelligence to Build the Personal Intelligences

Take a Walk in My Shoes Project

One of the themes of *To Kill a Mockingbird* is: don't judge others until you have walked in their shoes. With this in mind, ask the student body and other faculty members to bring in shoes that still have some wear in them. Request the shoes at least two weeks in advance of the unit to ensure a good assortment. Ask your guidance counselor for the name of your family services representative who could help you find a good charity to accept these shoes when you are finished.

Discuss the idea of putting yourself in someone else's "shoes" in order to understand them better. Decide how this idea fits into the novel *To Kill a Mockingbird* (1960). Ask each student to choose a pair of the shoes that were donated to the class and to imagine what kind of person wore them. Then ask them to write a story, or a descriptive essay, or a character sketch so that we as readers can get a better idea of the person who wore those shoes. The teacher should take a picture of each pair of shoes to attach to the student's essay, and a copy of the essay should be put inside the shoes to go with them when they are given to the charity. Essays should be peer evaluated once; later a final draft trait should be scored by the teacher.

This assignment, developed by Kathy Megyeri (1996) of Sherwood High School in Sandy Spring, Maryland, elicited imaginative and creative responses. One student wrote about a girl who had loved to dance in her little ballet slippers, but had tragically died of an illness. Another student wrote about a woman who was a prim and proper businesswoman by day, but wore her red, shiny dancing shoes to the nightclubs in the evening. One story was about a grimy little boy who loved suckers. The black, dirty athletic shoes had a partially eaten sucker stuck inside one of them. See Table 7.6 for an excerpt from a story "Cowboy Boots" by Janelle Spelich, a student at Bristol High School, Bristolville, Ohio.

TABLE 7.6: "COWBOY BOOTS"

Cowboy boots are hard shoes to fill. It takes a true country boy or girl to do it. The person who wore these boots was a rodeo man. He is the Lane Frost of a small town northeast of us called Kinsman . . . My cowboy is by far the best bull rider in Ohio. It's only a matter of time until he goes pro. He has been riding bulls since he was twelve years old; it's his life. However, since he's not in the pro league, he doesn't make much money, so he has to have another job. During the days he works on a farm doing odd jobs, such as bailing hay, cleaning stalls, grooming horses, and whatever else he's asked to do.

Knowing this, you can imagine what he looks like. After a hard day on the farm, he is dirty, smelly, and sweaty. He has hay everywhere, in his hair and beard, all over his clothes, and even in his boots. His beard isn't exactly a beard; it's more of a five o'clock shadow. His hair is short on top and to the middle of his neck. It looks really good under his black Wrangler hat. There is a horse hair band on his hat that matches his belt. He only wears wrangler jeans and has a big gold and silver belt buckle that he won at a rodeo. His boots were the ones I am giving you now. His father bought them for him before he left for the farm. When he works, he wears either a flannel shirt or a long sleeved shirt, but when he goes out and to rodeo, he has a white straw hat, brown boots, nice jeans, and a dressy button-down shirt. He looks really sharp when he dresses up, and even at work, but it's his face that catches your eye. He has deep caramel brown eyes and a smile that would melt an iceberg.

Wrap It Up

Verbal/Linguistic and Intrapersonal Intelligences

Reflective Journal

Each student should complete this unit with a reflective journal on his or her feelings about prejudices in our world. Allowing students the opportunity to examine their own values is part of the responsibility of education and should be taken very seriously. By studying the literature of the plights of mankind, students can and will develop an empathy for their fellow man that can only serve to make the world a better place in which to live. The literature suggested in this chapter represents only a small part of the literature that is available to teachers and students. I can only hope that this unit will provide the impetus for other teachers to seek out literature that speaks to their students about what it means to be tolerant of and empathetic toward our human condition, thereby nurturing the human spirit.

Young Adult Literature for Teaching Tolerance and Empathy Toward Others

Campbell, Bebe Moore (1993). *Your Blues Ain't like Mine.* New York: Ballantine Books.

Curtis, Christopher Paul (1995). *The Watsons Go to Birmingham—1963.* New York: Delacorte Press.

Davis, Ossie (1992). *Just Like Martin.* New York: Simon & Schuster Books for Young Readers.

Fenner, Carol (1995). *Yolanda's Genius.* New York: Simon & Schuster Children's Publishing Division.

Griffin, John (1960). *Black Like Me.* Boston: Houghton Mifflin Company.

Hamilton, Virginia (1974). *M. C. Higgins, The Great.* New York: Simon & Schuster.

Hurston, Zora Neale (1937). *Their Eyes Were Watching God.* New York: Harper & Row.

Krisher, Trudy (1994). *Spite Fences.* New York: Delacorte Press.

Lee, Harper (1960). *To Kill a Mockingbird.* New York: HarperCollins Publishers.

Levine, Ellen (1993). *Freedom's Children: Young Civil Rights Activists Tell Their Own Stories.* New York: G.P. Putnam's Sons.

Meyer, Carolyn (1993). *White Lilacs.* New York: Gulliver Books, Harcourt Brace & Company.

Taylor, Mildred D. (1976). *Roll of Thunder, Hear My Cry.* New York: Puffin Books.

Taylor, Theodore (1969). *The Cay.* New York: Avon Books.

Taylor, Theodore (1993). *Timothy of the Cay.* New York: Avon Books.

Thomas, Joyce Carol (1982). *Marked by Fire.* New York: Avon Books.

Wesley, Valerie Wilson (1993). *Where Do I Go from Here?* New York: Scholastic.

Wilkinson, Brenda Scott (1987). *Not Separate, Not Equal.* New York: HarperCollins.

Related Young Adult Nonfiction

Barr, Roger (1994). *The Importance of Malcolm X.* San Diego, CA: Lucent Books.

Beals, Melba Pattillo (1994). *Warriors Don't Cry: A Searing Memoir of the Battle to Integrate Little Rock's Central High.* New York: Pocket Books.

Duvall, Lynn (1994). *Respecting Our Differences: A Guide to Getting Along in a Changing World.* Edited by Pamela Espeland. Minneapolis, MN: Free Spirit.

Haskins, James (1993). *Black Music in America: A History through its People.* New York: HarperCollins/Harper Trophy Books.

Haskins, James (1992). *The Life and Death of Martin Luther King, Jr.* New York: William Morrow/Beech Tree Books.

Haskins, James (1992). *The March on Washington.* New York: HarperCollins.

Haskins, James (1994). *The Scottsboro Boys.* New York: Henry Holt & Co.

King, Coretta Scott (1993). *My Life with Martin Luther King, Jr.* New York: Penguin/Puffin Books.

Myers, Walter Dean. *Now is Your Time: The African-American Struggle for Freedom.* New York: HarperCollins.

Newman, Gerald and Layfield, Eleanor Newman (1995). *Racism: Divided by Color.* Berkley Heights, NJ: Enslow.

Parks, Rosa with Jim Haskins (1992). *Rosa Parks: My Story.* New York: Dial Books.

Perry, Bruce (1992). *Malcolm: The Life of a Man Who Changed Black America.* Station Hill Press.

Terkel, Susan (1996). *People Power: A Look at Nonviolent Action and Defense.* Lodestar Books/Dutton.

Walter, Mildred Pitss (1992). *Mississippi Challenge.* New York: Macmillan/Bradbury Press.

Weidhorn, Manfred (1993). *Jackie Robinson.* New York: Atheneum.

Wyman, Carolyn (1993). *Ella Fitzgerald: Jazz Singer Supreme.* Franklin Watt/Impact Books.

References

Atwell, N. (Ed.). (1990). *Coming to know: Writing to learn in the intermediate grades.* Portsmouth, NH: Heinemann Educational Books.

Boggeman, S., Hoerr, T., & Wallach, C. (1996). *Succeeding with multiple intelligences: Teaching through the personal intelligences: Another practical guide created by the faculty of the New City school.* St. Louis, MO: The New City School, Inc.

Carnes, J. (1995). *Us and them: A history of intolerance in America.* Montgomery, AL: Teaching Tolerance, A Project of the Southern Poverty Law Center.

Daniels, H. (1994). *Literature circles: Voice and choice in the student-centered classroom.* York, ME: Stenhouse Publishers.

Goleman, D. (1995). *Emotional intelligence.* New York: Bantam Books.

Lee, H. (1987). *To kill a mockingbird.* [Videotape]. MCA Home Video, Inc.

Megyeri, K. (1996, September). Take a walk in my shoes project. *N.E.A. Today, 15* (1).

Rock Hall of Fame (Nov. 2000). Keep on pushing: Popular music and the civil rights movement. http://www.rockhall.com/programs/institute.asp.

Rose, R. (1990) *Twelve angry men*. [Videotape]. MGM/UP Home Video, Inc.

Roberson, H. (1995). *The shadow of hate teacher's guide*. Montgomery, AL: Teaching Tolerance, A Project of the Southern Poverty Law Center.

The shadow of hate: A history of intolerance in America. (1995). [Videotape]. Charles Guggenheim, Producer. Narrated by Julian Bond. Montgomery, AL: Teaching Tolerance, A Project of the Southern Poverty Law Center, 40 minutes.

CHAPTER 8

New Ties, Unconventional Relationships with M. E. Kerr

Jackie Glasgow

Introduction

In *Frames of Mind* (1983), Howard Gardner examines two aspects of human nature: intrapersonal and interpersonal intelligences. According to Gardner, development of the intrapersonal intelligence begins with "access to one's own feeling life" (p. 239). One must discriminate among a range of emotions or feelings, label them, and be able to draw upon them as a means of understanding and guiding one's behavior. At its most advanced level, "intrapersonal knowledge allows one to detect and to symbolize complex and highly differentiated sets of feelings" (p. 239). This form of intelligence is highly developed in authors like Proust who can write introspectively about feelings, in people who undergo psychotherapy and come to a deep knowledge of their feelings, as well as in elders who draw on their wealth of inner experiences to advise others.

Whereas intrapersonal intelligence turns inward as individuals examine their feelings, the other personal intelligence turns outward to the behavior, feelings, and motivations of others. Gardner defines interpersonal intelligence as the "ability to notice and make distinctions among other individuals and, in particular, among their moods, temperaments, motivations, and intentions" (p. 239). This intelligence develops as young children learn to discriminate the moods of individuals around them. In an advanced form, "interpersonal knowledge permits a skilled adult to read the intentions and desires—even when these have been hidden—of many other individuals and, potentially, to act upon this knowledge" (p. 239). We see highly developed forms of this intelligence in political and religious leaders, in skilled parents and teachers, as well as individuals in other helping professions such as therapy and counseling.

With adolescence comes maturation of knowledge both of self and of others. In adolescence, individuals must bring together these two forms of personal knowledge into a larger and more organized sense, a sense of identity or a sense of self. As formulated by the psychoanalyst, Erik Erikson, identity formation is a process of an individual in coming to terms with his own personal feelings, motivations, and desires—including the powerful sexual ones beginning at puberty—needed to function effectively with a social context in which she/he has chosen to live.

Sexuality influences every aspect of our lives including family functioning, peer relationships, morality, and physical development. As adolescents come to terms with gender identity issues, they must sort out their emotions, social relationships, fantasies, and cultural expectations that accompany the physical changes in their bodies. Teenagers are often confused about their sexual identity, and this confusion often puts them at risk. If their feelings lead them into unconventional and controversial relationships, they can be isolated and alienated from their families and friends. While homosexuality may be experienced by only a few teenagers, nearly all young people wonder about the moral and social implications of experimenting with sexual activity. This unit will provide opportunities for students to explore sexuality and romantic relationships in young adult literature where their concerns can be addressed.

While the recommended books center on themes of coming to terms with homosexuality, they also are stories of love, coming–of–age, adventure, and self-discovery. Some of the characters are dealing with being gay or lesbian themselves, and others are dealing with gay or lesbian parents or friends. Kerr's books: *Night Kites* (1989), *Deliver Us from Evie* (1995) and *"Hello," I Lied* (1997) are not limited to issues of homosexuality. Kerr also touches on complications of friendships that cross socioeconomic and religious lines and on family dynamics when one important player in the family pulls out. While Kerr's books are the primary books for this unit, other books that give an honest portrayal of love developing in homosexual relationships may supplement the reading:

- Nancy Garden's (1982) *Annie on My Mind*
- Jacqueline Woodson's (1995) *From the Notebooks of Melanin Son*
- Francesca Lia Block's (1989) *Weetzie Bat*
- Isabelle Holland's (1972) *The Man Without a Face*
- Paula Fox's (1995) *The Eagle Kite*

The goal for this thematic unit is to affirm a healthy sexual identity by exploring themes of intimacy, trust, and fidelity in human relationships that might take unconventional forms departing from cultural norms. The young adult literature suggested in this unit gives adolescents a chance to explore and to question their own attitudes and beliefs about sexual orientation, as well as to raise awareness of issues confronting those individuals who choose homosexual affiliations. Generally speaking, adolescence is a time for sorting out their emotions. Young adults experience diverse and extreme feelings of curiosity, fear, guilt, and exhilaration as a part of normal development and hormonal changes. If they are victims of sexual exploitation, they have feelings of betrayal, horror, and trauma to sort out. If they cross cultural norms of sexual-orientation, they experience conflicts with family, friends and society in general. To help mitigate against isolation with these intimate issues and to examine stereotypes, the unit activities are designed to promote reflection and positive decision-making. Consciously projecting oneself into perspectives and experiences quite different from one's own enhances both empathy and critical thinking. Young adult literature provides a means for readers to experience and explore these important issues vicariously and then to discuss the sensitive issues within a safe context. Empathy provides an essential base for moral development, while critical thinking promotes understanding of complex issues. So, whether students are merely exploring their own sexuality or "coming out" with their unconventional relationships, the goal of this unit is to help them integrate these complex issues into a healthy perspective and to develop tolerance for those who might have different sexual orientations. See Table 8.1 for Activities to Explore Unconventional Relationships and Build the Personal Intelligences.

Overview of Unit Activities

In this unit, students explore their own sexual identity by creating a *report sack* about themselves. They find concrete objects to represent themselves, put them into a brown lunch bag, and explain the significance of the objects they chose to personify themselves. For another activity, students create a *coat of arms* for a favorite character in one of the Kerr books. Creating a *photo essay* is an activity which encourages students to take pictures that solve a problem or develop a theme. Another way they can express their feelings about a favorite character is to find appropriate, contemporary music and *create a dance* showing the mood changes and emotional conflicts of a main character. Students can explore moments of isolation and discovery in their lives through *journal writing, song writing,* and *poetic responses* to the books. They can compare and contrast characters through a polar appraisal activity. Through character mapping, students recreate the emotional relationships of the characters. The culminating activity for this unit will be to create and perform a readers' theater production of a scene from one of the books.

TABLE 8.1: ACTIVITIES TO EXPLORE UNCONVENTIONAL RELATIONSHIPS
AND BUILD THE PERSONAL INTELLIGENCES.

Multiple Intelligences	Interpersonal Intelligence	Intrapersonal Intelligence
Verbal/Linguistic	Compose a readers' theater script Complete writing frame for Coat of Arms Complete Story Discussion Grid	Complete a self-discovery journal Create poetic responses to passages Do an evoked response to a moving passage Create Bio Poems or I Am Poems
Logical/Mathematical	Compare and contrast a protagonist with an antagonist using a polar appraisal Create a character map showing emotional relationships Devise Split-Open Mind showing a dilemma	Create Split-Open Mind for a personal conflict Make a Venn Diagram for conventional vs unconventional relationships Develop analogies for characters in Kerr's books
Visual/Spatial	Create photo essay of a favorite character; Design Coat of Arms for a character; Create Story Portrait of a theme Create Story Board of main events	Compose a Photo essay or collage of healthy relationships Draw or paint abstract terms such as love, empathy, com-passion, tolerance or understanding
Musical/Rhythmic	Create soundtrack for a book; Collect love songs that explore differing perspectives; Research rock and roll songs mentioned in *Night Kites*	Create musical responses to characters, themes, and events Complete Rockin' the World Worksheet
Bodily/Kinesthetic	Create a dance showing the emotional conflicts of a main character; Perform readers' theater; Role play conflict resolution for Evie and Patty	Make a Report Sack to show your identity; Perform a monologue for a character with a tough decision to make; Mime Evie's responsibilities at home and conflict in leaving

Visual/Spatial Activity to Build the Personal Intelligences

Report Sack

The report sack is a versatile activity that can be used as the culminating activity of a literature unit since it focuses on the personality of the main character. In this case, the report sack is a way for students to be introspective and to assess their own personalities. Later, they may choose to make a report sack for their favorite character from one of the books. The first step is to brainstorm a list of personality traits that best describes the way students act and relate to others. Then ask students to choose at least six objects that represent those character traits. Challenge students to be selective in the information they share, just as Erick was in Kerr's *Night Kites* (1989), and with good reason. Students should elect only positive traits and images that make them look good. Ask students to put the objects in a standard brown paper lunch sack. They may decorate the sack if they feel inclined. They then write a one-page typewritten explanation of their object choices to include with the project when they share with the class. Ask students to give positive feedback to each other after they share in order to build confidence and trust with each other. See Table 8.2 for an example of the items that Erica Sprague used to describe herself to the class.

Reports sacks are effective for getting to know one another and for sharing honestly about personal values. Identity and cultural issues come out in the safety of discussing the concrete objects. This activity is motivating and good for building self-esteem and self-discovery which are important in developing intrapersonal intelligence.

TABLE 8.2: ERICA'S REPORT SACK

This is my self-report sack. Note that the items are not necessarily listed in order of significance.

Richard Scarry's *Funniest Storybook Ever*. This was my favorite book when I was little. The characters are naive, ignorant, and silly. Perhaps I am still fond of this book because of its realism.

Winnie-the-Pooh. This is my identity as portrayed by a bear. He is childlike enough to be brutally honest and he often admits his own weaknesses. I identify with that.

Bumper Sticker. Animals are a big part of my life. They are friendlier and more trustworthy than people, and I love them for it.

Finger Paint. I consider myself an immature artist and I have yet to develop my skills.

The boot. This is my adolescent attitude that I cannot let go. I am tough. I can withstand anything thrown my way. I am not feminine. I just am. Deal with it!

Bone necklace. This is representative of my native heritage and I'm really drawn to it.

The bracelet. This is from Mexico. A seven or eight-year-old girl made this and sold it to me for the equivalent of $1.00. She made this herself as a way to support her family. I will never forget that 80% of the world lives this way. I will never be a gringo again.

Verbal/Linguistic and Visual/Spatial Activities to Build the Personal Intelligences

Coat of Arms

If students need to think more creatively about themselves, the coat of arms activity will help them generate images metaphorically and visually. The activity is also very successful to activate the imagination and gain insight into the main character in a book, such as Erick, Pete, Dill or Niki from *Night Kites* (1989); Parr, Evie, or Patsy from *Deliver Us From Evie* (1995); or Lang from *"Hello," I Lied* (1997). According to Pugh, Hicks, and Davis (1997), "metaphorical ways of knowing endeavor to press established relationships between language and meaning into new fields through imaginative comparison" (p. 8). In this case the metaphor can guide students into the experience of others. By completing the writing frame for a coat of arms, students must imagine the character in a new way and must also give a reason for their choices. Then, they represent their rich images or symbols graphically on poster board in the shape of a shield or coat of arms. See Table 8.3 for the Writing Frame for the Coat of Arms designed by Olson and Schiesl (1996).

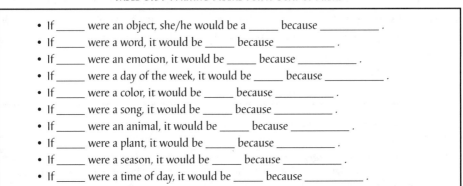

TABLE 8.3: WRITING FRAME FOR A COAT OF ARMS

- If _____ were an object, she/he would be a _____ because _____ .
- If _____ were a word, it would be _____ because _____ .
- If _____ were an emotion, it would be _____ because _____ .
- If _____ were a day of the week, it would be _____ because _____ .
- If _____ were a color, it would be _____ because _____ .
- If _____ were a song, it would be _____ because _____ .
- If _____ were an animal, it would be _____ because _____ .
- If _____ were a plant, it would be _____ because _____ .
- If _____ were a season, it would be _____ because _____ .
- If _____ were a time of day, it would be _____ because _____ .

Students may construct their coat of arms in the form of a shield on poster board using the metaphors created in the writing frame and/or use any new ideas that occur to them. Students should use whatever media they are most comfortable with: drawing, painting, magazine collage, photography, or computer clip art. They should also write a one page paper explaining their choices for the symbols and the media. Be sure to share the projects as a basis for discussion and reflection, noting the different insights about the character that students present.

Verbal/Linguistic Activity to Build Intrapersonal Intelligence

Evoked Response

Since the books in this unit are likely to evoke an emotional response, students can confront their emotions directly with this activity. After reading silently either the entire book or a particularly moving passage, ask students to select a section that especially touched them. Ask them to read the passage aloud into a tape recorder, so they can listen to the nuances of change in their voices. As they listen to the tape, ask them to record any emotion or reaction that surfaces in the reading of the passage. Ask students to use the following questions, suggested by Milner and Milner (1993), to help clarify their personal response:

- What tone shifts can you discern in your oral reading of the passage? What do they reflect about your feelings? Are your feelings constant throughout or do they vary?
- Do certain incidents or characters in the passage carry a particularly powerful emotional load? How do you respond to these incidents or characters?
- What seems to be emotionally the most intense point in the passage?
- What moments of ambivalent or mixed emotion do you find in the passage?
- What might be the reason for this uncertainty?
- What is the emotional resolution of the passage (if one exists)?
- What is your most prominent emotional response to the passage as a whole—anger, sorrow, joy, fear, vexation, disgust? Why? (p. 92)

Conclude by asking students to review their notes and consider whether they have written of *feelings* about the text, or if they have *explained* the text. Have them distill their writing to three basic responses to the story based on the answers to the questions above. Before submitting the tape and the paper, ask them to explain their choices to a partner to validate, expand, or alter their own reading of the story. Then have them select one word (it might be an emotion) that for them singularly captures their responses. Ask students to share with the class if the responses are not too personal.

Visual/Spatial Activity to Build the Personal Intelligences

Photo Essay

In order to explore some of the abstract themes related to this unit, give students the choice to create the photo essay either individually or collaboratively. Tell students that they are to collect photos that portray the development of healthy relationships with family and friends. Students should select a positive focus or theme from the ideas discussed in class such as: formation of friendships, aspects of commitment, identity crisis, tolerance of homosexuals, dealing with AIDS, overcoming alcohol, "coming out" issues, self-discovery, defending and asserting oneself in school, finding solace in spirituality, or locating community support for homosexuality. Students should take 20 to 25 photographs on either a conventional or digital camera that tells the story of their theme. Students should be reminded that although this is a "wordless" story, all good storytelling incorporates the use of an introduction, a body with supporting details, and a conclusion. The photo theme should make an assertion or point about relationships. Photos taken on the conventional camera should be mounted on a sheet of poster board in the proper sequential order. Photos taken on a digital camera could be displayed in a Power Point or other Multimedia Presentation. Collages from magazine or clip art are also appropriate. Students should be encouraged to use their imaginations in developing individual themes and should be supported with positive feedback after their presentation to the class. For students needing more structure, they can portray themes directly from Kerr's books such as: Erick's reactions to his brother's homosexuality in *Night Kites* (1989); Evie's identity issues and contention with her mother to act and dress in a more feminine manner in *Deliver Us from Evie* (1995); and, Lang Penner's resistance and confusion with "coming out" in *"Hello," I Lied* (1997).

Verbal/Linguistic and Musical/Rhythmic Activities to Build the Personal Intelligences

Love Songs

As students explore their relationships to family and friends, their feelings surface and want expression. Through writing and performing their songs, students can express the meaning of love, commitment, or other themes explored in this unit. For this assignment, even the most reluctant student can write the lyrics and then put the words to music. Begin by asking students to freewrite their ideas and feelings about a particular relationship to a friend or family member in which they struggle to express or understand their emotions. From the freewriting, ask students to form the lyrics for a song in chorus and verse and ask them to tap out the rhythmic pattern of the words, putting marks above the stressed syllables. If they can identify the poetic rhythms such as iambic, trochaic or anapestic, they can translate the meter used in writing music such as the waltz (3/4), march (4/4), swing (6/8). Then ask students to rewrite the words, elongating them to fit the rhythmic patterns. After formulating a tune for the song, ask them to visually represent the notes on newsprint where they put words higher or lower depending on the changes in pitch of the tune. Students who are musically literate should go ahead and place the notes in rhythmic patterns on staff paper. Give students colored markers or crayons to indicate the mood or feelings of the line, such as, red for passion, green for envy, yellow for cowardice, purple for longing. Next, ask the students to sing their songs into a tape recorder so they can find or compose an accompaniment. If they are musically inclined, they should compose the accompaniment and sing along with an instrument such as piano, guitar, or accordion. Other students may perform their songs along with a previously recorded accompaniment. Those musically literate students might also be willing to accompany other students who struggle with musical conventions or who do not play an instrument. See Table 8.4 for Maria's Folksong written by a student in Terry Murcko's eleventh grade English class.

TABLE 8.4: MARIA'S FOLKSONG

The Language of Love
Maria Guarracino

My parents could not show affection,
I-love-yous that I never heard,
But I learned this wasn't rejection;

The language of love had no words.
The language of love had no words.
They couldn't say what they meant.
The language of love had no words,
So I found out how to be silent.

None of my thoughts become verbal.
You claim that I do not care.
Know that my love is eternal;
Listen to my constant stare.

The language of love has no words.
You didn't see what I meant.
The language of love has no words;
I don't know how not to be silent.
I don't know how not to be silent.
I don't know how not to be silent.

Maria was one of the most reluctant students to attempt this assignment, but her message was poignant when she finally made it. As students learn to express personal themes in their music, they can extend this work through researching and responding to rock music mentioned in Kerr's novels.

Musical/Rhythmic Research and Response to Build the Personal Intelligences

Rockin' and Rollin' with M.E. Kerr

The importance of contemporary music to the themes of *Night Kites*, published in 1989, is evidenced by Nicki's rock trivia which permeates the text. Nicki sees her world as a grandiose music video, with family, friends, and acquaintances cast according to their physical likeness to rock icons. She refers to songs which reflect her attitudes and moods; however, in our times, the impact of her lyrical allusions becomes dated. The purpose of this activity is to research the messages of the songs that Kerr selected for creating mood in *Night Kites* (1989). The students will then combine this knowledge with their familiarity of contemporary music to create a more meaningful musical background for the novel.

Begin by asking students to bring in CD's and a copy of the lyrics for songs and groups mentioned in *Night Kites*. Divide the class into small groups of three to five, each group focusing on a particular preformer such as Sting or Bruce Springsteen. Alternatively, this activity can be done as a teacher-led class discussion on one song at a time. Instruct each group to listen carefully to the song(s) and to complete the worksheet. They may also research additional background, if appropriate. Then, each group will conclude with a presentation containing:

- Summary of the factual information contained in the songs.
- Explanation of any inferences, generalizations, conclusions, and points of view found in the songs, particularly those ways that Nicki compared to Erick.
- Statement of the group's points of view in regards to the other questions about the songs, particularly the ways songs as historical documents are important in understanding American society.

For *Rockin' the World Worksheet* go to Lesson 9 at the Rock and Roll Hall of Fame website (www.rockhall.com/programs/institute.asp and then click on Lesson Plans). As students prepare for the group presentation, they could create a scrapbook/photo album of the recording artist as a visual for their presentation.

After studying the rock artists in 1986, students can update the novel by proposing contemporary music and artists to replace the 1986 references. They should give explanations to support their choices. Students might even prepare tapes that include both selections of the music to share with the class. See Table 8.5 for Kandace Cleland's example of this assignment.

TABLE 8.5: KANDACE CLELAND'S UPDATED MUSIC FOR *NIGHT KITES*

1986	1996
Ric Ocasek "Jimmy, Jimmy"	Toad the Wet Sprocket "Woodburning"

The song Nicki refers to talks about the restless wanderings of Jimmy. Nicki says her father had those same feelings of wanting to run away. She also identifies with the confusion in the piece. "Woodburning" talks about the way people go from one relationship to another and never settle down. The loneliness of these patterns leave ashes of burnt wood behind. Nicki has been hopping from guy to guy. She is being consumed in the process. She also leaves a path of burned hearts behind her.

1986	1996
Billy Squires "Eye on You"	R.E.M. "Night Swimming"

The song Nicki refers to talks about the passionate feeling of a man for a woman. The song describes the obsession that people can have for each other. By focusing on the physical, people try to escape their personal trials. In "Night Swimming," a couple escapes the world by skinny dipping together. Since Nicki and Erick had their first experiences together in City By The Sea, this song makes a strong connection with the novel.

An alternative to this assignment, would be to ask students to study the music of gay and lesbian music groups such as the Indigo Girls, a Grammy award-winning folk-rock duo. Students could look for themes in the music that connect with one of the books in the unit or create a collage of musicians with alternative lifestyle choices.

Logical/Mathematical Activity to Build the Personal Intelligences

Character Map

In this assignment, students will probe characters and the story context by mapping them according to their relationships. They are not making comparisons so much as uncovering strong relationships between characters and how those relationships are webbed together to create a whole story (adapted from Milner and Milner, 1993, p. 94–95). If teaching character mapping for the first time, group students and give them newsprint and colored markers. Cut out circles that are three inches in diameter for the major characters and two inches in diameter for the minor characters. Then ask students to write the name of one character on an appropriately-sized circle. For *Night Kites* (1989), they should have a separate circle for each of the following characters: Erick Rudd, Pete Rudd, Nicki Marr, Dill Dilberto, Jack, Mr. Arthur Rudd, Grandpa Rudd, Mrs. Rudd, Mrs. Tompkins, Phil Kern, Mr. Bertie Dilberto, Mrs. Dilberto, Dill's Aunt Lana, Cap Marr, Annabel Poe Marr, and Jim Stanley. On the newsprint or posterboard, students begin arranging the circles according to the most obvious pairs or trios. Place them according to their relationship to the central character, their close personal relationship, or their antipathy for one another. After the cliques are established, ask students to make lines between the circles that visually connect the characters in some fashion. After students are satisfied with their arrangement of the characters, ask them to show the emotional relationships by coloring lines that connect one character to another (such as, red for anger, green for jealousy, yellow for cowardly, black for hate.). Ask them to make a key for their color-coding decisions. Then ask students to write a one-page paper discussing the placement of characters in the arrangement they chose. After students become more experienced in character mapping, ask them to replace the circles with symbols for each of the characters based on the character's personality, function in the story, or interests. For instance, symbols for Nicki might be a rock album, cigarette, or flashy model. Sometimes students add a context for the characters such as a sketch of the Kingdom by the Sea for Nicki's family. When they have finished, hang the students' character maps around the room and ask them to share their rationale for placement of the characters. Comparing character maps allows students to see the diverse ways characters relate to one another. This discussion should give students insight into the story and into the craft and content of fiction.

Split Open Mind

For this assignment, students must get into the mind of a character either to explore the changes they made after a traumatic event or to explore a central conflict facing the character. The assignment works equally well in helping students understand the horns of a dilemma that they might be struggling with in their own personal lives. In this case, students will get into the mind of Lang Penner, the main character in *"Hello," I Lied* (1997) by M. E. Kerr. When Ben Nevada asks Lang to describe himself using only one word, Lang replies, "Torn" (1997, p.8). He goes on to say that he is "torn between comfort and conformity" (1997, p. 8). This activity will help students understand the conflicts that Lang experienced as he considered "coming out" as gay which "tore" him between the comforts of his gay identity and the conformity to hide that identity.

Using a piece of newsprint or posterboard, ask students to draw a large head of a person. They don't need to include much detail except maybe ears, neck, a little hair. Drawing a line down the middle of the face and labeling the piece, "Lang Penner" and "Torn" as the subtitle and descriptor, label one side of the head, "Comfort" and the other side, "Conformity." Ask students to find examples in the text to support arguments for both sides of Lang's dilemma. For instance, on the comfort side, they might mention his contentment when he is with Alex. Lang and Alex like to do things together such as dine in restaurants, watch movies, swim at the beach, attend plays, or engage in secret love games together. On the conformity side, students should mention the dangers to homosexuals by homophobic reactions ranging from subtle insinuations to blatant accusations, to acts of violence. Lang and Alex encounter scorn, shunning, rejection, isolation, and assault during the course of their outings. At Alex's parents' twenty-fifth wedding anniversary party, Lang encounters Mrs. Southgate's objection to homosexual couples: She wants grandchildren and family gatherings. And Alex's father gives the lecture about AIDS. On the other hand, dating Brittany Ball and Huguette Haun are safer and won Lang social approval, but he has "to lie and pretend he was someone that he wasn't" (1997, p. 46). Lang is reluctant to accept Ben Nevada's deal to show Huguette around the Hamptons, because he "gets tired of the masquerade" (p. 47). Later, Lang goes into more detail about the artifice, evasion, subterfuge, and hiding that goes into being a closeted gay (p. 75). This activity helps students sort out the conflicts Lang is faced with if he decides to "come out" to his family and friends.

Verbal/Linguistic and Visual/Spatial Activities to Build the Personal Intelligences

Story Portrait

In this activity, students can work collaboratively to focus on the main point of a book and to represent their understanding in a one-page graphic design that resembles a picture or portrait. Students work in small groups equipped with posterboard and colored markers to discuss the main ideas in *"Hello," I Lied* (1997) by M. E. Kerr. This activity designed by Olson and Schiesl (Spring 1996), requires students to construct a frame for the picture, generate a symbol for the main idea, decide on a theme, and agree on a quote that supports the picture of the novel that they are presenting.

The first step is to draw a border or frame around the "portrait" based on a significant or important idea from the book. Encourage students to decorate the border with words or pictures that show an important aspect of the story. For *"Hello," I Lied*, one group of students chose to frame their portrait with the word, "Lies," since Lang is caught lying to everyone at one point or another in the story. Another group framed their picture with the symbols for male and female followed by question marks, showing the difficulty in making the choice. Another group did the same thing using the words, "gay" or "straight" for their border. Still another group framed their portrait with record albums of rock stars since they are mentioned throughout the text. Once the students have constructed the frame, they move on to a discussion of the "big idea" of the novel.

Inside the border, in the "portrait" area, ask students to draw a symbol for the big idea that they see as the main idea or message of the story. This symbol is open to the students' interpretation. For example, one group drew a heart that was torn down the middle and separated in two parts to symbolize Lang's feeling of being "torn" between comfort and conformity. Another group chose to draw an androgenous person with all the body parts centered in a heart to show that love is more important than sexual orientation. Another group drew two males and a female holding hands, alluding to the bisexual orientation or confusion that tormented Lang. Another group drew a boy bursting out of a heart to symbolize Lang's desire to "come out" gay. Another group, made a gold key chain with the words, "Paint Over It," as their symbol to represent a summer that Lang will never forget, but would paint over it by continuing his relationship with Alex. After generating a symbol that represents the "big idea" of the book, students are ready to write a statement of the author's theme of the story.

The next step is to ask students to write the theme or moral of the story that verbally expresses the symbolic idea they created. Most students described Lang's difficulties or obstacle in "coming out," his need to "paint over" his feelings for Huguette, or his desire to remain true to himself with Alex. The next step is to find a quote from the text that blends the symbol and the theme statement together in the framework of the portrait students are painting.

Ask students to find a quotation from the story that shows the big idea and write it somewhere else in the portrait to complete the picture. The group focusing on the bisexual behavior Lang exhibited chose the quote, "I think people who claim to be bisexual just can't admit they're queer. It's easier to say you're bi. That makes you halfway straight" (1997, p. 35). The group that sympathized with Lang's difficulties in dealing with his feelings for Huguette chose the quote, "Don't try to make everyone fit a mold" (p. 36). That group also included the words to the song, "Paint Over It" (p. 118). The group that tuned into Lang's difficulties in "coming out" chose the quote, "Every truth has two sides; it is well to look at both, before we commit ourselves to either" (1997, p. 86). Even though this was the summer that Lang says he loved a girl, he resolved his conflict by committing himself to the relationship with Alex which was permanent and satisfying to him.

Verbal/Linguistic and Logical/Mathematical Activity to Build the Personal Intelligences

Class Discussions and the Story Grid

This activity can be used with either short stories or with novels to generate students' reactions to the literature. The Story Discussion Grid developed by Yarick (1995, p. 13) can be completed individually in preparation for class discussion or done collaboratively to generate discussion in small groups. Later,

relationships? Although Gardner questions the ideal instruction in the personal realm, he does emphasize the fact that "one is a unique individual, who must grow up in a social context—an individual of feelings and striving, who must rely on others to furnish the tasks and to judge one's achievements—is an ineluctable aspect of the human condition and one firmly rooted in our species membership" (1983, p. 254). To the extent that we provide a context for personal knowledge to emerge, we can effect the proper kinds of discrimination students need to learn as they become more tolerant and compassionate human beings.

Young Adult Literature for New Ties, Unconventional Relationships

Bauer, Marion Dane, ed. (1994). *Am I Blue? Coming Out From the Silence.* New York: HarperCollins Publisher.
  In this first-ever collection of original stories devoted to the topic of growing up gay or lesbian, or with gay or lesbian parents or friends, sixteen prominent young adult authors offer original short stories about love, coming-of-age, adventure, and self-discovery. It features works by Lois Lowry, Francesca Lia Block, Bruce Coville, James Cross Giblin, M.E. Kerr, William Sleator, Jane Yolen, and eight others.

Block, Francesca Lia (1989). *Weetzie Bat.* New York: HarperCollins.
  In this modern fairy tale, Weetzie Bat and her Los Angeles friends, Dirk, Duck, and My-Secret-Agent-Lover-Man, portray the natural beauty of sex, the normalcy of a gay couple who are funny and foolish, and the fulfillment of Weetzie's three wishes.

Fox, Paula (1995). *The Eagle Kite.* New York: Laurel-Leaf Books.
  When he was 10, Liam smashed and buried the eagle kite his father had given him. It was the morning he saw his father on the beach with another man. Liam kept that memory hidden for three years until his mother told him his father was sick—from a blood transfusion. He father has AIDS and leaves home to live and then die in a cabin on the beach.

Garden, Nancy (1982). *Annie on My Mind.* New York: Farrar, Straus, Giroux.
  This book is a touching story about two teenage girls who fall in love with each other. Liza puts aside her feelings for Annie after the disaster at school, but eventually she allows love to triumph over the ignorance of people.

Garden, Nancy (1999). *The Year They Burned the Books.* New York: Farrar, Straus, Giroux.

When Wilson High Telegraph editor Jamie Crawford writes an opinion piece in support of the new sex-ed curriculum, which includes making condoms available to high school students, she has no idea that a huge controversy is brewing. Lisa Buel, a school board member, is trying to get rid of the health program, which she considers morally flawed— from its textbooks to its recommendations for outside reading. The newspaper staff find themselves in the center of the storm and things are complicated by the fact that Jamie is in the process of coming to terms with being gay; her best friend, Terry, also gay, has fallen in love with a boy whose parents are anti-homosexual. As Jamie's and Terry's sexual orientation become more obvious to other students, it looks as if the paper they're fighting to keep alive and honest is going to be taken away from them. Nancy Garden has depicted a contemporary battleground in a novel that probes deeply into issues of censorship, prejudice, and ethics.

Heron, Anne (ed.) (1995). *Two Teenagers in Twenty: Writings by Gay & Lesbian Youth.* Los Angeles, CA: Alyson Publications, Inc.

These stories give a realistic sense of what life is like for gay and lesbian teenagers based on research reporting statistics that two out of twenty teenagers are homosexual. Their stories emerged from newspaper ads and from the free pen pal service at Alyson Publications. Teens express themes of self-discovery, isolation and despair in "coming out" and dealing with family and friends.

Holland, Isabelle (1972). *The Man Without a Face.* New York: HarperCollins Children's Books.

Now a motion picture, this book tells the story of 14-year-old Charles, who develops an unusual relationship with a terribly scarred, mysterious man named Justin McLeod, his tutor for the St. Matthew school entrance exams.

Kerr, M. E. (1989). *Night Kites.* New York: HarperTrophy.
Seventeen-year-old Erick's comfortable and well-ordered life begins to fall apart when he is forced to keep two secrets: the identity of his new girlfriend and the nature of his brother's debilitating disease.

Kerr, M. E. (1995). *Deliver Us from Evie.* New York: HarperTrophy.
Narrated by her brother, Parr, this is the story of 18-year-old Evie, her Missouri farm family, and the turmoil created by Evie's love for the local banker's beautiful daughter.

Kerr, M. E. (1997). *'Hello,' I Lied.* New York: HarperCollins Publisher.
Summering in the Hamptons on the estate of a famous rock star, seventeen-year-old Lang, tries to decide how to tell his longtime friends

that he is gay, while struggling with an unexpected infatuation over a girl from France.

Wersba, Barbara (1997). *Whistle Me Home.* New York: Henry Holt and Company.

Noli, a smart, boyish teenage girl has fallen in love with T.J., the new boy at school. Cute, sensitive, and attentive, T.J. appears to be her soul mate, but much to Noli's dismay their intense relationship never becomes sexual. When T.J. finally confesses his homosexuality to her, Noli is both furious and crushed.

Woodson, Jacqueline (1995). *From the Notebooks of Melanin Sun.* New York: The Blue Sky Press, an imprint of Scholastic Inc.

Ever since Kristin, a pretty white lawyer, entered Mama's life, Melanin Sun, a 14-year-old African-American boy, fears that he and Mama are losing the special closeness they always shared as he struggles to come to terms with her homosexuality.

References

Gardner, H. (1983). *Frames of mind: The theory of multiple intelligences.* New York: Basic Books.

Milner, J., & Milner, L. (1993). *Bridging English.* New York: Macmillan Publishing Company.

Olson, C. B., & Schiesl, S. (1996, Spring). A multiple intelligences approach to teaching multicultural literature. *Language Arts Journal of Michigan, 12* (1), 21–28.

Pugh, S., Hicks, J. W., & Davis, M. (1997). *Metaphorical ways of knowing: The imaginative nature of thought and expression.* Urbana, IL: NCTE.

Rock and Roll Hall of Fame (Nov. 1998). *Rockin' the world worksheet.* (Lesson 9). http://www.rockhall.com/programs/institute.asp

Yarick, S. J. (1995). *The write course: A writing course for community college freshmen.* Ottawa, KS: The Writing Conference, Inc.

CHAPTER 9

Conformity vs. Individuality in Cormier's
The Chocolate War

Linda J. Rice

Introduction

"Be yourself" has become the motto of modern times; Robert Cormier reveals the dark side of individuality and the risks of non-conformity. Considered a classic in young adult fiction, *The Chocolate War* opens the door for introspection and classroom debate which come alive by incorporating the multiple intelligences. Through theme collages and dialogue journals students relate incidents of peer pressure from their own lives, empathize with characters from the novel, and explore the societal tension between individuality and conformity. Character Continua, Probe, and Focal Judgments activities nurture critical reflection and analysis, while music compositions and storyboards encourage students' artistic interplay with the text.

With the help of essays by Henry David Thoreau, Mohandas Gandhi, and Martin Luther King, Jr., students investigate the concept of civil disobedience in history, find contemporary examples, discuss its merits and difficulties, and subsequently examine Jerry's actions in the form of a synthesis paper. Poems by Martin D. Niemoller, Langston Hughes, and Gwendolyn Brooks, provide thematic links and opportunities to compose parallel poems which model the "master poets" style, but with content relevant to *The Chocolate War*.

Through character mapping and dramatic tableaux students explore and convey power structures and analyze in subsequent discussion how and why these structures have become so deeply imbedded in schools and other communities. To contrast the harsh realism with which Cormier ended *The Choco-late War*, students view Keith Gordon's film version of the novel and evaluate which one offers the more believable ending for protagonist Jerry Renault, questioning whether or not it pays to "disturb the universe." As a final celebration of individuality, students contract to complete projects of their choosing which show their understanding of some specific aspect of the novel. Illuminating the dangers of challenging the norm, discographies, original music compositions and raps, poetry collections, videos, time lines, maps, and panoramas are some of the ways in which students have celebrated their uniqueness in light of a young adult novel.

Visual/Spatial, Verbal/Linguistic Intelligences

Theme Collages

Students should be encouraged to look beyond any novel's plot level alone. Before they even begin reading *The Chocolate War*, students respond to one of six questions by creating a collage (see Table 9.1). The six questions taken from Bushman (1993), which draw on students' own life experiences, are designed to provide a glimpse into the novel's themes. While many students use magazines rich with pictures and words as their primary tool for completing the collage, others elect to draw or even relate a poem with which they are familiar in order to visually compose their answer to one of the thematic questions.

TABLE 9.1: THEMATIC QUESTIONS FOR COLLAGE

• Tell of an incident in which you were forced by an authority figure to do something that you didn't want to do.
• Relate an incident in which you were pressured by peers to do something.
• Tell of a time in which you were pressured by peers to do something.
• Tell of an incident in which you were bullied into doing something that you didn't want to do.
• Tell of a situation when you felt too restricted to act in a way that you really wanted to.
• What is something that you would be willing to fight for and why?

One student cut out pictures of cigarettes and alcohol and arranged them in collage-form on the page to show an incident when he felt pressured by peers. Another student, who drew two clocks, told of being forced by an authority figure to do something she didn't want to do. The hands of the first clock, pointing to one o'clock, read "Me" and had a universal "no" symbol drawn over it, while the hands of the second clock pointed to eleven and read "Mom." A student willing to protect children from abuse traced her own hand over a picture of a little girl. Finally, a student who had acted against the law by hunting deer out of season arranged on his collage a rifle and other hunting matter with the poem "Willard Fluke" from Edgar Lee Masters' *Spoon River Anthology*. The poem served as a further example of how a man had gone astray, but this time from the marriage law since he had an affair with a woman named Cleopatra.

This opportunity for students to exercise their artistic skills helps not only to frame the book's thematic context but also to "connect" it with students' lives.

Verbal/Linguistic, Interpersonal Intelligences

Dialogue Journals

Dialogue journals (Anson and Beach, 1995) encourage student writing and critical thinking on a daily basis. Students count off by two's to determine whether they will write about the odd- or even-numbered chapters of *The Chocolate War*. Each entry for a dialogue journal consists of one page—front and back—of notebook paper. Students fold a sheet of notebook paper vertically so that it is divided one-third on the left and two-thirds on the right. According to their assigned chapters, students write front and back on the two-thirds portion of the paper. Here, students may pose questions about their reading, such as asking about characters' feelings, or perhaps parallel occurrences with their own lives; they may reflect on thought-provoking aspects of plot, or even respond to specific quotes that intrigue them from the text. This journal writing ensures on-going reflection and establishes a written discourse among students. Students who have written about the even-numbered chapters will exchange journals with those who have written about the odd-numbered ones. The one-third of the paper is the area in which students respond to the insights of their peer partner. Through this process students express concurrence and difference, offer clarification, and extend their critical engagement with the text.

Logical/Mathematical, Visual/Spatial, Verbal/Linguistic Intelligences

Character Mapping

After reading the first 10 chapters and discussing the characters' goals and conflicts, students will create a character map as a means of exploring relationships in *The Chocolate War*. This activity may be framed in specific terms such as, "If the characters were a household appliance, which parts of that appliance would they be, and why? Choose 5-8 examples." This may also be expanded to include character relationships viewed as parts of a landscape, athletic event, building, or automobile (see Figure 9.1).

Students draw and label the character map and include a written rationale for their choices on a separate sheet of paper. While sharing these interpretations with their peers, thematic questions again rise, this should lead to a discussion of Jerry Renault's striving for individuality through his refusal to sell the chocolates, the Vigils' resistance to Jerry's act, then subsequent efforts to "make" him conform. Here, too, the question emerges: "who holds the power at Trinity?" As students examine this question and those related to corrupt authority figures, such as Brother Leon, the themes of individuality vs. conformity along with the risks of "disturbing the universe" suface. See Table 9.2 for the Explanation of Adam's Character Map.

FIGURE 9.1

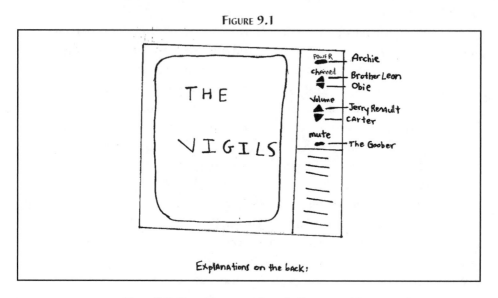

TABLE 9.2: EXPLANATION OF ADAM'S CHARACTER MAP

Archie is the power button because he is the most powerful character in the book. He can get others to do what he wants them to do.

Brother Leon is the up channel because he has control over all the kids in his class and he will take control of the school when the principal goes into the hospital.

Obie is the down channel because he directs the other kids a little bit. He is officially the secretary of the Vigils. He was pretty much Archie's right hand man.

Jerry is the down volume because he does not have as much power as the other kids. He is only a freshman. He is a skinny kid that is just trying to make the freshman football team.

Carter is the up volume because he had power. He is the president of the Vigils because the president was always a football player. He is very intimidating and nobody fooled around with him.

The Goober is the mute button because he didn't have much say on things. They said he was good Vigil bait because he did what anyone told him to do and never got his say on things. The Vigils wanted him to go into brother Eugene's room and loosen up the screws on everything for an assignment.

The Vigils are the screen because they are the centerpiece of the book. All of these boys make up the Vigils, and they say this group rules the school.

Visual/Spatial, Logical/Mathematical, Verbal/Linguistic Intelligences

Character Continuum

Having examined the characters of the novel through character mapping, students can delve into the comparative aspect of character analysis by creating a Character Continuum. This continuum begins with the selection of extremes such as Good and Evil, Merciful and Merciless, Generous and Greedy, and Inclusive and Exclusive. Once students have selected the extremes for their continuum, they begin to plot the characters of *The Chocolate War* in relation to one another. Although many students initially approach the continuum in a linear fashion, the artistry of it can grow by proposing that students arrange the "line" of the continuum in a symbolic form. For example, in conveying Good and Evil, one student began by drawing clouds around the word "Good" in which each of the "o's" was crowned by a halo. As the continuum progressed toward Evil, which appeared as a fiery home of Brother Leon beneath the earth, the line wound gracefully through Jerry's house and Trinity, into Room 19, and onto the football field, highlighting both characters and events from the story.

Supplying them with large sheets of banner paper seems to unroll the creative minds of students as they work on this activity, freeing them to think about the "big" picture of character interactions. And, to really ground this activity in the text, students should use quotes which illuminate why characters stand as they do on the scale of trait pairs. When symbolism, key words, quotes, and related illustrations merge, the character continuum brings new life to character analysis and provides ample room for discussing motives, virtues, and vices.

Verbal/Linguistic, Bodily/Kinesthetic, Interpersonal Intelligences

Tableaux

As readers of *The Chocolate War* will observe, Archie and Carter have different ways of intimidating Trinity students who have been dealt assignments by the Vigils. Archie, not involved in athletics because he despised the smell of sweat in the locker room, downplayed physical violence as a means to achieve compliance in the assignees running the Vigils' show with psychological intimidation. By contrast, Carter, the brutish athlete, resorted to physical blows, driving those who attempted to defy the Vigils into compliance. With this precept in mind, students explore ways that people attempt to impose their power on others and also discuss power as it is perceived and defined both in the novel and in today's world. Integral to this examination of power is Foucault's (1983) concept of "pastoral power" which is both individualizing and totalizing. Pastoral power is individualizing because it questions the status of the individual and asserts his or her right to be different; it is totalizing because it critiques anything that interferes with the "community ideal," therefore forcing the individual back to the group ideal. Therefore, as students look at Jerry Renault's right to be an individual and his decision not to participate in the school's annual sale, they also look at how the Vigils use Jerry's stance against him. During the roll call of chocolates, Brother Leon exemplifies the concept of pastoral power as he lauds those who have participated in the sale by calling them the "true sons of Trinity." Here too, students examine how corruption can ensue when too much power is invested in a dominant individual or group. Lord Acton's letter to Bishop Creighton dated April 5, 1887 and cited in Bartlett's (1992) provides the invitation for discussion he wrote: "Power tends to corrupt, and absolute power corrupts absolutely." Subsequent questions include: Who has the power in the novel? When and how does this evolve? To what extent is power conceived as a physical force? A psychological one? What type of power is more prevalent in today's world? How do students experience this in their lives.

As a transition from discussion to tableaux (Milner & Milner, 1993), students form small groups and make human tableaux to represent their concept of power through the course of the day's discussion. Before students pose their tableaux, they move their desks into a circle, leaving room in the middle for the human statues. As one group freezes in the center, the others observe and interpret it, analyzing the view of power represented. After each group shares its tableau, students return to their small groups where they are assigned several chapters from the book from which they are to select scenes for future tableaux. These incidents and the number of students necessary to pose the tableau, are written on note cards; for example: prepare Room 19 Assignment: two people. The teacher collects the note cards, turns them face down; a student draws a card and prepares the requested tableau. As the tableaux are posed, students review the events of the book. Before closing the activity, discussion resumes about the concept of power. To what extent is it physical and psychological? In what ways does power promote and inhibit individuality?

Verbal/Linguistic, Intrapersonal Intelligences

Character Probe

As its name suggests, the Character Probe (Milner & Milner, 1993) delves into the minds of the characters in order to "reflect on [their] actions, personality, and motivation" throughout the course of the novel. As students empathize with the characters' egotism or particular struggles and vulnerabilities, they convey their understanding in one of the following ways:

- write about the dreams and imaginings of a character

- organize a debate between two characters (this one can be done cooperatively)
- write a yearbook entry or newspaper article about the character
- exchange gifts between characters, making sure to note how the choice of gifts reveals the uniqueness of the characters involved
- select what would be a character's favorite book, magazine, work of art, and store
- compose several journal entries by the character

Several poignant incidents through which students may reflect on the actions, personalities, and motivations of characters are listed below:

- Brother Leon asking Archie (and, therefore, the Vigils) for help with the sale
- Archie acknowledging the existence of the Vigils in front of Brother Leon
- Gregory Bailey after being accused of cheating
- Archie's trouble creating assignments
- Brother Jacques after the "environment" assignment
- Jerry's decision, and subsequent torment, not to sell the chocolates

Students may elect to present their character probe activity in front of the class or exchange it for quiet sharing with another student. Finally, as a follow-up to this process of sharing, students may engage in debate over areas of disagreement regarding various characters, and critiquing or defending their motives. Furthermore, these empathetic probes, through deliberative conversation, become segues for further analysis of the prizes and prices of conformity.

Musical/Rhythmic, Verbal/Linguistic Intelligences

Musical Compositions and Connections

This component of *The Chocolate War* unit is designed to celebrate those students willing to share their ability to compose and perform music, while not intimidating those who do not possess this dominant intelligence. Students are invited to compose a song or rap which conveys their understanding of any aspect—character, plot, setting, conflict, theme—of the novel. Such compositions may be performed live or recorded and played on audio or video tape depending on students' comfort level. Lyrics to two original student compositions related to *The Chocolate War* appear on Table 9.3. The first was performed live in class, rap style, with background music from a CD that the students selected. The second was recorded on audio tape and consisted of vocals in alternative scream style, electric guitar, keyboard and percussion. A third noteworthy audio retold Cormier's story through a series of carefully selected lines from the text read over the background of an original keyboard composition, dramatized further with a ringing telephone and resonant psychotic-like laughter representative of the torment Jerry experienced at home.

Table 9.3: Lyrics for Students' Musical Compositions

Cortland Funktown Homeboys John Ameen, Josh Bolinger, Joe Shaker, and Brock Stefura	No More Tim Beaumont
We'll give it t'ya'll straight bout a war on candy Put your ear on the ground cause it's a real jim-dandy	I'm beside myself wanting to give in can't let you rule me I'll keep coming back with my cuts and scratch I won't let you fool me
They had no bloods and they had no crips the little Vigil club was a gang-land rip	
Bullying youngsters, they were urban pirates goin gainst the world of the priestly tyrants	CHORUS: No more! No more!
Chorus: Keep that candy handy, yea. Keep that candy handy. Keep that candy handy, yea. Keep that candy handy.	Never break my pride take a look inside won't sell your chocolates 14 years of age with this chocolate craze the image you create
Jerry was a modern James Dean, Bussin up Leon's chocolate scheme. He wasn't backing down, threw it in their face Leon said, "You's a disgrace to your race.	CHORUS
Leon poured on the pressure like a pitcher Telling Archie, "Make Trinity richa." The jive was stoppin', wasn't playin' no mo. Had Emile beat him down like a 2 dollar hoooo.	Chocolate war in disguise Vigils full of lies mask of foolish games you can knock me down go ahead break my crown never forget my name
Chorus: Jerry watch your back Cause they're coming to get ya Watch ya back, watch ya back Cause they're coming to get ya. (Twice)	CHORUS
Jerry was tired, he was ready for a face-off, going to the stadium, he was going to play tough. Him and Emile at the mercy of the crowd Never gonna walk away, just too proud.	
He took the fall a lot like Mr. Tyson, going against Emile, like fightin' a bison. Leon on the hill, Archie wasn't sweatin', was gonna be a great year, Archie was a bettin'.	
Chorus: Fight the power, Fight the power Do not let it getcha. (Four times)	

While the three examples convey a certain familiarity on the part of the student composers with the musical/rhythmic intelligence, this ability may prove to be intimidating to other students. So that all students may enjoy the opportunity to engage their musical senses with the novel, a second option exists for those who do not choose to compose and perform music. This option acknowledges students' ability to appreciate music and connect it with literature. Students simply choose a character, event, place, time, theme, or conflict from the novel, read it to the class, and then play the song they've found that helps express their understanding of it. Particularly important here is the reasoning students exhibit upon making this connection; therefore, explaining the connection in writing may help students to clarify their ideas.

Visual/Spatial, Logical/Mathematical, Verbal/Linguistic, Interpersonal Intelligences

Storyboarding

Moviemakers prepare storyboards before filming in order to map out the flow of a scene. Storyboarding is an art form that requires its creator to transform flat text into movie magic. In effect, storyboarding requires students to think like moviemakers in order to determine how they can best convey the story line. Storyboarding is a comprehensive task involving multiple intelligences and is time intensive, especially for amateurs. Storyboarding also, however, invests its artists with the power of interpretation since they determine what the eye sees and what the ear hears.

As a minimum, students will need four days to complete a basic storyboard. Table 9.4 shows that day one consists of an overview of terms and examples of how each is used, plus time for students to select groups and to choose a brief scene from the text which will provide the basis of their storyboard (Franek, 1996). A manageable storyboard, for completion in three to four fifty-minute class periods, will be limited to eight to twelve shots. See Figure 9.2 for Susan Watters's Storyboard.

As most shots are only held for a few seconds, the incidents students select for their storyboard should be one "tellable" in two to three minutes of film time. Some examples are: Jerry at home tormented by phone calls; Rollo's appearance before the Vigils; Carter announcing the rules of the raffle; Brother Jacques turning out the lights to end the fight and the ambulance whirring into the darkness. Designating specific chapters for each group is advisable in order to prevent overlap. Additionally, when students are asked to determine, then convey through their storyboard, what they believe the most "important, significant, poignant, or memorable" excerpt from their assigned chapters is through their storyboard a refreshing review of the novel emerges. For added challenge, students may put the storyboard to use by actually filming the plan they've created and sharing the production with the class.

TABLE 9.4: THE BASICS OF STORYBOARDING

Usual Elements of Storyboarding

I.   Production Notes (descriptions to appear on cover page before frames of storyboard begin)
    A   Characterization
    B.   Costumes
    C.   Location
    D.   Props
    E.   Lighting

II. Descriptive Essentials (to be listed with each frame of the storyboard)
    A.   Sound (voice-over narration, dialogue, sound effects, music)
    B.   Action (what happens in the frame—movement by characters or objects)
    C.   Interior/Exterior (is the shot filmed indoors or outside?)
    D.   Type of shot
    E.   Duration of shot
    F.   Direction to next shot (see camera movement and editing)

III. Key Terms/Types of Shots
    A.   LS *Long Shot*—(a relative term) a shot taken from sufficient distance to show a landscape, a building, a crowd
    B.   MS *Medium Shot*—(also relative) a shot between a long shot and a close-up that might show two people in full figure or several people from the waist up
    C.   CU *Close Up*—a shot of a face or an object that fills the screen completely
    D.   ECU *Extreme Close Up*—a shot of a small object like an eye or an ear or a marble, that fills the screen
    E.   *Reverse CU*—switch already established CU to other person's perspective

IV. Camera Angles
    A.   *High Angle*—looks down at what is being photographed (often from a crane shot, with camera mounted overhead)
    B.   *Eye Level*—approximates human vision—camera presents an object so that the line between camera and object is parallel to the ground
    C.   *Low Angle*—looks up at what is being photographed

V.   Camera movement
    A.   *Pan*—horizontal movement from a fixed base
    B.   *Tilt*—vertical movement from a fixed base
    C.   *Tracking (Dolly) Shot*—the camera moves through space on a wheeled truck (or dolly), but stays in the same place
    D.   *Boom*—the camera moves up or down through space
    E.   *Zoom*—not a camera movement, but a shift in the focal length of the camera lens to give the impression that the camera is getting closer to or farther from an object
    F.   *Arc*—camera moves in a circle

VI. Duration of Shots
    A.   *Subliminal*—a few frames
    B.   *Quick*—less than a second
    C.   *Average*—more than a second, but less than a minute
    D.   *Lengthy*—more than a minute

cont.

VII. Editing
  A. *Cut*—the most common type of transition in which one scene ends and a new one immediately begins
  B. *Fade-out/Fade-in*—one scene gradually goes dark and the new one gradually emerges from the darkness
  C. *Dissolve*—gradual transition in which the end of one scene is superimposed over the beginning of a new one
  D. *Wipe*—an optical effect in which one shot appears to "wipe" the preceding one from the screen
VIII. Technical Aspects/Technicians
  A. Dolly (track for camera, such as when following someone walking)
  B. Grip (person who runs the dolly)
  C. Boom (hanging camera)

FIGURE 9.2: SUSAN WATTERS'S STORYBOARD

Focal Judgments Activity

Paring the Focal Judgments (Milner and Milner, 1993) activity with the Storyboard is an effective way to incorporate analytical writing into *The Chocolate War* unit. The scene students depicted in their storyboard becomes that which they analyze through the Focal Judgments questions (see Table 9.5 for an example). In doing so, an added dimension of depth emerges to strengthen students' understanding of the novel.

TABLE 9.5: FOCAL JUDGMENTS ACTIVITY

For this assignment you will make personal judgments about the most important words, passages, and aspects of a text of literature.
<div align="center">Procedure</div>
1.   After reading the text, choose what you consider to be the most important word in it. Give your rationale for the choice, that is, tell why it is the most important word.

2.   Return to the text and select the most important passage. Reduce the passage to a three or four word phrase that captures the entire text. Compare your phrase with the work's title to see if the two call up the same meaning. Reflect on and write about the selected passage in terms of each of the following:
      most important words
      connection with total meaning
      links with other passages
      feeling and mood

3.   Write what you consider to be the most important aspect of the text. "Aspect" is purposely vague so as to allow you many possibilities. Tell why it is the most important aspect.

4.   When you have selected your word, passage, and aspect, examine the three for connections. Do this by answering the following questions:
      Does the passage represent the aspect? Explain.
      Does the word appear in the passage?
      In what ways are the three related to one another? Unrelated?
      Does the work's title connect to all three? Explain.

5.   Conclude with a brief statement that describes what this activity reveals to you about a text of literature.

Visual/Spatial, Verbal/Linguistic Intelligences

Report Sacks

Individually or in teams, students can assume the role of one character in *The Chocolate War* and collect a series of artifacts which illuminate the life, triumphs, and trials of that character. These items will each be accompanied with a notecard revealing their significance, and, if desired, a quote from the text supporting the importance of the items. Students combine the artifacts, note cards, and quotes in a Report Sack or Box decorated to include the character's name. Students may choose a variation on the container for the goods when relevant. For example, since Archie's assumed fear of drawing a black marble tempers the assignments he gives, one group placed their artifacts in a wooden box with a handle, designed as an oversized model of the box held by the Vigils. Another group emphasizing Brother Leon's obsession with the chocolate sale placed their items in a candy box, while the group representing Brian Cochran stored their artifacts in a miniature safe, to remind the class of Brian's role as treasurer of the sale.

Verbal/Linguistic, Logical/Mathematical, Interpersonal Intelligences

Parallel Poems

"We Real Cool" by Gwendolyn Brooks, "Children's Rhymes" and "I, Too, Sing America" by Langston Hughes, and "Yes, Virginia, There Was a Holocaust: Is Anybody Out There" by Martin D. Niemoller are four poems that provide striking thematic links to *The Chocolate War*. Students first read and discuss all four poems then write a parallel poem relating the themes of Brooks, Hughes, and Niemoller to Cormier's. When writing a parallel poem, students attend to the language patterns of poetry, especially rhyme and rhythm. See Table 9.6 for Michael Dann's parallel response to Langston Hughes' *I, Too, Sing America* found in Adoff (1997). Although parallel poems may be written independently, collaboration often results not only in more ideas, but in an increased willingness and enthusiasm to perform the new poem before the class. Students are particularly encouraged to recite their parallel poem in a manner which includes multiple voices. A mini lesson on Paul Fleischman's concept of *Poems for two Voices* also proves to be useful here.

TABLE 9.6: MICHAEL DANN'S PARALLEL POEM

Individuality
Michael Dann

I, too, am Individual

I shall not fall
Into conformity
And be led around
Like an animal In a pack.

Tomorrow,
I will break the mold
I will fight the current
And go against the grain.
Then people will say to me,
"You are different,
And I respect you."

I, too, am Individual
They know the importance of individuality
And they are aware of its price.

I, too, am Individual.

Verbal/Linguistic, Logical/Mathematical, Visual/Spatial, Interpersonal Intelligences

Civil Disobedience and Jerry Renault

Prior to today's activity, students should have viewed Gordon's *Chocolate War* and read Thoreau's "A Nonconformist" from *Civil Disobedience* and King's "Homage to Gandhi."

Divided into research teams, the class meets in the media center or library to further investigate the concept of civil disobedience. From their independent reading, students will know to pay particular attention to the influences of Henry David Thoreau, Mohandas Gandhi, and Martin Luther King, Jr. Each research group is to find at least one quote or example of civil disobedience from Thoreau, Gandhi, and King, but will need to extend their research to include other examples of the concept in action. The beauty of this activity is an expanded knowledge of history which students gain in the process. Lunch counter sit-ins, Kent State, and Tiananmen Square are just a few of the incidents students discover in their investigation. Students determine how they will present their findings—either through collage, handout with pictures, time lines or some other activity—and will compile a works cited page to practice appropriate documentation.

After each group shares its findings with the class as a whole, students link the principles of nonviolent resistance with Jerry's decision not to sell the chocolates and then they debate the validity of his choice. Finally, the discussion extends to an investigation of the following questions:

- What are valid causes for the practice of civil disobedience historically? In today's society?
- How does civil disobedience affect perceptions of power?
- To what extent do numbers of individuals involved influence the effectiveness of civil disobedience?
- What other factors such as society, government, and religion influence the effectiveness of civil disobedience?

Verbal/Linguistic, Logical/Mathematical Intelligences

Synthesis Paper

Synthesis writing is the art of bringing together seemingly unconnected writings and ideas into a cohesive whole. Rooted in high-order thinking and critical analysis, synthesis is one of the most challenging writing assignments for young adults; it is also one that has the best chance of ensuring authenticity in student writing, while enabling the teacher to check for understanding. For the synthesis paper, students are asked to write a thesis based on the theme they determine best links the works studied as part of *The Chocolate War* unit. Students must include: Cormier's novel; three of the four poems; insights from Thoreau, Gandhi, and King; the song of their choice; and a new contribution. The new contribution may be a story, poem, essay, song lyrics, or even a work of art, so long as students are able to establish its relevance to the thesis controlling their synthesis paper.

As a minimal guideline, students may think in terms of writing one well-developed paragraph per genre or concept. For example, after the introductory paragraph, students may write one paragraph about the poems, followed by another paragraph about the song, then one about the new contribution, and a concluding paragraph. More sophisticated writers should seek to interweave the genres, authors, and concepts throughout their synthesis. Whichever approach students take, however, their central task is to adhere to their chosen thesis, making sure each genre, author, and concept reinforces it. An example thesis in which the thinking student would be able to fit all of the works studied is: *History, literature, and music exemplify humanity's love of individuality, but also remind the scholar that nonconformity has its price.*

Verbal/Linguistic Intelligence

Comparing the Conclusions: Cormier's Novel vs. Gordon's Film

Viewing a film after reading the corresponding book sharpens the viewer's critical lens and naturally provides confidence to the critic rendering judgment on the film. Until the film reaches its conclusion, Keith Gordon's interpretation of *The Chocolate War* is true to the book. In the final fifteen minutes of Gordon's film, Archie, the arrogant victor of Cormier's novel, draws not a vindicating white marble, but an ominous black one. Archie, the "assigner-kept-in-check," enters the ring in place of Emile Janza. Not only does Jerry pound Archie to a knock-out victory, but the whole school, including the Vigils and Brother Leon, rises to its feet to applaud Jerry. The Vigils subsequently demote Archie to secretary and promote Obie to Assigner.

Gordon's interpretation, with a graphic account of Jerry's final blow to Archie's face from which several teeth are sent flying, is shocking to the reader expecting to see Jerry whisked away in an ambulance. After the "oohs" and "aahs" and "yeahs" subside from the student viewers, a need arises to confront Gordon and the liberty he has taken as a filmmaker. For here, the former notion of consequence relating to individuality vs. conformity, is turned upside down. The Jerry Renault who the reader might assume is dead because of his failure to conform and his defiance of the Vigils, is a hero of epic proportions. Cormier himself addressed his feelings about the movie's conclusion in a letter to Lakeview High School students. See Table 9.7 for Cormier's Letter. Today's task is simple—show the last fifteen minutes of the film, and let the debate begin.

TABLE 9.7: EXCERPT FROM ROBERT CORMIER'S LETTER, JANUARY 25, 1997

As far as the movie version of *The Chocolate War* is concerned, I am very distressed by the ending. I trusted the filming to a young director who had read the novel in high school and loved it. After years of trying to find the right film maker, I felt he could be trusted most of all, and gave him the film rights in an agreement involving a modest amount of money. Without consulting me, he drastically changed the ending. (A sad truth: when a writer signs a contract with a film maker, all control is given up—that's why it is so important to work with someone you trust, as I mistakenly did with Ken Gordon.).

Choice of the Multiple Intelligences

Contracting as a means of Celebrating Individuality!

As the culminating activity for *The Chocolate War* unit, students will con-tract with the teacher to create a project which exhibits their unique under-standing of an aspect from Cormier's novel. See Table 9.8 for format. Although the contract statement is simple, teachers aiming for specific criteria on which to base grades, will need to help students make their contracts precise and measurable. For instance, if a student contracts "to complete a scrap-book showing understanding of Jerry Renault's life and struggles at Trinity," the teacher can help make the contract more specific by asking the follow-ing questions: How many pages will the scrapbook include? How will the scrapbook be rooted in the text of *The Chocolate War* (suggest using quotes from the book)? What materials will make the scrapbook interesting (sug-gest pictures, letters, artifacts, etc.)? Students contracting to create videos may also be encouraged to write a script or create a storyboard. The teacher may ask those contracting "to make a map which will show the important places in the book" to make the map three-dimensional with materials like papier-maché and wood. Such suggestions tend to lift student projects to a more creative level where they are actually making the setting rather than just assembling it with the help of action figures and toy houses. Students creating discographies—collections of music—should include a typed list of song titles, performing artists, and either a quote or an incident from the book which parallels the music choice. Also advisable is limiting any one song excerpt to thirty seconds (or even fifteen seconds, which really forces students to use their critical thinking skills and be selective) and the whole tape to five minutes as this makes presentation time manageable and effi-cient. The primary focus of the culminating projects students contract to do, is celebrating individuality. The more varied the approaches to exhibiting understanding, the better to make the point that even in a system as struc-tured as a school, there is still room for creative expression.

TABLE 9.8: CONTRACT STATEMENT FORMAT

Student's Name: To show my understanding of _____,
                                              (Must be specific aspect of the novel—
                                              character, plot, setting, conflict, theme, etc.—
                                              not just the title)
 I will _____.
 (Be as specific as possible)

Conclusion

Cormier's vivid writing challenges the grand ideals upon which Americans have staked their future: that in speaking out, one will be heard; that in standing by one's principles, one will earn respect; that in being one's self, one will gain admiration. Having delved into the risks inherent in being a nonconformist through the variety of introspective and communal activities connected to *The Chocolate War* and other related texts, students have broadened their capacity to see the complexity of humankind. With a critical eye, they may see both uniqueness and injustice in the world. It is no accident that as a pioneer of young adult literature, Robert Cormier reaches into the lives of teenagers and dares to disturb their universe.

References

Anson, C. and Beach, R. (1995). *Journals in the classroom: Writing to learn.* Norwood, MA: Christopher-Gordon.

Attenborough, R. (1982). *Gandhi.* [Videotape]. Columbia Tristar Studios.

Bartlett, J., & Kaplan, J. (Eds.). (1992). *Familiar quotations* (16th ed.). (p. 521). Boston: Little, Brown.

Brooks, G. (1997). "We real cool" in A. Adoff (Ed.). *I am the darker brother: An anthology of modern poems by African-Americans* (p. 22). New York: Simon & Schuster.

Bushman, K. P. (1993). Dealing with the abuse of power in *1984* and *The chocolate war.* In J. R. Kaywell (Ed.). *Adolescent literature as a compliment to the classics,* Vol. 1. (p. 217). Norwood, MA: Christopher-Gordon.

Cormier, R. (1985). *Beyond the chocolate war.* New York: Alfred A. Knopf.

Cormier, R. (1974). *The chocolate war.* New York: Dell.

Franek, M. (1996). Producing student films: Shakespeare on screen. *English Journal* (p. 50–54). In A. Wilder and A. B. Teasley, "How to read a movie: Strategies for active viewing in high school English classes." In C. Cox (Ed.). *Media literacy: Classroom practices in the teaching of English.* Urbana, IL: NCTE.

Fleischman, P. (1988). *Joyful noise: Poems for two voices.* New York: Harper Trophy.

Foucault, M. (1983). *The subject and power.* In H. L. Dreyfus and P. Rainbow (Eds.).

Michel Foucault: Beyond structure and hermeneutics. (p. 211–214). Chicago: University of Chicago Press.

Gordon, K. (1989) *The chocolate war.* Video produced by M.C.E.G.

Hughes, L. (1997). "I, too, sing America" in A. Adoff (Ed.) *I am the darker brother: An anthology of modern poems by African Americans* (p. 122). New York: Simon & Schuster.

Hughes, L. (1999). Children's rhymes. In *Langston Hughes: Poems.* Selected and edited by D. Roessel. New York: Knopf.

King, Jr., M. L. (1973). from "Homage to Gandhi." In *The United States in literature* (p. 174C). Glenview, IL: Scott, Foresman.

Masters, E. L. (1962). *Spoon river anthology.* New York: Macmillan.

Milner, J., & Milner, L. (1993). *Bridging English.* New York: Macmillan.

Niemoller, M. D. *Yes, Virginia, there was a Holocaust: Is anybody out there?* Statement. http://www.rogertaylor.com/samples/918.htm

Thoreau, H. D. (1973). From *Civil disobedience.* In *The United States in literature* (p. 145–151C). Glenview, IL: Scott, Foresman.

CHAPTER 10

Preservation of Self and the Environment with Will Hobbs

Jackie Glasgow

Introduction

In his book, *The Disciplined Mind: What all Students Should Understand* (1999), Howard Gardner eloquently argues that the purpose of K–12 education should be to enhance students' deep understanding of truth, beauty, and goodness as defined by their various cultures. Whereas few would deny that the primary purpose of schooling is the inculcation of knowledge and truth, the role of schools as primary communicators of beauty and goodness is much less certain. In American society, religious and moral instruction has been the task of the home, the church, or the relevant institution elsewhere in the community. Organizations like the Boy and Girl Scouts, after-school clubs, and summer camps often step into this breach. The context that made a "virtue-oriented" education possible has disintegrated throughout the world and is especially tenuous in modern and postmodern societies like the United States. However, Gardner believes that "education must continue to confront truth (and falsity), beauty (and ugliness), and goodness (and evil), in full awareness of the problematic facets of these categories and disagreements across cultures and subcultures" (1999, p. 35). According to Gardner, the academic disciplines remain the best way to pursue this mission. In the English and Language Arts classroom, one way to pursue the vision of the true, the beautiful, and the good is with Will Hobbs and his contributions to young adult literature, along with Joseph Bruchac and other Native American authors. See the Annotated

Bibliography at the end of the chapter for resource materials.

In the presence of nature's great mountains, canyons, and rivers, human conflicts and tensions diminish. As the human soul is quieted, there is room to contemplate and discover the self. Hobbs believes that "there is a part of the human heart that longs for wild places. We yearn for the connection to nature that helped form our consciousness over the millennia. Our sense of beauty derives from natural forms; our sense of adventure and discovery, in books and in real life, finds ready fulfillment on the grandest stage of them all, the outdoors" (Donelson and Nilsen, 1997, p. 138). With this admiration and respect for humans in the outdoors, one might suspect that Will Hobbs is endowed with an extra measure of Howard Gardner's Naturalist Intelligence. Gardner describes the naturalist as the individual who "is able to recognize flora and fauna, to make other consequential distinctions in the natural world, and to use this ability productively [in hunting, in farming, in biological science]" (1995, p. 206). Hobbs, himself, as well as the characters in his books enjoy the outdoors, love animals, and are comfortable with nature. They demonstrate the ability to discern, identify and classify plants and animals as they generally survive in remote, rugged wilderness areas of Canada, Alaska, and the Western United States. In this unit, students will have opportunities to nourish and develop their naturalist intelligence as they explore spiritual themes of natural beauty, spiritual journey, identity formation, survival, and preservation of the environment within both the naturalistic settings and adventures of Hobbs' books and in their own back-yards.

Utilizing Gardner's Multiple Intelligences for a Deep Understanding of Truth, Beauty and Morality in the Environment: Responding to Hobbs' *Bearstone, Beardance* and/or *The Big Wander*

Gardner asserts, "It is important that a culture identify the truths, beauties, and virtues that it values, and that it then dedicate resources to inculcating their understanding in young learners" (1999, p. 245). He admits that deep understanding is difficult to achieve, but if education is to achieve greater success with more individuals, it must attempt to overcome the obstacles. Gardner's research has also shown that individuals possess different kinds of minds and represent information and knowledge in idiosyncratic ways. This unit is designed to accomplish both purposes—to help students utilize their multiple intelligences by gaining a deep understanding of environment described in the works of Will Hobbs, Joseph Bruchac and other native writers. See Table 10.1 Activities for Deep Understanding of the Environment Utilizing the Multiple Intelligences.

Intrapersonal, Visual/Spatial, and Verbal/Linguistic Intelligences

Secret Naming Ceremony

Create the atmosphere of a cave by darkening the room and playing mood music such as a selection from Resphigi's *The Pines and Fountains of Rome,* "The Pines Near a Catacomb" while someone reads dramatically from *Bearstone* beginning on page 14. Stop reading on page 16 when Cloyd gives himself the secret name. At this point ask students to create their own secret name or nickname that personally describes them. Students could then make their own badge, banner, or headdress to represent their new identity. After selecting a name, ask students to bring in or make an object that is as significant to them as is Cloyd's bearstone to him. Describe its significance by some means such as an essay, short story, poem, song, creative dance; or videotape a dramatic presentation which is indicative of the secret name and object. Students may choose either to share with the class or only with the teacher.

An extension of this lesson would be to create a "life map" of significant events in the students' lives and make a poster board presentation including photographs or objects. They should focus on their strengths just as a business world would "sell" itself and list some weaknesses and strengths of Cloyd. Students should list three of their weaknesses and then write an obtainable goal for each one. Sealing the goals in an envelope, they will open it in one month and write a journal entry or share their progress with someone. With this information, students could create a pamphlet titled "Marketable Me." If technology is available, students could make a brochure using Print Shop's Presswriter or other user-friendly software. If appropriate, students could use the information for a job search or for advertising their services for babysitting, lawn care, house or room painting, or other services for which they are qualified and in which they are interested.

After discussing the Native idea of a circle and reading "The Circle" by Nancy Wood (1993), ask students to use her poem as a template for one of their own. See Table 10.2 for the template.

TABLE 10.1: ACTIVITIES FOR DEEP UNDERSTANDING OF THE ENVIRONMENT USING THE MULTIPLE
INTELLIGENCES FOR SEEKING TRUTH, INSPIRED BY BEAUTY, AND MAKING MORAL DECISIONS

Intelligences	Activities Seeking Truth	Inspired by Beauty	Moral Decisions
Verbal/ Linguistic	Research laws for endangered species Author study on Hobbs or Bruchac Write winter survival stories	Create a bear story or folktale Write and tell myths and legends	Write a new law to support your view of endangered species
Logical/ Mathematical	Design a tepee Figure how many hides cover a tepee Calculate grizzlies in CO Create a timeline for Cloyd's adventures Compare heights of horse and burro Make topographical map for Cloyd	Design a ranch Solve gold mining problems Find and make a best recipe for peach cobbler Create hieroglyphics Design obstacle course to train for mountain climbing	Determine the populations of hunted animals in your area. At what point is hunting an animal justified?
Visual/Spatial	Create totems Prepare museum of Ute artifacts Create a travel brochure for excursion in the novel Make a project cube of scenes from novels Create a Ute mural of history and culture Decorate room to resemble a cave	Design dream catchers Send postcards from Cloyd to sisters Design mobiles Make a picture book for a Ute legend Design a T-shirt for Cloyd Paint landscapes Create a photo essay of the beauty in your life	Create Navajo sandpaintings to attract good or dispel evil Create a photo essay of your life
Bodily/ Kinesthetic	Sew a Native American outfit Design a Sweat Hogan Build a fence similar to Cloyd's Make a scavenger hunt to a gold mine Make obstacle course to train for mountain climbing or for saving bears and mustangs	Perform a Ute Dance Hike in a park near you Camp or backpack Go fishing Do an Outward Bound Adventure Try basket weaving	Do project for Dine CARE Participate in Annual Ute Bear Dance Tap maple trees and collect sap to make syrup candy and sugar

cont.

Musical/ Rhymthic	Create a dance for your totem Research bear dances Make and tune a Ute drum Research Ute chants Create a song summarizing the plot of one of the novels	Perform a bear dance Perform a drum routine Perform Ute chants Compose tunes for legends Create a sound track for bear sighting Create music for hogans	Sponsor a beardance-a-thon to preserve bears Provide music for Annual Ute Bear Dance
Naturalist	Study environmental issues and endangered species in your geo-graphical area Study types of bears Study Outward Bound Program Study hunting laws for your State	Write poems that respect nature Keep a journal while hiking fishing or camping Design your own Outward Bound Experience	Form Ecology Club Design gun control reforms Design hunting reforms
Interpersonal	Study Ute culture and compare with cultures represented in the classroom	Debate hunting as a sport Study conflict resolution models	Role-play conflict resolution for Cloyd vs. Walter Rusty Ursa
Intrapersonal	Select a valuable object or totem Create a "life map" for yourself Create a pamphlet "Marketable Me" List strengths and weaknesses of Cloyd and compare with your own	Journal your dreams and visions Act out Cloyd's experience in the cave Write about your favorite place write a "circle" poem	Write a law that supports your view of hunting Conduct a secret naming ceremony
Existential	Compare and contrast Ute values with mainstream values Study Pantheism Consider the issues of extinction and take a position on preserving endangered species	Examine your beliefs about nature Design a plan to preserve some aspect of the environment	Meditate in a sweat Hogan Conduct *Blessingway* and *Enemyway* Ceremonies according to your own beliefs

TABLE 10.2: TEMPLATE FOR "THE CIRCLE" POEM

"The Circle"
All is a circle within me.
I am _____.
I am _____.
I am _____.
I am _____.
All is a circle within me.
I have (seen) _____.
I have (seen) _____.
I have (seen) _____.
All is a circle within me.
I have (gone) _____.
I have (gone) _____.
I have (gone) _____.
Now (all) _____.
Now (all) _____.

An art project for this cave experience would be for students to redecorate the room to resemble a cave, papering all of the walls and creating their own hieroglyphics. Students could retell Cloyd's story by painting pictures of important scenes in his life that show how he feels about his history and culture. One wall could be a pictorial interpretation or listing of the cultural differences between Cloyd and the various cultures represented in the classroom. Another place on a wall could be used to create common signs or words from different tribal languages. Along the ledges of the cave, students could make a museum of objects that represent the Ute Nation. See Table 10.3 for Assessment Rubric for Artistic Products.

Interpersonal and Naturalist Intelligences

Conflict Resolution

Violence is a growing problem in schools, society, and the workplace. We need to set aside time to help young people control their anger, manage conflicts, and become peacemakers. English teachers can teach conflict resolution skills to resolve issues raised in the context of literature, allowing students to practice in a nonthreatening, safe environment. In *Bearstone* (1989), there are scenes in Cloyd's life that lend themselves for discussion and role-play to help students become tolerant of different characters' views and to solve destructive conflicts that arise in the stories. Cloyd has difficulty managing his anger at being sent to Walter's ranch; he resents working long hours; he is enraged when Walter permits Rusty to hunt on his property; and he becomes violent when Rusty kills the bear. Walter Landis must manage his rage and broken heart when he discovers his wife's peach trees have been destroyed. Ursa is committed to protecting the grizzlies as an endangered species. In order to resolve the conflicts peaceably so that the agreements are mutually beneficial, students need a model for positive negotiation. Johnson and Johnson (1995) suggest that by taking a problem-solving approach, players can avoid win-lose negotiations that are exemplified by Cloyd, Rusty, Walter, and Ursa in *Bearstone* (1989).

TABLE 10.3: ASSESSMENT RUBRIC FOR ARTISTIC PRODUCTS

	Quality (5)	Acceptable (4)	Not Yet (1-3)
Assessment Rubric for Artistic Products Student's Name: Artistic Project:			
Effective Use of Elements of Art			
1. Used interesting lines to create imagery	_____	_____	_____
2. Used creative shapes to create imagery	_____	_____	_____
3. Used effective colors to create imagery	_____	_____	_____
4. Used focal/vanishing points to create art	_____	_____	_____
5. Used a variety of textures (rough, smooth, shiny)	_____	_____	_____
6. Used empty space effectively	_____	_____	_____
Effective Use of Principles of Art			
1. Used balance to create a desirable effect	_____	_____	_____
2. Used variety and contrast to create an impression	_____	_____	_____
3. Used repetition (rhythm) to create an effect	_____	_____	_____
4. Used emphasis to make a point	_____	_____	_____
5. Used movement	_____	_____	_____
6. Used unity (harmony) to create an impression	_____	_____	_____
Content			
1. Project completed as assigned	_____	_____	_____
2. All criteria of assignment met	_____	_____	_____
3. Elements and principles blended well to create a message	_____	_____	_____
4. Used care in producing product	_____	_____	_____
Overall Grade for Product			

Problem-solving negotiations have characteristics that distinguish them from other types of conflict management strategies such as win-lose and compromise strategies. Johnson and Johnson (1995) provide a six step model for negotiating a conflict of interest that assumes that both parties give consent to the negotiation and agree to participate in arriving at a mutually beneficial solution to the problem that will strengthen a long-term cooperative relationship:

- Describe what each person wants.
- Describe how each person feels.

- Exchange reasons for positions.
- Understand each other's perspective.
- Invent options for mutual benefit.
- Reach a wise agreement. (p. 52)

According to Johnson and Johnson (1995), the heart of negotiating is meeting the goals of the other person while meeting your goals. The success of negotiating depends upon finding out what the other person really wants and showing that person a way to get it while you get what you want (p. 59). A wise agreement is one that meets the legitimate needs of all participants and is considered to be fair by everyone involved. Whether planning a debate, panel discussion, or role-play, these six steps provide a framework for students to become cooperators in resolving conflicts as partners, rather than as adversaries.

One of the central issues producing conflict in *Bearstone* (1989) concerns attitudes about hunting as a sport. In order to solve the conflicts between Rusty, Walter and Cloyd, divide the class into groups according to their interests in order to generate arguments appropriately representative of the various positions. One group could represent Rusty and his desire to shoot the grizzly. Another group could represent Walter's permission for hunters to hunt his land. Another group could explore Cloyd's position of the bear as totem. Another group could represent Ursa's position as wildlife biologist for endangered species. Another group might research gun control legislation, hunting licenses, and/or reasons for hunting seasons. When research is complete and each group is well prepared, create a talk show, panel discussion or debate discussing the hunting issue. Another outcome would be to design role-plays based on key scenes in the book: Cloyd's anger at Walter for granting Rusty permission to hunt on the ranch, Walter's confrontation with Cloyd after the destruction of the peach trees, and Rusty's confrontation with Cloyd in hunting grizzlies. An extension to the lesson would be to have students research and write a new law that would enforce their viewpoint on the hunting issue. They might hold a mock congressional debate and vote on the proposed law.

Naturalist, Bodily/Kinesthetic, Musical/Rhythmic, Intrapersonal, and Existential Intelligences

Make a Model Hogan

In the *Big Wander* (1992), Navajo Sam Yazzie, builds a sweat hogan from three long forked sticks of green willow that he found by the river. He must purify himself before he can talk to Clay about the difficult issues concerning his father. Sam feels that if he prepares himself in the right way, everything will be all right. He will fast, meditate, play his drum, and chant. One of the songs he sings is about *Bik'é hozoni*, the trail of beauty:

Beauty before me, with it I wander.

Beauty behind me, with it I wander.

Beauty below me, with it I wander.

Beauty above me, with it I wander.

Beauty all around me, with it I wander.

On the beautiful trail I am, with it I wander. (Hobbs, 1992, p. 87).

The literal meaning of hogan is "the place home." It is built in a specially chosen place for the purpose of housing Navajo ceremonies. Usually the hogans are made of wood or mud in a round shape, like the sun and the ceremonial basket, and the entrance faces east in order to catch the first rays of dawn. Within the hogan the children and grandchildren are taught all of the stories of the origin of the hogan and the respect and care that is necessary for it.

Students might be interested in researching more about the various Navajo ceremonials held within the hogan. The *Blessingway* is used to ensure good luck, good health and prosperity. The *Enemyway* is used to exorcise the ghosts of aliens, violence and ugliness and is derived from old ceremonials used to protect warriors from the ghosts of those they had killed. The *Holyway* ceremonies may last anywhere from one night to nine nights and are for the purpose of purification, dispelling evil (or ugliness) and the attraction of good. *Sandpaintings* both attract good and dispel evil. Artistic students may want to try making their own sandpaintings after researching the Navajo technique. See http://hanksville.org/voyage/navajo/sandpaintings.php3 for information. Many of the songs or chants used in the ceremonies are accompanied with a rattle. Each chant has its own origin legend that describes how the Holy People have the ceremonial to the Earth Surface People. Some of these chants are available through Canyon Records Productions, 4143 N. 16th St., Suite 6, Phoenix, AZ 85016. The phone number is 1-800-268-1141.

To personalize this experience, students might think of special places they like to go in order to restore peace and harmony within themselves. Do they have a time-out place? Do they engage in any rituals that help them clear their minds and focus on issues concerning them? What music is important to calm them down or help them think? Do they prefer quiet and solitude? How long might they spend in this environment?

Will Hobbs suggests a writing activity about a favorite place. He suggests that students think of a natural setting that they feel very strongly about—a lake, a pond, a meadow, a mountainside, a spot in a city park. They then visit it in person or in memory, and make a list of impressions that come from their five senses. After that, they should think of an animal that lives in the special place; in what manner are they, or their character, changes through an encounter with the creature.

Naturalist, and Bodily/Kinesthetic Intelligences

Dinè CARE (Citizens Against Ruining our Environment)

Dinè CARE—Dinè being the Navajo word for "the people", is an all-Navajo environmental organization, based within the Navajo homeland. They strive to educate and advocate for their traditional teachings in order to protect and provide a voice for all life in the Four Sacred Mountains in Utah, Colorado, Arizona, and New Mexico. They promote alternative uses of natural resources that are consistent with the Dinè philosophy of Beauty Way. Their main goal is to empower local and traditional people to organize, to speak out, and to determine their own destinies. At present, their main projects are uranium issues, forest conservation, recycling, and monitoring the progress of a ten year forest management plan proposed by the Navajo Nation Forestry Department and the Bureau of Indian Affairs.

For this project, students should consider both the environmental issues and endangered species indigenous to their geographical area: such as city, town, countryside, home, school, or work. Students might break into groups according to the issues that interest them. After researching the issue, they design and implement an action plan. What can they to do improve, beautify, and prevent further ruination? Suggestions might be tree planting, yard cleanup, mural painting, gardening, litter control, bird houses, letters to companies contributing to pollution, among others. They then select an animal indigenous to their community and take a field trip to its habitat. Researching ways to protect that animal or other animals from becoming endangered species and write poems about the environment could be presented to elementary students in your district. They might join the Dinès in organizing projects, speaking out against destruction, and taking responsibility for their own destinies. They might create an Ecology Club for their school that addresses the environmental issues of their area. Students might invite speakers from various environmental issues groups to discuss issues raised either by the books or ones of their choosing. They might organize a "Beardance-a-thon" to raise funds for the club's projects.

Naturalist, Bodily/Kinesthetic, Logical/Mathematical, Interpersonal, Intrapersonal, and Existentialist Intelligences

Outward Bound

During World War II, German U-boats targeted British merchant shipping with terrifying accuracy. The frigid waters of the North Sea claimed hundreds of seamen, with the greatest number of casualities among younger sailors, who were presumably more fit. German-born educator Kurt Hahn was commissioned to find the reason for this imbalance. Hahn soon realized that the younger inexperienced seamen weren't as well prepared for the rigors of survival in the open sea as were the older, more seasoned sailors. *They gave in to panic. They gave out.* Fear led quickly to exhaustion in the cold water. *Then they gave up.* Hahn established a program of rugged training to help these young recruits develop mental toughness, which he believed was as necessary for survival as physical endurance. They needed confidence. They needed the presence of mind to overcome panic. Above all, they needed to learn to rely not on life preservers, but on themselves.

The name Hahn chose for his program was nautical jargon familiar to every sailor. It referred to the moment when a ship leaves its safe harbor for the unknown dangers and adventure of the open sea. At this moment the ship was said to be "*outward bound.*" Today, fifty-five years after Kurt Hahn's success, Outward Bound is an international organization with over fifty schools and centers on five continents. There are five wilderness schools and two urban centers in the United States. Since the first school was established in 1961, over 400,000 people have participated in their programs.

Outward Bound courses are designed to help people develop confidence, compassion, and a lasting relationship with the natural environment. The Outward Bound community knows firsthand the importance of respecting the natural world and understanding its potential dangers. They are not a survival school. They do offer, however, a rugged adventure in the wilderness—whether on the sea, rivers, mountains, or deserts—during which a person receives unparalleled training in wilderness skills. Personal growth is central to the Outward Bound experience. People prepare physically, mentally, and emotionally to become fit team members which results in the camaraderie and interdependence necessary for a team to achieve its goals. When ready, the adventure begins into unfamiliar territory where people apply newfound knowledge and skills. Teammates and instructors provide the emotional support for the experience which is the basis for the Outward Bound motto: "to serve, to strive, and not to yield" See http://outwardbound.org for more information.

Some students may be interested in joining one of the Outward Bound adventures, but classes may choose to design their own Outward Bound experience into nature providing a challenge, retreat, and an opportunity for self-discovery. Select an area nearby for an overnight or weekend trip such as a state or national park, river, lake, bluffs, farmland that might be appropriate for the skills of students. Set goals and implement activities to develop the physical, mental, and social training needed to successfully complete the adventure. Discuss equiment, food, clothing, and shelter requirements. Students could choose to build a tepee of the Ute Indian tribe. Using their logical mathematical skills, students would need to determine the slant height of the tepee, the circumference of the sector circle, the area of the circle and the total surface area. How many hides or simulated material will be needed to cover the structure? Why didn't people use bear hide for their tepee fabric instead of elk or buffalo hide? Discuss safety issues and learning outcomes. How will those outcomes be assessed—journals, portfolios, narratives, and/or adventure stories? Determine the costs and ways to raise the funds for the trip. If this experience is out of the question, consider an alternative: create an obstacle course to train for the endurance and physical fitness needed to handle the bears and mustangs as well as Cloyd and Clay did.

Bodily/Kinesthetic and Logical/Mathematical Intelligences

Obstacle Course

This lesson is designed to create an obstacle course based on endurance and physical fitness that main characters Clay from *The Big Wander* (1992), and Cloyd from *Bearstone* (1989) and *Beardance* (1993) needed to help the bears and the mustangs. Some students might prefer to demonstrate the design, construction, and training needed for the fence building that Cloyd had to learn. Students could make a maze and provide a training program to Walter's gold mine, Pride of the West, as another alternative for developing a fitness program.

Divide students into groups. Each group should design an obstacle course based on Cloyd's challenge to save the grizzlies and/or Clay's quest to find his uncle and to join him in saving the mustangs. For example, students may have Cloyd climbing a mountain (running up stairs), then shimmying along a ledge of a cliff (balancing across a beam). They must determine which muscle groups are needed to succeed at the obstacle course and they need to determine which activities, preparation, or training are needed to succeed at the course. For example, if the group determines that the participant will be using hamstrings, then it must also determine what activities will strengthen those muscles, such as leg extensions or squats. The students must actually set up the course and have another group run through it. Optionally it may be established as a timed competition.

This lesson could also be extended across the curriculum. For example, the physical education teacher could help students choose appropriate training or actually run the students through the needed training. The science teacher could help the students see the different muscles that are used. The health teacher could bring nutrition and wellness into the activity, and the math teacher could design a project using the times of the students on the course by having them find the mean and average. Classes could also take a field trip to a nearby park or field, for example, to set up the obstacle course in a more natural environment.

Combines all the Multiple Intelligences

Annual Ute Bear Dance

After researching the Ute history and culture, students simulate the Annual Ute Bear Dance as the culminating activity for the unit. They construct the Bear Dance Corral, make Ute musical instruments, prepare food, create songs and tell legends, prepare winter survival stories, make costumes, and practice the bear dance.

The origin of the Bear Dance relates to the time when two brothers were out hunting in the mountains and as they became tired, they lay down to rest. One of the brothers noticed a bear who was standing upright facing a tree and seemed to be dancing and making a noise while clawing the tree. The one brother went on hunting while the other brother continued to observe the bear. The bear taught the young man to do the same dance and the song that went with the dance. He told the young man to return to his people and teach them the dance and songs of the bear.

The Annual Ute Bear Dance, held when the first thunder in the spring is heard, is a social dance everyone enjoys. According to some of the elders, this was usually around the middle of March. Even though the original meaning of the Bear Dance has been dropped by modern people, the practice still survives because everyone is so ready to be outside after a long winter. Traditionally, the men prepared the Bear Dance corral. The women prepared food and the family's clothes worn during the dance. The storyteller related the family's way of life and how they survived the winter. Ute legends or stories told at the Bear Dance are reminders of the times when the elders asked the hunters to go out and gather meat. As they were out hunting, they encountered some small people who ran into the rocks in the hills. They told the elders about them and the elders told them that they were called cliff dwellers, which according to archaeologists were called Anasazi, the ancient ones. The songs, according to legends, show respect for the spirit of the bear and show that respect to the bear spirit makes one strong. The Bear Dance was one way in which people could release their tensions and become strong for the spring planting. The men and women, as they entered the corral, would wear plumes which, at the end of the fourth and final day, they would leave on a cedar tree at the east entrance of the corral. According to the Utes, "leaving the plume on the tree was to leave your troubles behind and start your life anew." For more information see http://www. southern-ute.nsn.us/culture/bear.html.

To begin planning an Annual Ute Bear Dance, divide students into groups according to their interests; they might research and prepare the corral, the music (songs, dances, instruments), the food (could be peach cobbler among other traditional foods), the games, the costumes, the stories, and legends. Students should set goals, create timelines, and determine the costs of their group's project. This would be a good time to teach social skills and group dynamics to help students work efficiently and effectively in producing their contribution to the ceremony. For additional resources go to the Oyate Website: http://www.oyate.org/. Oyate, the Dakota word for people, is a Native organization which disperses resource materials by and about Native peoples.

The storytelling group's job is to create a series of legends or myths to perform at the ceremony. They might begin by reading Hobbs' *Beardream* (1997) to stimulate ideas for stories that respect the Ute culture, the environment, and especially, the bear. Students could write their own survival stories, create a bear story, and/or retell an Indian folklore tale. Students could also share here their poems and stories earlier written about their secret names and special objects. Their stories could also be spinoffs from the novel. Use the rubric in Table 10.4 to generate ideas for their stories.

TABLE 10.4: RUBRIC FOR GENERATING STORIES

Significant event in the Book	Describe how the character felt during this event	Describe your feelings as you were reading this section.	What if . . .	The character's feelings would have been?	Rewrite the ending to this story according to the "What if" scenario
1. 2. 3. 4. 5.					

In addition to storytelling, this group could create a play or drama based on a specific event or conflict in the novels. A puppet show portraying the ecology themes would be motivating to present at the ceremony and might also be taken on the road to elementary classrooms.

Meanwhile, another group could prepare the corral and design games and sports to be played at the big event. They need to select an appropriate time and setting for the ceremony that is outdoors, if possible. This group could design a scavenger hunt based on Cloyd's hunt for the Grizzly or

Walter's hunt for gold. Board games might be constructed to focus on wild animals living in the mountains, a topographical map for solving dilemmas from the novel, or gold mining such as Pride of the West. They could play charades highlighting various scenes from the book. They might incorporate an obstacle course to rebuild their strength for hunting, mountain climbing, and planting crops. They could design a maze that leads to the Pride of the West. Students could design and build a Ute tepee and other cultural artifacts to display at the ceremony and set the stage for the big event.

Choose a Master of Ceremonies to coordinate the agenda for the Bear Dance and a Head Singer to lead the chants and drums. Both of these positions are a great honor suggesting they have distinguished themselves in leadership and knowledge of many songs. The Head Singer has the first and last word and has complete control of what goes on at the drum and, therefore, at the dance floor. Songs are started with a lead line sung by the Head Singer. This lets the drum and the dancers know what song is coming next. After the lead line, the drums begin playing, and everyone joins in. At this point the dancers begin to dance. The loud beats during the songs, sometimes called "Honor Beats" are a time for dancers to honor the drum. Liquor is never permitted at the drum. Women usually do not sit at the drum; rather, if they do sing, they usually sit behind the men singers. If a special song is requested, those asking for the song should donate to the drum. At the end of the ceremony, the Head Singer divides up the money among the singers according to their ability and support in carrying the load that made his job easier For more information do a web search on drum etiquette.

Students could compose a tune for the bear song sung by Cloyd on p.185 of *Beardance* (1993). Students could then compose other chants that detail sighting a bear, observing their feeding habits, care of their young, exploring their habitats, hibernation in winter, and hazards to their well-being. Traditional chants could be followed by a narrative poetic summary of the plot using the same format. See Table 10.5 for an example of a student product written by workshop participants. The contrived authentic Ute tune is: O-o- Ah- Si- Wah- O- Knees. It means: "Yellow Hair Standing on End." The purpose is to celebrate the sighting of a bear.

Once the chants are written and learned, have students build or borrow other instruments such as flutes and drums to accompany the music. Research the importance of the drum in the life of a Native American. Often the whole culture centers around the drum which brings the heartbeat of our Earth Mother to the ceremony for all to feel and hear. Drumming brings everyone back into balance. Whether dancing, singing, or just listening, people around the drum can connect with Spirit. Search for or see Drum Etiquette for more information on the web. Once the instruments are made and rhythms established, they should begin choreographing the Bear Dance. The dance could be typical of the Ute dance, or be an original aerobic routine; regardless of the form chosen, the dance should be learned by everyone attending the event.

TABLE 10.5: CHANT FOR SIGHTING A BEAR

"O-o- Ah- Si- Wah- O- Knees" or
"Yellow Hair Standing on End"

Cloyd came to Walter's house
Who was sad, he lost his spouse
Cloyd ran off to be alone
In a cave he found Bearstone

His only friend, Blueboy, a horse
The mountains' lure, his driving force
Built a fence out in the sun
To seek the mountains when he's done

A hunter came and killed a bear
Cloyd chopped peach trees in despair
Went to grandma's but won't stay
Will work with Walt another day
Off to find the vein of gold
That Walter wants, he's getting old

In the mine Walt nearly dies
Cloyd must reach a compromise
A grizzly's death he does not tell
Will stay with Walter 'til he's well
That's the end, there ain't no more
Read the book, it's at the store.

Young Adult Novels Written by Will Hobbs

Hobbs, Will (1988). *Changes in Latitudes.* New York: Atheneum (Simon & Schuster).

Hobbs, Will (1989). *Bearstone.* New York: Atheneum (Simon & Schuster).

Hobbs, Will (1991). *Down River.* New York: Atheneum (Simon & Schuster).

Hobbs, Will (1992). *The Big Wander.* New York: Atheneum (Simon & Schuster).

Hobbs, Will (1993). *Beardance.* New York: Atheneum (Simon & Schuster).

Hobbs, Will (1995). *Kokopelli's Flute.* New York: Atheneum (Simon & Schuster).

Hobbs, Will (1996). *Far North*. New York: Morrow Junior Books.

Hobbs, Will (1997). *Beardream*. Illustrator: Jill Kastner. New York: Atheneum (Simon & Schuster).

Hobbs, Will (1997). *Ghost Canoe*. New York: Morrow Junior Books.

Hobbs, Will (1997). *River Thunder*. New York: Delacorte Press.

Hobbs, Will (1998). *Howling Hill*. Illustrator: Jill Kastner. New York: Morrow Junior Books.

Hobbs, Will (1998). *The Maze*. New York: Morrow Junior Books.

Hobbs, Will (1999). *Jason's Gold*. New York: Morrow Junior Books.

Annotated Bibliography of Young Adult Literature by or about Native Americans

Alexie, Sherman (Spokane/Coeur d'Alene) (1993). *The Lone Ranger and Tonto Fistfight in Heaven*. Berkeley, CA: Oyate.

With wrenching pain and wry humor, Alexie presents contemporary life on the Spokane Reservation.

Alexie, Sherman (Spokane/Coeur d'Alene) (1995). *Reservation Blues*. Berkeley, CA: Oyate.

The tale of Coyote Springs, an all-Indian Catholic rock-and-roll band, blends narrative, visions, songs, and dreams to describe the effects of Christianity on Indian people today.

Bruchac, Joseph (Abenaki) (1997). *Lasting Echoes: An Oral History of Native American People*. New York: Avon Books.

Bruchac tells the histories of seven generations of Native American people. From Lakota to Apache to Abenaki, from Geronimo to Sitting Bull to lesser-known voices, this book is the moving story of the American Indian peoples as seen through their own eyes.

Bruchac, Joseph (Abenaki) (1993). *Dawn Land*. Golden, CO: Fulcrum Publishing.

This book unfolds in the time after the last glaciation, about ten thousand years ago. Here the People of the Dawn Land live in harmony with animals and the land—until their peace is threatened by evil. Young Hunter, one of the finest sons of the village, is chosen by the elders to venture out and face the mysterious threat.

Bruchac, Joseph (Abenaki) (1995). *Long River*. Golden, CO: Fulcrum Publishing.

This book is a sequel to Dawn Land. Young Hunter, now a grown man and husband, is once again chosen to face ominous threats to his community. With help from his wife, best friend and his faithful dogs, he struggles to save his people.

Bruchac, Joseph (Abenaki) (1993). *Flying with the Eagle, Racing the Great Bear*. Berkeley, CA: Oyate.

Bruchac tells 16 stories about the transition from boyhood to manhood—leaving home, leaving the protection of his mother and father, and going out to prove to himself that he can survive and grow.

Bruchac, Joseph (Abenaki) (1998). *The Heart of a Chief*. New York: Dial.

This story deals with some of the many issues confronting Native young people today, on and off the reservation: Indian "mascots," leadership, and alcohol abuse. This story realistically portrays a loving extended Indian family trying to deal with alcoholism.

Coel, Margaret (1998). *The Story Teller*. New York: Berkley Prime Crime.

When the Arapaho storyteller discovers that a sacred tribal artifact is missing from a local museum, an investigation begins. The lost treasure: a one-of-a-kind ledger book and the only eyewitness account of Arapaho history on the plains set the scene for solving this mystery.

Conley, Robert J. (Cherokee) (1992). *Mountain Windsong: A Novel of the Trail of Tears*. Berkeley, CA: Oyate.

In weaving together song, legend, and historical documents, Conley tells the love story of two ordinary people caught up in the removal from their traditional lands and brings to life the suffering and endurance of the Cherokee people.

Grutman, Jewel H. and Mattaei, Gay (1997). *The Ledgerbook of Thomas Blue Eagle*. New York: Lickle Publishing Inc.

While Tomas Blue Eagle is a fictional character, the book describes the life of a Sioux boy who attended school in the East to learn about the world of the white man. It chronicles the clash of two completely different cultures in America toward the end of the last century using white man's words and the Indians' picture stories.

Hogan, Linda (Chickasaw) (1995). *Solar Storms*. Berkeley, CA: Oyate.

A hurt and rebellious teenager, scarred in face and spirit, sets out to search for her birth family, her mother, and herself. Reunited with her adopted great-grandmother, great-great-grandmother, and the woman who adopted her mother, this family of women sets off by canoe on a journey to their ancestral homeland in the far North, where a hydroelectric dam project threatens the existence of two indigenous nations.

Hubbard, Jim (Ed.) (1994). *Shooting Back from the Reservation*. Berkeley, CA: Oyate.

Given a camera, some film, and a short course in photography, children from reservations in Arizona, Minnesota, New Mexico, South Dakota, and Wisconsin give back to the reader a camera's-eye view of their lives in black and white photos.

Hunter, Sally (Anishinabe) (1996). *Four Seasons of Corn: A Winnebago Tradition*. Berkeley, CA: Oyate

In this addition to the "We Are Still Here" series, 12-year-old Russell, Hunter's grandson, learns how to grow and dry corn from his Hochunk (Winnebago) grandfather.

King, Sandra (Ojibway) (1993). *Shannon: An Ojibway Dancer*. Berkeley, CA: Oyate.

Shannon, who is 13-years old, invites readers to accompany her and her friends as they hang out at the mall, play video games, fix each other's hair, and work on their outfits for the powwow.

Meyer, Carolyn (1994). *Rio Grande Stories*. New York: Gulliver Books, Harcourt Brace & Company.

This book gives voice to 15 seventh graders of diverse cultures and peoples of New Mexico, who decide to write and sell a book. Told in chapters that alternate between stories about the students and their own contributions to their book, Meyers' collection celebrates the lives of Native American, African-American, Hispanic, Anglo, and homeless students.

O'Dell, Scott (1992). *Sing Down the Moon*. New York: Yearling Books.
The Spanish slavers were an ever present threat to the Navajo way of life. This historical novel is about a young girl, Bright Morning, who is kidnapped and enslaved by Spaniards and then rescued by her husband-to-be.

Regguinti, Gordon (Ojibway) (1992). *The Sacred Harvest: Ojibway Wild Rice Gathering*. Berkeley, CA: Oyate.

For 11-year-old Glen Jackson, this warm late summer day was one he had waited for all year. It was the first time his father would take him out to gather mahnomin, the sacred food of the Ojibway people. This was the day he would become a wild ricer.

Roessel, Monty (Navajo) (1993). *Kinaaldá: A Navajo Girl Grows Up*. Berkeley, CA: Oyate.

This is the story of 13-year-old Celinda McKelvey's puberty ceremony as she takes on the honor and responsibilities of womanhood.

Sawyer, Don (1988). *Where the Rivers Meet*. Berkeley, CA: Oyate.
Through the wisdom of a grandmother, a Shuswap teenager, grieving after the suicide of a close friend, finds inner strength which points the way towards true values and recovery, for herself and her people.

Slipperjack, Ruby (Ojibway) (1987). *Honour the Sun.* Berkeley, CA: Oyate. This is the diary of a carefree child, who grows into womanhood and experiences despair as she sees her mother and her friends succumb to alcohol. As a 16-year-old, she returns home for a summer visit and realizes her mother's words will always guide her.

Taylor, Drew Hayden (Ojibway) (1990). *Toronto at Dreamer's Rock / Education is Our Right.* Berkeley, CA: Oyate
These two one-act plays examine the problems facing Native youth today. In *Toronto*, a teen's magical encounter with two member of his nation—one from the past and one from the future—make him aware of what it means to be Indian. In *Education*, the Minister of Indian Affairs is confronted by the Spirits of Education Past, Present, and Future.

References

Donelson, K., & Nilsen, A. P. (1997). *Literature for today's young adults* (5th ed.). New York: Longman.

Gardner, H. (1999). *The disciplined mind: What all students should understand.* New York: Simon & Schuster.

Gardner, H. (1995, November). Reflections on multiple intelligences: Myths and messages. *Phi Delta Kappan, 7,* 200–209.

Johnson, D. W., & Johnson, R. T. (1995). *Reducing school violence through conflict resolution.* Alexandria, VA: Association for Supervision and Curriculum Development.

Outward Bound. http://outwardbound.org.

Oyate Native Organization. http://www.oyate.org/

Resphigi, O. The pines near a catacomb. *The pines and fountains of Rome.*

Sandpaintings. http://hanksville.org/voyage/navajo/sandpaintings. php3.

Ute bear dance. http://www.southernute.nsn.us/culture/bear.html.

Wood, N. (1993). The Circle. In *Spirit walker.* New York: Doubleday.

CHAPTER 11

Confronting Environmental Threats with Robert O'Brien

Mary Hostetler with Jackie Glasgow

Introduction

It is an unfortunate fact of life that young people today are faced with the knowledge that many nations around the world have at their control weapons of global destruction. But far from paralyzing with fear, this unit will provide a basis for teaching today's youth how they can influence tomorrow's future. It was, after all, public opinion that put an end to slavery, child labor, and segregation.

The primary text that we will use for this unit is Robert O'Brien's *Z for Zachariah* (1987), a book that confronts the nuclear threat. The book is about 16-year-old Ann Burden, who manages to survive a nuclear war sheltered in a protected valley. She raises chickens, plants a garden, and keeps a journal of her activities, hoping someday to find other survivors like herself. After a year of existing on her own, a stranger approaches her valley. Although excited at first, she soon realizes the tyrant that he is and plans a way of escape. This book is paired with the classic novel describing the nuclear holocaust, *Hiroshima* by John Hersey (1985). Other young adult literature introduces students to the horrors of biological and chemical warfare in the Persian Gulf: Kerr's (1993) *Linger* and Westfall's (1992) *Gulf.* Jane Yolen and Bruce Coville (1998) tell a story about two teenagers who face the world ending in fire in *Armageddon Summer.* Survival, isolation, and conflict arising from some global catastrophe, whether through environmental disaster or war, has been explored well in nonfiction also. Isaac Asimov and Frederik Pohl (1991) provide an excellent background of other dangers to our environment that threaten man's existence; *Our Angry Earth* contains a hopeful message regarding mitigation of the situation. Through a series of collaborative and individual activities provided in this unit, students will gain an understanding not only of threats to the environment, but also they will learn to handle antagonistic relationships with people and the planet, while at the same time learning the importance of self-reliance. The activities for this unit will incorporate Howard Gardner's five important principles that guided Arts PROPEL assessment efforts.

In his book, *Multiple Intelligences: the Theory in Practice* (1993), Howard Gardner recommends new principles and assessment procedures for Arts PROPEL, a pilot approach to teaching and assessing in the arts and humanities. The implications of Arts PROPEL are also appropriate for English and language arts classrooms. These principles can serve as guidelines for teachers interested in changing their assessment procedures. When students learn in diverse ways, traditional paper-and-pencil evaluations will not necessarily document their achievement. Here are five Arts PROPEL assessment principles adapted from Gardner's (1993) research and the ASCD Multiple Intelligences Series (1994, pp. 5–8) by Linda and Bruce Campbell:

- *Assessment Captures Growth over Time*—Portfolios, Reader Response Logs, Writer's Notebooks, and Journals with reflective statements encourage students to actively reflect on their growth as an aspect of ongoing classroom learning.
- *Assessment is Multidimensional*—Rather than limiting assessment to written tests, students can demonstrate their learning through multimodal representations of knowledge such as projects, performances, role-play, music, or demonstrations.
- *Assessment Informs Instruction*—Assessment informs instruction when grading criteria are established by both teachers and students working together to determine them. High standards in any classroom should address both the knowledge of content and the processes of thinking and learning.
- *Informal Assessment is Important*—Teachers assess their students' progress through both formal and informal measures. Informal observations based on class discussion, small group activities, and conferences can be made explicit through observation checklists and/or teacher journal entries.
- *Students are Active Self-Assessors*—Howard Gardner emphasizes the importance of students' evaluating their strengths and weaknesses, articulating what they have learned, and recognizing how they have applied thinking and learning. When students reflect on their work,

they assume an active role in the learning process by constructing their understanding of the subject matter. Intrapersonal forms of assessment can occur through student journals or portfolios, peer-assessment sessions, checklists, exhibitions, or informal discussion with other students and the teacher.

When teachers extend these five principles of assessment into classroom practices, assessment reflects the teaching and learning process and requires students to critique their own achievement. These principles contain three critical dimensions of assessment that Gardner recommends with major curriculum units or projects: (1) *content and skill assessment*—which is what we use most often in school today; (2) *interpersonal assessment*—where students receive feedback from their peers, teacher, parents, community members, and knowledgeable experts in the field; and (3) *intrapersonal assessment*—where students reflect on the quality and process of their work (ASCD, p. 29). See Table 11.1 for Activities to Assess Student's Learning about Environmental Threats.

After reading *Z for Zachariah* (1987), students will construct a visual/spatial representation of Ann's world showing which areas are safe and which are dangerous. Since radios and telephones are dead, students who are musically inclined will enjoy a chance to analyze song lyrics with a theme of peace or destruction and compose songs reflecting the perspectives of Ann or Loomis. One very beneficial activity to foster the naturalist and bodily/kinesthetic intelligences will be to learn survival skills that may be invaluable in any number of emergency situations. Oral activities will nurture interpersonal and intrapersonal intelligences. In a Socratic Seminar, students will discuss issues of domestic abuse and the controversy surrounding the stockpiling of nuclear weapons. The follow-up activity for the discussion will be a verbal/linguistic activity which asks students to write a different ending to O'Brien's book that shows ways that Ann and Loomis resolve their hostility. To learn the concepts presented in *Our Angry Earth* (1991), students will work collaboratively to create an *Environment Letter Book*. Students will then create a portfolio of current environmental issues, solutions, and personal actions that reflect a focus of their choosing such as water pollution, poisons in the air or on the land, or weapons of mass destruction, including nuclear, biological and chemical warfare. Nature lovers will enjoy exploring their local watershed and representing the beauty in an art form. After reading literature about the dropping of the atomic bomb in 1945, students will design the culminating activity for this unit which takes place at a local bomb shelter—i.e., the school boiler room—where students simulate the experience of an air raid on Hiroshima.

TABLE 11.1: ACTIVITIES TO ASSESS STUDENT'S LEARNING ABOUT ENVIRONMENTAL THREATS

Intelligences	Content and Skill Assessment	Interpersonal Assessment	Intrapersonal Assessment
Verbal/ Linguistic	Write a letter from Ann to her mother Write letters to the United Nations banning nuclear weapons Write watershed poetry Make environmental Letter Book for *Our Angry Earth* Create an original metaphor for themes in the book	Lead a Socratic Seminar on stockpiling or using nuclear weapons Demonstrate peer editing skills for letter writing and watershed poetry Learn assertive and nonassertive responses for conflict situations Plan bomb shelter simulation	Pack your favorite books for the bomb shelter Keep a survival journal Reflect on Anne's independence Reflect on Anne's decision to leave the valley Write the next chapter of *Z for Zachariah* that resolves the hostility Write reflective paper for bomb shelter simulation
Logical/ Mathematical	Make a timeline of the book Make Ann's daily schedule Figure how long it takes to do various jobs by hand Estimate food consumption and regeneration Describe how to survive skills Figure out where the book takes place	Compare book to domestic abuse cases In groups, Make a Venn Diagram for the interests and characteristics of Ann and Loomis Compare modern life with electricity to Amish life without electricity	Reflect on your own interests and compare them with Ann and Loomis Reflect on your own daily schedule and compare it with Ann's Reflect on schedule and food supply for bomb shelter simuation
Visual/ Spatial	Create watershed art after the field trip Make a collage of a theme in the book Watch a movie with a similar theme	In groups, create a map of the valley based on details in the book Design record jacket for a musical album for Ann or John Evaluate the productivity of the group Make lanterns for loved ones who died in a bombing or at war	Illustrate your Portfolio of Threats and Solutions to the Environment Illustrate a metaphor I llustrate Environmental Letter Book Create an object, sculpture or painting for Hiroshima Peace Museum
Bodily/ Kinesthetic	Plan activities for air raid simulation Demonstrate survival skills Model conflict resolution strategies Explore a local watershed	Role play conflict resolution for Ann and Loomis Create an air raid simulation In groups, brainstorm action projects	Pack your bag for the bomb shelter Learn survival skills for an imminent catastrophe Design personal action project Fold paper cranes for Sadako's statue
Musical/ Rhythmic	Play "Hit" Game Make instruments from natural objects Collect peace songs Play folk songs that warn of catastrophic events	In small groups, analyze song lyrics with a theme of peace or destruction In groups, play "Hit" Game	Write songs imitating sounds in nature Compose songs reflecting the perspectives of Ann or Loomis
Naturalist	Learn about edible foods in the wild List natural objects that serve as tools or other uses Study the effects of radi- ation on the environment Study characteristics of your watershed	In groups, Create a portfolio of current environmental issues In groups, Generate solutions to current environmental issues	Reflect on your personal beliefs and actions to preserve the environment Prepare survival kit for emergencies

Visual/Spatial and Mathematical/Logical Assessments

Map the Valley

In order to understand the limits of Ann's world, ask them to create a map of the valley area where she lived in *Z for Zachariah* (1987). Ask students to choose the materials they will need for the map: poster board, markers, plaster of paris, papier maché, paints, or other artistic mediums. Begin the map by considering from which direction Ann observed Loomis' approach. She first saw smoke over Claypole Ridge which was about fifteen miles away (p. 2). Beyond Claypole Ridge was Ogdentown (p. 2) where Ann went to school and where the library was when she wanted more books to read. From Burden Hill, place Dean Town (p. 8), where Ann was to attend Teacher's College, to the west of the Amish farms which are south of the Valley (p. 8). For even more detail, add Route Number 9 at County Road 793 that leads to her valley (p. 4). Since the Amish were the main customers there place Klein's store in the valley on a road that they would travel from their farms to the store.

This store plays a central role in the story since that is where Ann found most of her food, clothing, and miscellaneous needs. More difficult decisions in making the map are where to place the main house, garden, and cave where Ann hid to watch Loomis's arrival (p. 11). Next, students must decide how to place the roads and rivers through the valley. There was one stream full of living organisms and Burden Creek which was contaminated; both flow into a pond and out the other side where both are dead (p. 39). Later, after John Loomis helped her get the tractor going, place the field where Ann's father hadplanted melons, pumpkins, and squash that she now considers plowing (p. 94). Then, place the church where Ann went to pray when she thought Loomis would die (p. 119). After placing the church on the map, decide how to represent other hiding places where Ann stayed in her flight from Loomis. When students have finished their maps ask them to use clues from the book to figure out where in the United States they think the valley, itself, might be located: cold winters, Amish neighbors, frost in November, ten weeks walk from Ithaca, New York in a southerly direction.

Verbal/Linguistic, Interpersonal, Logical/Mathematical Assessments

Character Study

In many ways, Ann and Loomis are distinctly different from each, but they also share several commonalities in coping with their situation as lone survivors of nuclear war. Organize students in small groups giving them newsprint and colored markers to make a Venn Diagram—two overlapping circles with differences on the outside sections and similarities in the middle section—representing their discussion. Students should brainstorm a list of interests for Ann that might include: music, piano playing, books, fishing, farming, journal writing, religious beliefs, teaching children, knowledge of the outdoors. A list describing Loomis might include: scientist, mechanical propensity, atheist, technical knowledge, knowledge of radiation, draftsman, domineering personality. Then ask students to list the characteristics and interests they both share such as: reading, sharp-shooting, resourcefulness, independence, and survival skills. Students should display their Venn Diagrams and share them with the rest of the class.

Verbal/Linguistic, Logical/Mathematical, Bodily/ Kinesthetic, and Intrapersonal Assessments

"How to". . . *Survive: Process Paper and Demonstration*

Both Ann and Loomis exhibit numerous skills necessary for survival in a world without electrical power, running water, or other human beings. Students can choose from a list of survival skills taken from *Z for Zachariah*, adding to it as they see fit, then writing a paper and demonstrating one of those skills. They must learn about and show some part of the process to the class. Personalize a life without electricity, running water, or petroleum fuels. Have students choose from the following list or think up one of their own:

- How to build a fire and cook a meal
- How to prepare the soil, plant the seeds, and maintain a garden
- How to kill, clean, and cook an animal in the wild
- How to obtain, test, and purify water
- How to recognize and utilize plants, herbs, berries, nuts, etc. for health and healing
- How to make flour from grains (wheat, barley, etc.)
- How to treat injuries on the trail (lacerations, sprains, breaks, hypothermia, heat stroke)
- How to recognize and treat the stages of radiation sickness
- How to generate fuel from natural sources (i.e., manure to methane)
- How to camp in a cave (equipments, tools, clothing, food, first aid, etc.)
- How to preserve fruits, vegetables, nuts for the winter
- How to make sugar from maple sap, cane, or other natural sweeteners

Students may not be able to demonstrate the whole process in the classroom, but they can bring enough equipment to articulate and demonstrate the process they have learned.

Verbal/Linguistic, Musical/Rhythmic, Visual/Spatial Assessments

"Hit"

This game capitalizes on students' familiarity with popular music. Organized into teams of five or six, students develop a record jacket cover for a "hit" musical album that either Anne Burden or John Loomis could have logically written. The cover is divided into various parts, each part a separate task which, is assigned to a different team member. This game was developed by Gary Salvner (1991) for the Youngstown State English Festival.

Since the only musical instrument in the valley is Ann's piano and she doesn't play that very well, here is a game that will stimulate students' imaginations about the music Ann or Loomis may have enjoyed had there been radio and television working in their lives. Students should choose either Ann or Loomis and brainstorm their physical description, personalities, interests, important events, important objects and important places in the book. Then they will decide what kind of music Anne or Loomis would probably write and sing: rock, soul, gospel, heavy metal, rhythm and blues, country, rap, classical. Students will compose words for songs based on their personal experiences, and will create a clever title for the album which captures the spirit and background of this new performer.

Next students design, illustrate, and write the album or compact disc cover for this record. They should fold a heavy piece of paper in half and then in half again so that the album cover has four panels. The following are placed in each of those four panels:

- Front Cover: Design an appealing sketch or design which captures the theme and spirit of the album along with the name of the singer/songwriter and the album title. The title of the hit single from this album should be copied on the line in the upper right-hand corner of the cover.
- Page 2: Because their character is new to popular music, page two contains a paragraph introducing her/him. It might contain background biographical information from the work, an explanation of why this person became a singer/songwriter, a description of the kind of music contained in the album, and a comment on why this performer has suddenly become so popular.
- Page 3: Since one of the songs from this album has also become a hit single, choose which title will be the hit and write out the lyrics of the song. Song lyrics usually describe a person, place, or thing important to the songwriter, or they tell the story of an experience he or she had. They may rhyme, but don't have to; may have stanzas or verses; and may include refrains.

- Back Cover: The back cover should contain the titles of eight songs that have been written and performed by the main character—all about her/his own experiences. Four titles will be listed under "Side One," and the other four under "Side Two." Be sure that the titles reveal something about the contents of the songs.
- Memo: Print your names and fill in the name of your album and of your singer/songwriter and turn it in to identify your work.

Encourage groups to perform their "hit" songs if they are interested in composing the music and accompaniment for the pieces. See Table 11.2 for Mary's Hit List, Table 11.3 for the Hit Tune for Ann Burden, and Figure 11.1 for Front and Back Cover Designs for Hit Game.

Table 11.2: Mary's Hit List

Side 1	Side 2
Keepin' Hope Alive	*Tell Me I'm Not the Only One*
Lonely	*A Sign From the West*
Like the Phoenix (We'll Rise)	*The Solitude (Is Deafening)*
On My Own (Again)	*I Will Survive!*

Table 11.3: Mary's Gospel Hit Tune: A Sign From the West

A Sign From the West	
A sign came from the west one day A glimpse of a bird in flight Not in the valley, but from beyond Oh, what an awesome sight!	A sign came from the west one day And now my faith's restored! Now there's so much to be prepared, No longer time to be bored!
Chorus It means there's other life out there It means I'm not alone! It means someday we'll start anew A world of our own!	Chorus It means there's other life out there It means I'm not alone! It means someday we'll start anew A world of our own!

FIGURE 11.1: FRONT AND BACK COVER DESIGN FOR HIT GAME

Verbal/Linguistic, Intrapersonal and Interpersonal Assessments

Writing A Letter

Ask students to pretend they are Ann in O'Brien's *Z for Zachariah*. As Ann, they might write a letter to another character in the story describing how they felt about Loomis and his behavior toward them from the moment he entered the valley. They may write as Ann at the time she met Loomis in the valley or may choose to project themselves into the future when she would be looking back on her decision to leave him. As students describe their thoughts and feelings about the incident, they should use at least one metaphor to describe themselves (Ann) from the text and at least one metaphor of their own. They should write their letters in standard friendly letter form: greeting, body, closing; as well, they should be sure to use correct spelling, punctuation and sentence structure to make their letters impress the audience.

To help students think about their thoughts and feelings about Loomis, ask them to complete the Character Response Chart (See Table 11.4). This chart requires students to make a list of Loomis' actions, determine whether Ann's responses were passive or assertive, and decide what they would have done differently. To get started, initiate a discussion on passive and assertive behaviors. According to Johnson and Johnson (1997), people can *assert* their wants, needs, and goals directly to another person in an honest and appropriate way that respects both themselves and the other person. On the other hand, people who are *nonassertive* or passive, say nothing, give up their interests, and keep their wants, needs and desires to themselves (p. 356). Point out that Loomis was often *aggressive* when he hurt Ann to get his needs and desires met.

The letter and character chart are activities that have been adapted from Olson and Schiesl (1996, P. 27).

TABLE 11.4: CHARACTER RESPONSE CHART

John Loomis	Ann Burden		Me
What John did . . . Passive and Assertive behaviors	Ann's Nonassertive response	Ann's Assertive response	What I Would Do If I Were Ann?
1. 2. 3. 4. 5.			

In this activity, students should mention 8-10 of Loomis' behaviors. Even though he was mostly passive as Ann nursed him back to health during his serious illness, he became more assertive as he recovered. The passive behaviors might include examples of times when he was sick and stayed in his tent (p. 47–58), when he moved to David's room (p. 58–66), when he began walking around (p. 69), and when he figured out how to pump gasoline for the tractor (p. 70, 91). The assertive behaviors might include the time when he shot her chicken (p. 17), when he fired shots at the house breaking her parents' bedroom windows (p. 106–107), when he grabbed her hand and pulled her towards him (p. 161), when he attacked her in the night (p 174), when he tied up her dog (182), when he took the tractor key and padlocked the store (p. 204–206), when he shot her (p. 219), when he burned her belongings in the cave (p. 233), or when he hunted her like an animal (p. 228–234). Students should also note Ann's reactions to Loomis's behavior. What changes occur in her responses that lead her to the final confrontation with Loomis before she leaves the valley? How would the students' responses be the same as or different from Ann's? After students have sorted through their thoughts and feelings, they should be ready to create an original metaphor.

Verbal/Linguistic and Visual/Spatial Intelligences

Original Metaphor

Before asking students to create similes and metaphors for John and Ann, ask them about themselves. What animal are they most like? What plant are they most like? What shape are they most like? What food are they most like? Once students have explored figures of speech to represent themselves, ask them to find similes and metaphors in O'Brien's text, and then create their own original metaphor for John or Ann. The following are student examples:

- Ann is the lily in the valley. (Shamel)
- Ann feels like winter, cold and windy. (Allison)
- Loomis is a hawk in search of prey. (Cao)
- Loomis shoots Ann like a deer. (Rachel)
- Loomis tracks Ann down like a hunter stalking its prey. (Mary)

Ask students to draw their metaphor and provide examples from the text that support their critical thinking. If they are troubled by the assignment, encourage them to compose their metaphor based on behaviors from the character response chart. With these prewriting activities, students are ready to write the letter from Ann to another character. Will they choose to write the letter to Ann's mother, father, or brother? Students should choose the audience they prefer. See Table 11.5 for a sample letter from Ann to her mother.

TABLE 11.5: SAMPLE LETTER FROM ANN TO HER MOTHER

Dear Mother,

In writing these periodic letters to you, I keep the hope alive that you made it to a safe shelter somewhere and we will someday be reunited. It somehow comforts me to think of you. I'd like to think that you would be proud of the way I have survived here on my own and have become more or less self-sufficient (with the great help of Klein's General Store.)

Just as I was finally getting used to surviving by myself in our valley, my world was turned upside down with the arrival of Mr. John Loomis. I hope you understand and concur regarding my decision to leave the valley. Mr. Loomis made it impossible for both of us to stay. With him hunting me down as if I were an animal, I had no choice but to go. I hope one day to return to our valley. Not just to offer Mr. Loomis a second chance, but most importantly to see if you have somehow miraculously returned and to let you know where I went and that I am fine.

As always - loving you and missing you,
Ann

Naturalist, Bodily/Kinesthetic, Verbal/Linguistic and Visual/Spatial Intelligences

Exploring a Watershed: Creating Art and Poetry

In *Z for Zachariah* (1987), distinguishing the polluted river from the clean was a matter of life and death for Ann and Loomis. Asimov and Pohl (1991) address the shortage and pollution of the water we drink in Chapter 10 of their book, *Our Angry Earth*. Protecting our water is critical for life both now and in the future. In that regard, the following activities ask students to explore their watershed, initiate a service project, and respond to the issues by writing poetry or composing a piece of art or sculpture.

A watershed is an area of land that catches rain and snow, which then drains into a marsh, stream, river, or lake. Everyone lives in a watershed, which come in all shapes and sizes. They can include cities, farms, forests and deserts or combinations of many kinds of terrain and habitat. Everyone and everything in our watershed are part of the same natural and cultural community. Our life and ideas and attitudes are shaped, in part, by our watershed. In turn, we influence what happens in our watershed by our everyday activities.

Begin by locating the natural water sources in your community and geographical location. Research the condition of the lakes, rivers, creeks, and wells in your area. Then, help students arrange a visit to one of these waterways either collectively as a class field trip, or individually with their families. Students should take notes and make sketches of what they observe, feel, smell, and hear during a period of silence and meditation. If repeated visits are possible, they should observe and record changes that occur over a period of time. Engage students in a brainstorming session to decide ways that they might contribute to the preservation of their water. From the list, choose a service project. It could be activities such as monitoring the water quality, planting a tree, gardening or cleaning up a creek. When the project is complete, ask students to use the "raw data" they have collected to write poetry or to create a piece of art or sculpture. Share the results with your school and community to raise the consciousness of maintaining pure water. If interested, you may submit the poetry and art to the River of Words Environmental Poetry and Art Contest for children 5–19 years of age. The poetry is judged by Robert Hass, U.S. Poet Laureate, and the art by Germaine Juneau, Director of the International Children's Art Museum. The contest is sponsored by International Rivers Network & The Library of Congress Center for the Book which can be located at http://www.irn.org for more information about watersheds, watershed projects, or the contest.

Amish Society

While reading *Z for Zachariah,* it is almost impossible not to imagine oneself in Ann's situation, and to question how self-sufficient people could be if faced with the loss of electricity. While it may seem like a virtual impossibility, one need look no further than today's Amish society to see that people do live quite well without electricity or other outside power sources. The Amish have the security of knowing their survival is dependent not on outside sources, but on what they grow and produce with their own efforts from their own land. Louis Bromfield, the Pulitzer Prize-winning author and conservationist, once said that the family farmer "has a security and independence unknown to any other member of society."This is the case with the Amish, a largely self-sufficient sect of Christian people, who prefer farming as their chosen livelihood. For them, even more than for most farm families, working the land is more than an occupation; it is a way of life. The Amish delight in life's simple pleasures such as a hand-pieced quilt, a well-tended garden, or a delicious homegrown, home-cooked meal. The tapestries of their lives are made up of the threads of family, community, hard work, cooperation and obedience to God and to family. Satisfaction comes from the sweat of their brow and a sincere belief that simpler is better. Here life moves at a slower pace and time is measured more by the seasons than by the clock.

Activities that study the lifestyle of the Amish can be as simple as reading a work of historical fiction such as Yoder's *Rosanna of the Amish* (1940), or as involved as a project outfitting an Amish-style household using Lehman's Non-Electric catalog. Additional lessons and group projects could involve churning butter or making ice cream with old-fashioned wood crank butter churns or ice cream makers, which are readily available. A culminating group activity could be a field trip to an Amish community. There are currently 150,000 Amish living in 230 communities in 21 states and Canada (Garrett, 1996). Many of these communities welcome groups to stop and see the fixtures and appliances of a working house or farm.

See the annotated bibliography of selected Amish and Amish-Mennonite literature. These books accurately portray the lifestyle and beliefs of the Amish. In the fictional works, the story lines may be somewhat unrealistic, but the details of day-to-day Amish life and their religious beliefs are authentic.

All the Multiple Intelligences

Life in a Bomb Shelter

The culminating activity for this unit is a simulation that requires students to spend at least twenty-four hours in a bomb shelter. According to Canady and Rettig (1996), one of the advantages of simulations is that "students learn by using a wide range of communication skills: negotiating, arguing, interviewing, note-taking, drafting, editing, organizing, public speaking, and listening" (p. 144). In order to develop these communication goals and nurture their multiple intelligences, organize students in groups to make arrangements for shelter, food, equipment, personal belongs, character assignments, and debriefing activities appropriate for developing the simulation. The skills students learn in this simulation may help them survive other dangers such as tornadoes, hurricanes, floods, earthquakes, blizzards, and even air pollution alerts.

Instead of simulating isolation of an underground laboratory for three months living on freeze-dried army rations like John Loomis in *Z for Zachariah*

(1987, p. 63), students in this stimulation will experience at least some of the effects of living in the bomb shelter during an air raid on Hiroshima, Japan, August 6, 1945. After reading John Hersey's (1989) *Hiroshima* and Nevil Shute's (1989) *On the Beach*, and Cruit and Cruit's (1982) *Survive the Coming Nuclear War: How to Do It*, students will plan a simulation that takes place in a bomb shelter; they will assume survivor roles during the air raid when the atomic bomb was dropped. In preparing for the simulation, students will have to make critical choices about living conditions and deal with social conflict with diverse people in a confined and restricted situation.

One group will be in charge of securing the bomb shelter. Ask students to research atomic bomb shelter requirements that will provide safety from radioactive fallout. In the end, their task may be as simple as obtaining the high school boiler room; but students should know the criteria for safety from heat, fire, and radiation that result from the explosion. See Cruit and Cruit, 1982, Chapter 6 for helpful information. The group must decide how many people can secure shelter there in the upcoming, "emergency" situation and make sure there is room for everyone. This group must also decide the duration of the emergency condition. How long will they stay in the shelter? Under what conditions might someone leave? What will be the rules of conduct? What about restroom privileges and other personal emergencies? Will there be electricity? What will be the light source? This group might go so far as to plan some special sound and lighting effects for air raid sirens and bomb explosions, if they want to make the simulation more realistic. In addition to securing permission to use the "bomb shelter," this group will also be in charge of obtaining permission slips from parents, administrators, and/or community members.

After the number of participants and the duration of the simulation has been determined, another committee can begin planning the food for the shelter. Even though students may only spend 24 hours in their shelter, ask this group to plan for at least a two-week period. Since the food must be stored away in the bomb shelter ahead of time for an emergency situation, this group must research appropriate rations. Since there will be no electricity or phones lines available, what foods would be appropriate and realistic? How much food will they need and how much will it cost? What foods will be safe to eat? What about safe drinking water? Chapter 7 of Cruit and Cruit (1982) discusses plans for stockpiling appropriate foods and amount of food per person. Students should plan for two weeks, but actually provide food for the 24 hour period of the simulation through solicitation or fund-raising activities.

The responsibility of another group is to determine the shelter equipment and supplies. In a crowded fallout shelter, sanitation will be vital. This group will plan sanitation measures and also determine other equipment necessary for survival in the shelter such as tools, games, cooking equipment, garbage bags, radiation-measuring equipment, and first aid kits. Again, see Cruit and Cruit (1982) for a discussion of a well-equipped shelter. The group also needs to determine what personal belongings students can bring to the bomb shelter in the emergency created in the simulation. Even though B-29 bombers had been spotted, most people in Hiroshima were caught unaware when the bomb was dropped, and few made it to a shelter. Since these people had such little warning, what possessions were they able to bring with them? This group will decide the limits—will candy, granola bars, walkmans, CD players, radios, laptops, change of clothes, pillows, blankets, sleeping bags, giga pets, cell phones, and book bags be permitted?

The critical part in planning for this simulation is orchestrating the role play. This group's responsibility is to cast class members as A-Bomb survivors so that everyone has a story to tell in the bomb shelter. The list of survivors can include characters from: Hersey's (1985) *Hiroshima,* Yolen and Coville's *Armageddon Summer* (1998), and Shute's (1989) *On the Beach*; characters from the children's literature such as Nobuo Tetsutani in *Shin's Tricycle* (1995), Zoo Keepers in *Faithful Elephants* (1988), Sadako in *Sadako and the Thousand Paper Cranes* (1977), Mii in *Hiroshima No Pika* (1980), Sachi in Yep's *Hiroshima* (1995), Morimoto in *My Hiroshima* (1987); and from internet resources such as "Voices of A-Bomb Survivors," "Miyoko's Room," "A Child's Experience," "Children of Hiroshima," "Short Story: Children of the Cloud," "The Spirit of Hiroshima" by Miyolo Matsubara. These characters and information can be accessed at http://www.csi.ad.jp/ABOMB/hibakusha.html. Once students have their role assignments, they can begin researching the stories they will tell in the bomb shelter. Information will be more plentiful for some characters than others, but the following are some questions to guide the character search:
- How old were you, who did you live with and where did you live?
- What was your life like before the bomb was dropped?
- Where were you when the B-29's flew over head?
- What happened to you when the explosion occurred?
- What will you do after leaving the bomb shelter?
- What do you want to tell the world?

In addition to casting the roles for the simulation, this group will plan the schedule of events. They will schedule meals, games, individual presentations, and invite guest speakers, if appropriate.

Sample Character Study: Mary's role is to play an 18-year-old college freshman named Sarah. Away from home for the first time, eldest child Sarah is a responsible and level-headed young woman. Sarah and her roommate, who have become good friends, are walking across campus on their way back from dinner when they hear emergency sirens and bombs going off in the distance. With nothing but their backpacks, they decide to go straight to the nearest fallout shelter. With the bombs getting steadily closer, the girls reach the shelter just before the doors are locked and sealed.

Another group can organize the debriefing session that follows the simulation. As this experience is likely to be intense, students will benefit from an experience that allows them to express their emotions of sadness, grief, fear, guilt, and/or frustration. Options for debriefing might include responding to the discussion questions, writing a self-reflection paper, or simulating commemorations held on August 16th in Hiroshima every year. Activities might include folding paper cranes to be placed at the foot of Sadako's statue in the Hiroshima Peace Park. Creating an object, sculpture or painting for the Hiroshima Peace Museum might help some students express their feelings. Other students may feel more like composing music, dancing, or writing about their experiences during the simulation. In Japan lanterns, lit and set afloat on the seven rivers flowing through Hiroshima, are inscribed with the names of loved ones who died in the bombing. This activity might bring closure to the bomb shelter experience. In any case, students should be encouraged to voice their opinions about the atomic bomb. Do they agree with the Japanese and millions of others that it should never happen again, or do they feel that dropping the bomb was justified? What do these students want to tell the world?

Young Adult Literature

Asimov, Isaac and Pohl Frederik (1991). *Our Angry Earth*. New York: A Tom Doherty Associates Book.

This book presents the destructive forces that threaten our environment based on scientific research and then provides ways we might ameliorate the situation, creating a healthier environment for the third millenium.

Crow Dog, Mary (1994). *Lakota Woman*. Harperperennial Library.
This is the powerful autobiography of Mary Brave Bird, who grew up in the misery of the South Dakota reservation. Rebelling against the violence and hopelessness of reservation life, she joined the tribal pride movement in an effort to bring about much-needed changes.

Godrey, Martyn (1989). *The Last War*. New York: Collier Macmillan Publishing.

Brad was one of the "lucky" ones who survived the war living in his parents' house with his electric generator and stored food. He believed in a future until he met Angel, who showed him the reality of living in a world where man and animal struggle to survive.

Hersey, John (1985). *Hiroshima*. New York: Vintage Books, A Division of Random House.

Hersey tells the story of those who survived the city of Hiroshima which was destroyed by the first atom bomb ever dropped on a city. This edition also includes a final chapter written after Hersey returned to Hiroshima four decades later in search of the people whose stories he had told.

Kerr, M. E. (1993). *Linger*. New York: Harper/Trophy.

16-year-old Gary Peel is left at home to work at Ned Dunlinger's restaurant, while his older brother, Bobby, joins the army to fight in the Gulf War. Gary's narrative of the home scene is interspersed with journal entries from Bobby. Gary is caught between his boss's prejudice, the affair of his boss's daughter, and his brother's correspondence and return from the war.

Lawrence, Louise (1985). *Children of the Dust*. New York: Harper & Row Publishers.

After a nuclear war devastates the earth, a small band of people struggles for survival in a new world where children are born with strange eyes and even stranger beliefs and ways. Lawrence traces the fate and evolution of three generations of one family that survives in the ash-covered land that affirms life in the aftermath of the nuclear war.

O'Brien, Robert (1987). *Z for Zachariah*. New York: Aladdin Paperbacks, and imprint of Simon & Schuster, Children's Publishing Division.

Ann Burden has lived alone in a protected valley after a nuclear war. She was relieved to see a person arrive into her valley until she realized that he was a tyrant and that somehow she must escape.

Shute, Nevil (1989). *On the Beach*. New York: Ballantine Books.

A novel about the survivors of an atomic war, who face an inevitable end as radiation poisoning moves toward Australia from the North.

Westall, Robert (1992). *Gulf*. New York: Scholastic, Inc.

Tom watches his younger brother, Andy, change from a normal kid with a vivid imagination to a young boy who empathizes so strongly with the Persian Gulf conflict that he becomes a mentally unstable. He assumes the personality of an Iraqi fighter named Latif who speaks Arabic and fights against Americans to the degree that he must be hospitalized until the war is over.

Yolen, Jane and Coville, Bruce (1998). *Armageddon Summer*. New York: Harcourt Brace & Company.

14-year-old Marina and 16-year-old Jed fall in love when they find each other after joining the Believers on top of Mount Weeupcut, Massachusetts to await the end of the world prophesied by Reverend Raymond Beelson scheduled to occur on July 27, 2000.

Children's Literature

Coerr, Eleanor (1977). *Sadako and The Thousand Paper Cranes*. Illustrated by Ronald Himler. New York: Bantam Doubleday Dell Books for Young Readers.

Sadako Sasaki was just two when the atom bomb was dropped on her home city of Hiroshima. Ten years later she developed leukemia. Facing long days in bed, Sadako spent the time folding paper cranes; the legend holds that if a sick person folds 1,000, the gods will make him or her well again.

Kodama, Tatsuharu (1995). *Shin's Tricycle*. Illustrated by Noriyuki Ando. New York: Walker and Company.

This is a true story of a father and his son, Shin, who pleaded for a tricycle during a war when there was no metal for toys. An uncle found him a bike which Shin was riding with his best friend, Kim, when the bomb was dropped on Hiroshima. The children were buried with the tricycle. Later, the tricycle was resurrected and displayed in the Peace Museum in Hiroshima.

Maruki, Toshi (1980). *Hiroshima No Pika*. New York: Lothrop, Lee & Shepard Books.

This book is a retelling of a mother's story of what happened to her family, especially 7-year-old Mii, as they fled for safety during the Flash that destroyed Hiroshima in 1945 in hopes that such a disaster would never again recur anywhere in the world.

Morimoto, Junko (1987). *My Hiroshima*. New York: Viking.

The author and illustrator, Junko Morimoto, was a high school student when the bomb was dropped. Through this personal narrative, she tells about her daily life in Japan before the war, the horrors of surviving the holocaust with her family, and the contrasts between the past and the present. Her photos and drawings elicit compassion and empathy for the victims.

Tsuchiya, Yukio (1988). *Faithful Elephants: A True Story of Animals, People and War*. Illustrated by Ted Lewin. Boston: Houghton Mifflin Company.

A Zookeeper in the Tokyo Zoo tells the story of the army's command to kill the wild animals—keeping them from running the streets should the city be bombed. The caretakers weep and pray that the war will end and save the three performing elephants.

Yep, Laurence (1995). *Hiroshima: A Novella*. New York: Scholastic, Inc. Yep recounts the devasting day when the bomb was dropped on Hiroshima from both the airmen's and the school children's point of view. 12-year-old Sachi later came to the United States for healing of her body, then returned to Japan to heal her emotions.

Young Adult Literature of the Amish and Amish-Mennonites

Borntrager, Mary Christner (1991). *Daniel*. Scottdale, PA: Herald Press. One in a series called "Ellie's People", these books are suitable for younger readers, ages about 9 through 12. Daniel struggles to work and keep his family together after his wife mysteriously disappears. A string of bad luck puts Daniel at odds with the church and he is shunned. This book conveys well the unbending rules of the Amish religion.

Borntrager, Mary Christner (1992). *Reuben*. Scottdale, PA: Herald Press. Another in the "Ellie's People" series, young Reuben deals with the familiar dilemma between peer pressure and obeying one's parents.

Lewis, Beverly (1997). *The Shunning*. Minneapolis, MN: Bethany House. In the first book of a trilogy, Katie Lapp discovers a devastating secret about her past on the eve of her marriage. That secret, along with her own philosophical differences with her Amish faith, leads her to an extremely difficult decision.

Lewis, Beverly (1997). *The Confession*. Minneapolis, MN: Bethany House. This is the second book in the "Heritage of Lancaster County" series. After discovering that she was adopted, Katie Lapp searches for her birth mother. Along the way, she must try to decide who she truly is. This book, along with the first one, shows the severity of the rules of the Amish faith. It does a good job of comparing and contrasting the Amish and Mennonite religions.

Lewis, Beverly (1998). *The Reckoning*. Minneapolis, MN: Bethany House. The last book in Lewis' trilogy, this one is a little more sympathetic towards the Amish than the first two books. In this book, Katie Lapp must decide whether to return to her Amish family and their way of life. Or can she find peace and happiness in her new life?

Yoder, Joseph W. (1940). *Rosanna of the Amish*. Scottdale, PA: Herald Press. A true story of an Irish orphan girl raised by the Amish in 19th century Pennsylvania, the book delves into the reasons for many Amish customs and practices. This book is as popular with the Amish today as when it was written almost 50 years ago.

References

Campbell, L., & and Campbell, B. (1994). *The multiple intelligences series facilitator's guide*. Alexandria, VA: ASCD.

Canady, R. L., & Rettig, M. D. (Eds.). (1996). *Teaching in the block—Strategies for engaging active learners*. Larchmont, NY: Eye on Education.

Cruit, R., & Cruit, R. (1982). *Survive the coming nuclear war: How to do it*. New York: Stein and Day Publishers.

Environmental Poetry & Art Contest. *River of words*. International Rivers Network & The Library of Congress Center for the Book. PO Box 4000-J, Berkeley, CA 94704 or http://www.irn.org.

Gardner, H. (1993). *Multiple intelligences: The theory in practice*. New York: BasicBooks.

Garrett, O. A. (1996). *The guidebook to Amish communities across America*. Kalona, IA: Hitching Post Enterprises.

Johnson, D., & Johnson, F. (1997). *Joining together: Group theory and group skills*. Boston: Allyn and Bacon.

Lehman (1998). *Non-electric catalog*. One Lehman Circle, P.O. Box 321, Kidron, OH 44646-0321

Olson, C. B., & Schiesl, S. (1996, Spring). A multiple intelligences approach to teaching multicultural literature. *Language Arts Journal of Michigan, 12* (1), 21–28.

Salvner, G. (1991). Hit. In *Literature festival: Ten cooperative learning games designed to stimulate literary analysis*. El Cajon, CA: Interaction Publishers.

Multiple Intelligences Survey

Walter McKenzie, Surfaquarium Consulting
http://surfaquarium.com/MIinvent.htm

Part I

Complete each section by placing a "1" next to each statement that you feel accurately describes you. If you do not identify with a statement, leave the space provided blank. Then total the column in each section.

Section 1

_____ I enjoy categorizing things by common traits

_____ Ecological issues are important to me

_____ Hiking and camping are enjoyable activities

_____ I enjoy working on a garden

_____ I believe preserving our National Parks is important

_____ Putting things in hierarchies makes sense to me

_____ Animals are important in my life

_____ My home has a recycling system in place

_____ I enjoy studying biology, botany and/or zoology

_____ I spend a great deal of time outdoors

_____ TOTAL for Section I

Section 2

_____ I easily pick up on patterns

_____ I focus in on noise and sounds

_____ Moving to a beat is easy for me

_____ I've always been interested in playing an instrument

_____ The cadence of poetry intrigues me

_____ I remember things by putting them in a rhyme

_____ Concentration is difficult while listening to a radio or television

_____ I enjoy many kinds of music

_____ Musicals are more interesting than dramatic plays

_____ Remembering song lyrics is easy for me

_____ TOTAL for Section 2

Section 3

_____ I keep my things neat and orderly

_____ Step-by-step directions are a big help

_____ Solving problems comes easily to me

_____ I get easily frustrated with disorganized people

_____ I can complete calculations quickly in my head

_____ Puzzles requiring reasoning are fun

_____ I can't begin an assignment until all my questions are answered

_____ Structure helps me be successful

_____ I find working on a computer spreadsheet or database rewarding

_____ Things have to make sense to me or I am dissatisfied

_____ TOTAL for Section 3

Section 4

_____ It is important to see my role in the "big picture" of things

_____ I enjoy discussing questions about life

_____ Religion is important to me

_____ I enjoy viewing art masterpieces

_____ Relaxation and meditation exercises are rewarding

_____ I like visiting breathtaking sites in nature

_____ I enjoy reading ancient and modern philosophers

_____ Learning new things is easier when I understand their value

_____ I wonder if there are other forms of intelligent life in the universe

_____ Studying history and ancient culture helps give me perspective

_____ Total Section 4

Section 5

_____ I learn best interacting with others

_____ The more the merrier

_____ Study groups are very productive for me

_____ I enjoy chat rooms

_____ Participating in politics is important

_____ Television and radio talk shows are enjoyable

_____ I am a "team player"

_____ I dislike working alone

_____ Clubs and extracurricular activities are fun

_____ I pay attention to social issues and causes

_____ TOTAL Section 5

Section 6

_____ I enjoy making things with my hands

_____ Sitting still for long periods of time is difficult for me

_____ I enjoy outdoor games and sports

_____ I value non-verbal communication such as sign language

_____ A fit body is important for a fit mind

_____ Arts and crafts are enjoyable pastimes

_____ Expression through dance is beautiful

_____ I like working with tools

_____ I live an active lifestyle

_____ I learn by doing

_____ TOTAL Section 6

Section 7

_____ I enjoy reading all kinds of materials

_____ Taking notes helps me remember and understand

_____ I faithfully contact friends through letters and/or e-mail

_____ It is easy for me to explain my ideas to others

_____ I keep a journal

_____ Word puzzles like crosswords and jumbles are fun

_____ I write for pleasure

_____ I enjoy playing with words like puns, anagrams, and spoonerisms

_____ Foreign languages interest me

_____ Debates and public speaking are activities I like to participate in

_____ TOTAL for Section 7

Section 8

_____ I am keenly aware of my moral beliefs

_____ I learn best when I have an emotional attachment to the subject

_____ Fairness is important to me

_____ My attitude effects how I learn

_____ Social justice issues concern me

_____ Working alone can be just as productive as working in a group

_____ I need to know why I should do something before I agree to do it

_____ When I believe in something I will give 100% effort to it

_____ I like to be involved in causes that help others

_____ I am willing to protest or sign a petition to right a wrong

_____ Total for Section 8

Section 9

_____ I can imagine ideas in my mind

_____ Rearranging a room is fun for me

_____ I enjoy creating art using varied media

_____ I remember well using graphic organizers

_____ Performance art can be very gratifying

_____ Spreadsheets are great for making charts, graphs and tables

_____ Three dimensional puzzles bring me much enjoyment

_____ Music videos are very stimulating

_____ I can recall things in mental pictures

_____ I am good at reading maps and blueprints

_____ TOTAL for Section 9

Part II

Now carry forward your total from each section and multiply by 10 below:

Section	Total Forward	Multiply	Score
1		X10	
2		X10	
3		X10	
4		X10	
5		X10	
6		X10	
7		X10	
8		X10	
9		X10	

Part III

Now plot your scores on the bar graph provided:

100									
90									
80									
70									
60									
50									
40									
30									
20									
10									
0	Sec 1	Sec 2	Sec 3	Sec 4	Sec 5	Sec 6	Sec 7	Sec 8	Sec 9

Part IV

Key

Section 1 – This reflects your Naturalist strength

Section 2 – This suggests your Musical strength

Section 3 – This indicates your Logical strength

Section 4 – This illustrates your Existential strength

Section 5 – This shows your Interpersonal strength

Section 6 – This shows your Kinesthetic strength

Section 7 – This indicates your Verbal strength

Section 8 – This reflects your Intrapersonal strength

Section 9 – This suggests your Visual strength

Learning Difficulties Checklist

Armstrong, Thomas (1993). *7 Kinds of Smart: Identifying and Developing Your Many Intelligences.* New York: Penguin Books USA Inc., pp. 172–175. Used by permission of Plume, a division of Penguin Putnam Inc.

Logical/Mathematical:

_____ I have difficulty keeping my checkbook balanced.

_____ I get easily confused when someone is explaining a scientific concept to me.

_____ I frequently make errors when computing simple arithmetic.

_____ I have difficulty in school mastering postarithmetic subjects like algebra or trigonometry.

_____ I avoid the business page of a newspaper because economic or financial news confuses me.

_____ I still count on my fingers or use some other concrete method when calculating numbers.

_____ I usually get stumped when working on a brain-teaser requiring logical thinking in a puzzle book.

Other Logical-Mathematical Difficulties: _____

_____

_____

Spatial:

_____ I find it hard to see clear images in my mind's eye.

_____ I sometimes don't recognize the faces of people who should be familiar to me.

_____ I have difficulty finding my way around an unfamiliar town or building.

_____ I sometimes have problems telling right from left.

_____ My drawings of people are still at the stick-figure level.

_____ I have (had) a hard time in geometry class.

_____ I'm color-blind or have other difficulties distinguishing shades of color.

_____ I have difficulty copying simple shapes and designs on a sheet of
paper.
Other Spatial Difficulties: _____

_____

_____

Linguistic:

_____ I frequently experience problems understanding what I read.
_____ I have difficulty translating my thoughts into written words.
_____ I often don't pronounce new words that way they should be
pronounced.
_____ I often have a hard time coming up with the right word to describe
an object, situation, or concept.
_____ I'm still reading at an elementary-school level because of my
difficulty in decoding the printed word.
_____ I have problems telling the difference between subtle sounds in the
language ("b" and "p," "th" and "sh," etc.)
_____ I am frequently corrected by others (or am afraid of being
corrected) for ungrammatical phrases in my speaking or writing.
Other Linguistic Difficulties:_____

_____

_____

Musical:

_____ I have a hard time carrying a tune.
_____ I have difficulty keeping time to a rhythmic piece of recorded
music.
_____ I have problems recognizing musical passages that seem to be
familiar to my family and friends.
_____ I find it difficult to enjoy listening to music.
_____ There are only a very few songs (or no songs) that I can actually
remember.
_____ I would have a hard time naming the musical instrument a piece of
music was being played on (e.g., cello versus violin).
_____ I would have a difficult time matching my voice with a note on a
piano.
Other Musical Difficulties: _____

_____

_____

Bodily-Kinesthetic:

_____ I'm "all thumbs" when it comes to doing something that requires delicate fine-motor coordination (sewing, crafts, etc.)

_____ I'm uncoordinated on the athletic field.

_____ I have a hard time learning new dance steps.

_____ I'm resistant to touching things in my surroundings.

_____ I have a hard time expressing concepts through my body (in charades, acting, mime, etc.)

_____ I'm relatively unaware of my body most of the time.

_____ I'm clumsy when engaged in simple physical actions like walking, making the bed, or setting the table.

Other Bodily-Kinesthetic Difficulties: _____

_____

Interpersonal:

_____ I'm painfully shy when meeting new people.

_____ I get into frequent misunderstandings or disputes with others.

_____ I often feel hostile or defensive toward others.

_____ I frequently have a hard time feeling empathy for other people.

_____ In a time of crisis I would be virtually without any social support.

_____ I go through life generally unaware of the interpersonal interactions going on around me.

_____ I have a problem "reading" other people's moods, intentions, motivations, and temperaments.

Other Interpersonal Difficulties: _____

_____

Intrapersonal:

_____ I frequently feel a sense of low self-worth.

_____ I have little sense of where I'm going in my life.

_____ I'm generally unaware of how I'm feeling from moment to moment.

_____ I'm often afraid of being abandoned or engulfed my people whom I'm intimate with.

_____ I dislike spending time alone.

_____ I sometimes have feelings of unreality—as if I didn't really completely exist.

_____ I get easily disturbed by simple events in my life.

Other Intrapersonal Difficulties: _____

_____

Bibliography

Children's Literature and Picture Books

Armstrong, J. (1993). *Steal away to freedom*. New York: Scholastic.

Bartoletti, S. C. (1996). *Growing up in coal country*. New York: Houghton Mifflin.

Beatty, P. (1992). *Who comes with cannons?* New York: Morrow Junior Books.

Boyd, C. D. (1987). *Charlie Pippin*. New York: Macmillan.

Bunting, E. (1990). *The wall*. New York: Clarion.

Coerr, E. (1977). *Sadako and the thousand paper cranes*. New York: Dell.

Connell, K. (1993). *Tales from the Underground Railroad*. A. Haley (Ed.). Austin, TX: Raintree Steck-Vaughn.

Donnelly, J. (1991). *A wall of names: The story of the Vietnam veterans memorial*. New York: Random House.

Elish, D. (1993). *Harriet Tubman and the Underground Railroad*. Brookfield, CT: Milbrook Press.

Ferris, J. (1989). *Go free or die: A story about Harriet Tubman*. Minneapolis: Carolrhoda.

Fleischman, P. (1985). *I am Phoenix: Poems for two voices*. New York: Harper & Row.

Fleischman, P. (1988). *Joyful noise: Poems for two voices*. New York: Harper & Row.

Freedman, R. (1994). *Kids at work: Lewis Hine and the crusade against child labor*. New York: Clarion Books.

Gilson, J. (1992). *Hello, my name is Scrambled Eggs*. New York: Simon and Schuster.

Hobbs, W. (1997). *Beardream*. New York: Atheneum Books for Young Readers.

Hobbs, W. (1998). *Howling Hill*. New York: Morrow Junior Books.

Hopkinson, D. (1993). *Sweet Clara and the freedom quilt*. New York: Knopf.

Hunter, S. H. (1996). *The unbreakable code*. Flagstaff, AZ: Northland Publishing Company.

Johnson, D. (1993). *Now let me fly: The story of a slave family*. New York: MacMillan.

Johnson, L. W. (1995). *Escape into the night: The riverboat adventures, no. 1*. Minneapolis: MN: Bethany House.

Kent, D. (1995). *The Vietnam women's memorial*. Danbury, CT: Children's Press.

Kodama, T. (1995). *Shin's tricycle*. New York: Walker and Company.

Kristof, J. (1993). *Steal away home*. New York: Scholastic.

Lawrence, J. (1997). *Harriet and the promised land*. New York: Aladdin Paperbacks.

Levine, E. (1992). *If you traveled on the Underground Railroad*. New York: Scholastic.

Maruki, T. (1980). *Hiroshima no Pika*. New York: Lothrop, Lee & Shepard Books.

Monjo, F. N. (1993). *The drinking gourd: A story of the Underground Railroad*. New York: HarperCollins.

Morimoto, J. (1987). *My Hiroshima*. New York: Viking.

Nhuong, H. Q. (1982). *The land I lost: Adventures of a boy in Vietnam*. New York: HarperCollins.

Paterson, K. (1988). *Park's quest*. New York: Puffin Books.

Porter, C. (1993). *Meet Addy: An American girl*. Middletown, WI: Pleasant Company.

Rappaport. D. (1991). *Escape from slavery: Five journeys to freedom*. New York: Harper Collins Juvenile Books.

Ringgold, F. (1993). *Aunt Harriet's underground railroad in the sky*. New York: Crown.

Smucker, B. C. (1979). *Runaway to freedom: A story of the Underground Railroad*. New York: Harper & Row.

Stein, C. (1997). *The story of the Underground Railroad*. Chicago: Children's Press.

Tran, K. T. (1987). *The little weaver of Thai-Yen village*. San Francisco: Children's Book Press.

Tsuchiya, Y. (1988). *Faithful elephants: A true story of animals, people and war*. New York: Trumpet Club.

Winter, J. (1992). *Follow the drinking gourd*. New York: Knopf.

Yep, L. (1995). *Hiroshima: A novella*. New York: Scholastic.

Young Adult Literature

Alexie, S. (1993). *The Lone Ranger and Tonto fistfight in heaven*. Berkeley, CA: Oyate.

Alexie, Sherman. (1995). *Reservation blues*. Berkeley, CA: Oyate.

Asimov, I., & Pohl, F. (1991). *Our angry earth*. New York: Tom Doherty Associates.

Bachrach, S. D. (1994). *Tell them we remember: The story of the Holocaust*. Boston: Little, Brown.

Balgassi, H. (1997). *Tae's sonata*. New York: Clarion Books.

Balgassi, H. (1996). *Peacebound trains*. New York: Clarion Books.

Barr, R. (1994). *The importance of Malcolm X*. San Diego, CA: Lucent Books.

Bauer, M. D. (Ed.). (1994). *Am I blue? Coming out from the silence*. New York: HarperCollins.

Beals, M. P. (1994). *Warriors don't cry: A searing memoir of the battle to integrate Little Rock's Central High*. New York: Pocket Books.

Bennett, C. (1998). *Life in the fat lane*. New York: Delacorte Press.

Berenbaum, M. (1993). *The world must know: The history of the Holocaust as told in the United States Holocaust Memorial Museum*. Boston: Little, Brown.

Bial, R. (1995). *The Underground Railroad*. New York: Houghton Mifflin Publishers. Block, F. L. (1989). *Weetzie Bat*. New York: HarperCollins.

Borntrager, M. C. (1991). *Daniel*. Scottdale, PA: Herald Press.

Borntrager, M. C. (1992). *Reuben*. Scottdale, PA: Herald Press.

Brooks, G. (1997). We real cool. In A. Adoff (Ed.). *I am the darker brother: An anthology of modern poems by African Americans* (p. 22). New York: Simon & Schuster.

Bruchac, J. (1993). *Dawn land*. Golden, CO: Fulcrum Publishing.

Bruchac, J. (1993). *Flying with the eagle, racing the great bear*. Berkeley, CA: Oyate.

Bruchac, J. (1998). *The heart of a chief: A novel*. New York: Dial Books for Young Readers.

Bruchac, J. (1997). *Lasting echoes: An oral history of Native American people*. New York: Avon Books.

Bruchac, J. (1995). *Long River*. Golden, CO: Fulcrum Publishing.

Campbell, B. M. (1993). *Your blues ain't like mine*. New York: Ballantine Books.

Card, O. S. (1999). *Ender's shadow*. New York: Tor.

Carter, A. R. (1998). *Up country*. New York: Scholastic.

Choi, S. N. (1991). *Year of the impossible goodbyes*. Boston : Houghton Mifflin.

Choi, S. N. (1993). *Halmoni and the picnic*. Boston: Houghton Mifflin.

Choi, S. N. (1993). *Echoes of the white giraffe*. Boston: Houghton Mifflin.

Choi, S. N. (1994). *Gathering of pearls*. Boston: Houghton Mifflin.

Choi, S. N. (1997). *The best older sister*. New York: Bantam Books.

Christopher, J. (1967). *The white mountains*. New York: Simon and Schuster.

Coel, M. (1998). *The story teller*. New York: Berkley Prime Crime.

Conley, R. J. (1992). *Mountain Windsong: A novel of the Trail of Tears*. Berkeley, CA: Oyate.

Cormier, R. (1974). *The chocolate war*. New York: Pantheon.

Cormier, R. (1985). *Beyond the chocolate war*. New York: Alfred A. Knopf.

Crew, L. (1991). *Children of the river*. New York: Laurel Leaf.

Crow Dog, M., & Erdoes, R. (1991). *Lakota woman*. New York:

HarperPerennial.

Curtis, C. P. (1995). *The Watsons go to Birmingham—1963*. New York: Delacorte Press.

Cushman, K. (1995). *The midwife's apprentice*. New York: Clarion.

Cushman, K. (1995). *Catherine, called Birdy*. New York: Harper Trophy.

Davis, O. (1992). *Just like Martin*. New York: Simon & Schuster Books for Young Readers.

Duvall, L. (1994). *Respecting our differences: A guide to getting along in a changing world*. Pamela Espeland (Ed.). Minneapolis: Free Spirit.

Fenner, C. (1995). *Yolanda's genius*. New York: Simon & Schuster Children's Publishing Division.

Fleischman, P. (1988). *Joyful noise: Poems for two voices*. New York: Harper Trophy.

Frank, A. (1967). *The diary of a young girl*. New York: Doubleday.

Fox, P. (1995). *The eagle kite*. New York: Laurel-Leaf Books.

Fox, P. (1991). *The slave dancer*. New York: Yearling Books.

Garden, N. (1982). *Annie on my mind*. New York: Farrar, Straus, & Giroux.

Garden, N. (1999). *The year they burned the books*. New York: Farrar, Straus, Giroux.

Godrey, M. (1989). *The last war*. New York: Collier Macmillan Publishing.

Graff, N. P. (1993). *Where the river runs: A portrait of a refugee family*. New York: Little, Brown, and Company.

Griffin, J. (1960). *Black like me*. Boston: Houghton Mifflin.

Grutman, J. H., & Mattaei, G. (1997). *The ledgerbook of Thomas Blue Eagle*. New York: Lickle Publishing.

Hamilton, V. (1974). *M. C. Higgins, the great*. New York: Simon & Schuster.

Hamilton, V. (1984). *The house of Dies Drear*. New York: Macmillan.

Hamilton, V. (1995). *Many thousand gone: African Americans from slavery to freedom*. New York: Knopf.

Hamilton, V. (1997). *The mystery of Drear house*. New York: Scholastic.

Hansen, J. (1986). *Which way to freedom?* New York: Avon Books.

Haskins, J. (1992). *The life and death of Martin Luther King, Jr.* New York: William Morrow/Beech Tree Books.

Haskins, J. (1992). *The march on Washington*. New York: HarperCollins.

Haskins, J. (1993). *Get on board: The story of the Underground Railroad*. New York: Scholastic Publishers.

Haskins, J. (1993). *Black music in America: A history through its people*. New York: HarperCollins/Harper Trophy Books.

Haskins, J. (1994). *The Scottsboro boys*. New York: Henry Holt & Co.

Heron, A. (Ed.). (1995). *Two teenagers in twenty: Writings by gay & lesbian youth*. Los Angeles: Alyson Publications.

Hersey, J. (1985). *Hiroshima*. New York: Vintage Books.

Hesse, K. (1997). *Out of the dust*. New York: Scholastic.

Hinton, S. E. (1997). *The outsiders*. New York: Puffin.

Hobbs, W. (1988). *Changes in latitudes*. New York: Atheneum.

Hobbs, W. (1989). *Bearstone*. New York: Atheneum.

Hobbs, W. (1991). *Down river*. New York: Atheneum.

Hobbs, W. (1992). *The big wander*. New York: Atheneum.

Hobbs, W. (1995). *Kokopelli's flute*. New York: Atheneum.

Hobbs, W. (1996). *Beardance*. New York: Camelot.

Hobbs, W. (1996). *Far north*. New York: Morrow Junior Books.

Hobbs, W. (1997). *River thunder*. New York: Delacorte Press.

Hobbs, W. (1997). *Ghost canoe*. New York: Morrow Junior Books.

Hobbs, W. (1998). *The maze*. New York: Morrow Junior Books.

Hobbs, W. (1999). *Jason's gold*. New York: Morrow Junior Books.

Hogan, L. (1995). *Solar storms*. Berkeley, CA: Oyate.

Holland, I. (1972). *The man without a face*. New York: HarperCollins Children's Books.

Houston, J. W., & Huston, J. D. (1974) *Farewell to Manzanar: A true story of Japanese American experience during and after World War II internment*. New York: Bantam Books.

Hubbard, J. (Ed.). (1994). *Shooting back from the reservation*. Berkeley, CA: Oyate.

Hunter, S. (1996). *Four seasons of corn: A Winnebago tradition*. Berkeley, CA: Oyate.

Hurston, Z. N. (1937). *Their eyes were watching God*. New York: Harper & Row.

Kerr, M. E. (1989). *Night kites*. New York: HarperTrophy.

Kerr, M. E. (1995). *Deliver us from Evie*. New York: HarperTrophy.

Kerr, M. E. (1997). *"Hello," I lied*. New York: Harpercrest.

Kerr, M. E. (1993). *Linger*. New York: Harper/Trophy.

King, C. S. (1993). *My life with Martin Luther King, Jr.* New York: Penguin/Puffin Books.

King, Jr., M. L. (1973). From "Homage to Gandhi." In *The United States in Literature* (p.174C). Glenview, IL: Scott, Foresman.

King, S. (1993). *Shannon: An Ojibway dancer*. Berkeley, CA: Oyate.

Klass, D. (1994). *California blue*. New York: Scholastic.

Klein, G. W. (1995). *All but my life*. New York: Hill and Wang.

Koehn, I. (1990). *Mischling, second degree: My childhood in Nazi Germany*. New York: Puffin Books.

Krisher, T. (1994). *Spite fences*. New York: Delacorte.

Lasky, K. (1986). *The night journey.* New York: Puffin Books.

Lawrence, L. (1985). *Children of the dust.* New York: Harper & Row Publishers.

Lee, H. (1988). *To kill a mockingbird.* New York: Warner Books.

Lee, M. G. (1994). *Finding my voice.* New York: Laurel-Leaf Books.

Lee, M. G. (1994). *Saying goodbye.* Boston: Houghton Mifflin.

Lee, M. G. (1995). *If it hadn't been for Yoon Jun.* New York: Avon Books.

Lee, M. G. (1996). *Necessary roughness.* New York: HarperCollins Juvenile Books.

Lee, M. G. (1998). *Night of the chupacabras.* New York: Avon Books.

Lee, M. G. (1999). *F is for fabuloso.* New York: Avon Books.

Leitner, I. (1992). *The big lie: A true story.* New York: Scholastic.

Levine, E. (1993). *Freedom's children: Young civil rights activists tell their own stories.* New York: G.P. Putnam's Sons.

Lewis, B. (1997). *The confession.* Minneapolis, MN: Bethany House.

Lewis, B. (1997). *The shunning.* Minneapolis, MN: Bethany House.

Lewis, B. (1998). *The reckoning.* Minneapolis, MN: Bethany House.

Livo, N. J., & Cha, D. (1991). *Folk stories of the Hmong: Peoples of Laos, Thailand, and Vietnam.* Englewood, CO: Libraries Unlimited.

Lowry, L. (1990). *Number the stars.* New York: Yearling Books.

Lowry, L. (1993). *The giver.* Coldwater, MI: Houghton Mifflin.

Masters, E. L. (1962). *Spoon River anthology.* New York: Macmillan.

Matas, C. (1996). *After the war.* New York: Simon & Schuster.

Matas, C. (1993). *Daniel's story.* New York: Scholastic.

Meyer, C. (1994). *Rio Grande stories.* New York: Gulliver Books.

Meyer, C. (1993). *White lilacs.* New York: Gulliver Books.

Mori, K. (1995). *Shizuko's daughter.* New York: Henry Holt.

Myers, W. D. (1991). *Fallen angels.* New York: Scholastic.

Myers, W. D. (1991) *Now is your time: The African-American struggle for freedom.* New York: HarperCollins.

Newman, G., & Layfield, E. N. (1995). *Racism: Divided by color.* Berkeley, NJ: Enslow.

Nolan, H. (1994). *If I should die before I wake.* New York: Harcourt Brace.

O'Brien, R. (1987). *Z for Zacharia.* New York: Aladdin Books.

O'Dell, S. (1992). *Sing down the moon.* New York: Yearling Books.

Orgel, D. (1988). *The devil in Vienna.* New York: Puffin.

Parks, R., & Haskins, J. (1992). *Rosa Parks: My story.* New York: Dial Books.

Perry, B. (1992). *Malcolm: The life of a man who changed Black America.* Barrytown, NY: Station Hill Press.

Paulsen, G. (1995). *Nightjohn.* New York: Laurel-Leaf Books.

Paterson, K. (1991). *Lyddie.* New York: Lodestar Books.

Petry, A. (1993). *Harriet Tubman: Conductor on the Underground Railroad.* New York: HarperTrophy.

Philbrick, R. (1993). *Freak the mighty.* New York: Scholastic.

Rapp, A. (1997). *The buffalo tree.* New York: HarperCollins.

Regguinti, G. (1992). *The sacred harvest: Ojibway wild rice gathering.* Berkeley, CA: Oyate.

Reiss, J. (1990). *The upstairs room.* New York: HarperCollins.

Richter, H. P. (1987). *Friedrich.* New York: Puffin Books.

Roessel, M. (1993). *Kinaaldá: A Navajo girl grows up.* Berkeley, CA: Oyate.

Rogasky, B. (1988). *Smoke and ashes: The story of the Holocaust.* New York: Holiday House.

Rossell, S. (1990). *The Holocaust: The fire that raged.* New York: Franklin Watts.

Sachar, L. (1998). *Holes.* New York: Farrar, Straus and Giroux.

Sawyer, D. (1988). *Where the rivers meet.* Berkeley, CA: Oyate.

Sender, R. M. (1986). *The cage.* New York: Macmillan.

Shusterman, N. (1996). *Scorpion shards.* New York: Tor Books.

Shute, N. (1989). *On the beach.* New York: Ballantine Books.

Siegal, A. (1994). *Upon the head of the goat.* New York: Puffin Books.

Slipperjack, R. (1987). *Honour the sun.* Berkeley, CA: Oyate.

Speigelman, A. (1991). *Maus.* New York: Pantheon Books.

Spinelli, J. (1990). *Maniac Magee.* New York: HarperCollins.

Spinelli, J. (1997). *The library card.* New York: Scholastic.

Stuart, J. (1976). *The thread that runs so true.* New York: Simon & Schuster.

Taylor, D. H. (1990). *Toronto at Dreamer's Rock: Education is our right.* Berkeley, CA: Oyate.

Taylor, M. D. (1976). *Roll of thunder, hear my cry.* New York: Puffin Books.

Taylor, T. (1969). *The cay.* New York: Avon Books.

Taylor, T. (1993). *Timothy of the cay.* New York: Avon Books.

Temple, F. (1993). *Grab hands and run.* New York: Orchard Books.

TenBoom, C. (1971). *The hiding place.* New York: Bantam Books.

Terkel, S. (1996). *People power: A look at nonviolent action and defense.* New York: Lodestar Books/Dutton.

Thomas, J. C. (1982). *Marked by fire.* New York: Avon Books.

Uchida, Y. (1996). *The bracelet.* New York: Paper Star.

Uchida, Y. (1984). *Desert exile: The uprooting of a Japanese-American family.* Seattle: University of Washington Press.

Uchida, Y. (1993). *A Jar of dreams.* New York: Aladdin Books.

Uchida, Y. (1995). *The invisible thread: An autobiography.* New York: Beech Tree Paperback.

United States Holocaust Memorial Museum. (1996). *Historical atlas of the Holocaust*. New York: Macmillan.

Voigt, C. (1995). *Jackaroo*. New York: Turtleback.

Volavkova, H. (Ed.). (1993) *I never saw another butterfly: Children's drawings and poems from Terezin Concentration Camp 1942-1944*. New York: Schocken.

Walter, M. P. (1992). *Mississippi challenge*. New York: Macmillan/Bradbury Press.

Weidhorn, M. (1993). *Jackie Robinson*. New York: Atheneum.

Wersba, B. (1997). *Whistle me home*. New York: Henry Holt and Company.

Westfall, R. (1992). *Gulf*. New York: Scholastic.

Wesley, V. W. (1993). *Where do I go from here?* New York: Scholastic.

Wiesel, E. (1986). *Night*. New York: Bantam Books.

Wilkinson, B. S. (1987). *Not separate, not equal*. New York: Harper & Row.

Woodson, J. (1995). *From the notebooks of Melanin Sun*. New York: Blue Sky Press.

Wyman, C. (1993). *Ella Fitzgerald: Jazz singer supreme*. New York: E. Watts.

Yep, L. (1990). *Dragonwings*. New York: Cornerstone Books.

Yep, L. (1993). *Dragon's gate*. New York: HarperCollins.

Yep, L. (1995). *Mountain light*. New York: Harper & Row.

Yep, L. (1996). *The serpent's children*. New York: Harper Trophy.

Yep, L. (1997). *Child of the owl*. New York: Harper and Row.

Yep, L. (1998). *The imp that ate my homework*. New York: HarperCollins.

Yep, L. (1999). *The cook's family*. New York: Paper Star.

Yoder, J. W. (1940). *Rosanna of the Amish*. Scottdale, PA: Herald Press.

Yolen, J., & Coville, B. (1998). *Armageddon summer*. New York: Harcourt Brace & Company.

Yolen, J. (1988). *The Devil's arithmetic*. New York: Viking Penguin.

References

About Face. *Facts on body image, appearance, SES, ethnicity, and the thin ideal*: http://www.about-face.org/resources/facts/

Applebee, A. N. (1993). *Teaching literature in the secondary school*. Urbana, IL: NCTE.

Applebee, A. N. (1981). *Writing in the secondary school: English and the content areas*. Urbana, IL: NCTE.

Armstrong, T. (1994). *Multiple intelligences in the classroom*. Alexandria, VA: Association for Supervision and Curriculum Development.

Armstrong, T. (1993). *7 kinds of smart: Identifying and developing your multiple intelligences*. New York: Penguin Books.

Atwell, N. (Ed.). (1990). *Coming to know: Writing to learn in the intermediate grades*. Portsmouth, NH: Heinemann Educational Books.

Bigelow, B. (1997, October). The human lives behind the labels. *Phi Delta Kappan, 79:2, 112–119*.

Blockson, C. L. (1994). *The Underground Railroad*. New York: Berkeley Pub. Group.

Boggeman, S., Hoerr, T., & Wallach, C. (1996). *Succeeding with multiple intelligences: Teaching through the personal intelligences: Another practical guide created by the faculty of the New City School*. St. Louis, MO: The New City School.

Butterfield, F. (1986, August 3). Why Asians are going to the head of the class. *New York Times*, pp. 18–19.

Cambodia : http://www. Cambodia-web.net/index.htm.

Campbell, L., & Campbell, B. (1994). *The multiple intelligences series facilitator's guide*. Alexandria, VA: ASCD.

Campbell, L., Campbell, B., & Dickinson, D. (1996). *Teaching & learning through multiple intelligences*. Needham Heights, MA: Allyn & Bacon.

Canady, R. L., & Rettig, M. D. (Eds.) (1996). *Teaching in the block: Strategies for engaging active learners*. Larchmont, NY: Eye on Education.

Carnes, J. (1995). *Us and them: A history of intolerance in America*. Montgomery, AL: Teaching Tolerance, A Project of the Southern Poverty Law Center.

Chapman, C. (1993). *If the shoe fits … How to develop multiple intelligences in the classroom*. Arlington Heights, IL: IRI/Skylight Training and Publishing, Inc.

Coffin, L. (1997). *Reminiscences of Levi Coffin, the reputed president of the Underground Railroad*. Richmond, IN: Friends United Press.

Colman, P. (1994). *Mother Jones and the march of the mill children*. Brookfield, CT: The Millbrook Press.

Colman, P. (1995). *Strike! The bitter struggle of American workers from colonial times to the present.* Brookfield, CT: The Millbrook Press.

Coolio, (Performer). (1995). *Gangsta' paradise.* (Compact Disc Recording). New York: Tommy Boy Records.

Cooter, R. B. (1989). Thematic units for middle school: An honorable seduction. *Journal of Reading, 32* (8), 76–81.

Crankshaw, E. (1997, November). The east and west of origami. Http://fly.hiwaay.net/~ejcranks/arth193b.html

Cruit, R., & Cruit, R. (1982). *Survive the coming nuclear war: How to do it.* New York: Stein and Day Publishers.

Currie, S. (1997). *We have marched together: The working children's crusade.* Minneapolis, MN: Lerner Publications Company.

Daniels, H. (1994). *Literature circles: voice and choice in the student-centered classroom.* York, ME: Stenhouse Publishers.

Donelson, K. L., & Nilsen, A. P. (1997). *Literature for today's young adults.* (5th ed.). New York: Longman.

Drew, B. (1968). *A northside view of slavery The Refugee: or Narratives of Fugitive Slaves in Canada.* Westport, CT: Greenwood Publishing Group.

Dunning, S., & Stafford, W. (1992). *Getting the knack: 20 poetry writing exercises.* Urbana, IL: NCTE.

Elbow, P. (1990). *What is English?* New York: Modern Language Association.

Environmental Poetry & Art Contest. *River of words.* International Rivers Network & The Library of Congress Center for the Book. PO Box 4000-J, Berkeley, CA 94704 or http://www.irn.org

Eye of the storm. ABC News Documentary. The Center for Humanities, Inc., Box 1000, Mount Kisco, New York 10549

Faggella, K., & Horowitz, J. (1990, September). Different child, different style. *Instructor,* 49-54.

Gardner, H. (1983/1993a). *Frames of mind: The theory of multiple intelligences.* New York: Basic Books.

Gardner, H. (1991). *The unschooled mind: How children think and how schools should teach.* New York: Basic Books.

Gardner, H. (1993). *Creating minds: An anatomy of creativity seen through the lives of Freud, Einstein, Picasso, Stravinsky, Eliot, Graham, and Gandhi.* New York: Basic Books.

Gardner, H. (1993b). *Multiple intelligences: The theory and practice.* New York: Basic Books.

Gardner, H. (1995, November). Reflections on multiple intelligences: Myths and messages. *Phi Delta Kappan,* 7, 200-209.

Gardner, H. (1995, December). "Multiple intelligences" as a catalyst. *English Journal,* 84 (8), 16-18.

Gardner, H. (1999). *The disciplined mind: What all students should understand.* New York: Simon and Schuster.

Garrett, O. A. (1996). *The guidebook to Amish communities across America.* Kalona, IA: Hitching Post Enterprises.

Goleman, D. (1995). *Emotional intelligence.* New York: Bantam Books.

Graff, N. P. (1993). *Where the river runs; A portrait of a refugee family.* New York: Little Brown and Company.

Haiku. (1994). *Microsoft Encarta.* Funk & Wagnalls Corporation. Microsoft Company

Hansen, E. (Ed.). (1993). *The Underground Railroad: Life on the road to freedom.* Carlisle, MA: Discovery Enterprises.

Harris, K., & Harris, R. *Music of the Underground Railroad.* Chatham Hill Games, Box 253, Chatham, NY 12037. (800-554-3039)

Harvey, P. (1997, Summer). Sweatshop definition. *Rethinking Schools, 11* (4), 16.

Hoerr, T. (1996). The naturalist intelligence. In Boggeman, Hoerr & Wallach. *Succeeding with multiple intelligences: Teaching through the personal intelligences.* St. Louis, MO: The New City School, Inc.

How Seventeen undermines young women: http://fair.org/extra/best-of-extra/seventeen.html

Hoyt-Goldsmith, D. (1996). *Migrant worker: A boy from the Rio Grande valley.* New York: Holiday House.

Johnson, D., & Johnson, F. (1997). *Joining together: Group theory and group skills.* Boston: Allyn and Bacon.

Johnson, D. W., & Johnson, R. T. (1995). *Reducing school violence through conflict resolution.* Alexandria, VA: Association for Supervision and Curriculum Development.

Kagan, S. (1994). *Cooperative learning.* San Juan Capistrano, CA: Kagan Cooperative Learning.

Keyser, C. (1988). *The price you pay* (film) http://www.aems.uiuc.edu/html/results.las

Khmer art and sculpture. http://www.lonelyplanet.com.au/dest/sea/camb.htm

Khmer cuisine. http://www.lonelyplanet.com.au/dest/sea/camb.htm

Kielburger, C. (October 1998). *Free the Children.* http://freethechildren.org

Killing us softly: Advertising' image of women: http://www.mediaed.org/catalog/media/softly.html

Lang, R. (1988). *The complete book of origami: Step-by-step instructions in over 1000 diagrams.* New York: Dover.

Lazear, D. (1994). *Multiple intelligence approaches to assessment.* Tucson, AZ: Zephyr Press.

Lazear, D. (1991). *Seven ways of teaching.* Palatine, IL: IRI/Skylight Publishing, Inc.

Lee, H. (1987). *To kill a mockingbird.* [Videotape]. MCA Home Video, Inc.

Lewis, J. P. (1995). *Black swan, white crow.* New York: Atheneum Books for Young Readers.

Lehman (1998). *Non-electric catalog.* One Lehman Circle, P.O. Box 321, Kidron, OH 44646-0321

McDonald's/Disney linked to sweatshops. (1998, October) http://www.nlcnet.org/resources/resources.htm

McKenzie, W. (1999–2000). *Multiple intelligences survey.* Surfaquarium Consulting. http://surfaquarium.com/MIinvent.htm

Me, S. (1987). "I Am Poem." In Ron Padgett (Ed.). *The teachers & writers handbook of poetic forms.* New York: Teachers and Writers Collaborative.

Megyeri, K. (1996, September). Take a Walk in My Shoes Project. *N.E.A. Today, 15* (1).

Meinbach, A. M., Rothlein, L., & Fredericks, A. D. (1995). *The complete guide to thematic units: Creating the integrated curriculum.* Norwood, MA: Christopher-Gordon Publisher, Inc.

Milner, J., & Milner, L. (1993). *Bridging English.* New York: Merrill.

Montroll, J. (1985). *Animal origami for the enthusiast.* New York: Dover Publications.

Nieto, S. (1996). *Affirming diversity: The sociopolitical context of multicultural education.* New York: Longman.

Olson, C. B., & Schiesl, S. (1996, Spring). A multiple intelligences approach to teaching multicultural literature. *Language Arts Journal of Michigan, 12* (1), 21-28.

Outward Bound. http://outwardbound.org

Oyate Native Organization. http://www.oyate.org/

Puff Daddy. (Performer). (1997). *Victory.* (Compact Disc Recording). New York: Bad Boy Records.

Randlett, S. (1961). *The art of origami: Paper folding, traditional and modern.* New York: Dutton.

Reflections of gender studies in the media: http://www.childrennow.org/media/

Resphigi, O. The Pines Near a Catacomb. *The Pines and Fountains of Rome.*

Rock Hall of Fame (Nov. 2000). Keep on pushing: Popular music and the civil rights movement. http://www.rockhall.com/programs/institute.asp.

Rose, R. (1990) *Twelve angry men.* [Videotape]. MGM/UP Home Video, Inc.

Roberson, H. (1995). *The shadow of hate teacher's guide.* Montgomery, AL: Teaching Tolerance, A Project of the Southern Poverty Law Center.

Rosenblatt, L. (1995). *Literature as exploration.* (5th ed.). New York: Modern Language Association.

Salvner, G. (1991) Hit. In *Literature festival: Ten cooperative learning games designed to stimulate literary analysis.* El Cajon, CA: Interaction Publishers.

Sandpaintings. http://hanksville.org/voyage/navajo/sandpaintings. php3

Stepto, M. (1994). *Our Song, Our Toil: The Story of American Slavery as Told by Slaves* (ed.). Brookfield, CT: Milbrook Press.

The shadow of hate: A history of intolerance in America. (1995). [Videocassette]. Charles Guggenheim (Producer). Narrated by Julian Bond. Montgomery, AL: Teaching Tolerance, A Project of the Southern Poverty Law Center.

Shangri-Las. (Performer). (1988). *Leader of the pack.* (Compact Disc Recording). Venice, CA: Dominion Records.

Smith, W. (Performer). (1997). *Men in black* (Compact Disc Recording). New York: Columbia.

Shearer, C. B. (1996). *The MIDAS: A guide to assessment and education for the multiple intelligences.* Columbus, OH: Greyden Press.

Short, K., & Harste, J. (1996). *Creating classrooms for authors and inquirers.* (2nd ed.). Portsmouth, NH: Heinemann.

Smagorinsky, P. (1995, February). Constructing meaning in the disciplines: Reconceptualizing writing across the curriculum as composing across the curriculum. *American Journal of Education, 103,* 160-185.

Smagorinsky, P. (1995, December). Multiple intelligences in the English class: An overview. *English Journal,* 84 (8), 19-26.

Smagorinsky, P., & Coppock, J. (1994). Cultural tools and the classroom context: An exploration of an alternative response to literature. *Written Communication, 11* (3), 283-310.

Smith, J. (1992). *The frugal gourmet on our immigrant ancestors: Recipes you should have gotten from your grandmother.* New York: Avon.

Steam. (Performer). (1989). *Na na hey hey kiss him goodbye.* (Compact Disc Recording). Santa Monica, CA: Rhino Records.

Tomorrow we will finish. (1994). [Videotape]. Maryknoll, NY: Maryknoll World Productions, PO Box 308, Maryknoll, NY 10545-0308. Tel: 800-227-8523.

Ujeli: Child bride in Nepal. (1992). [Videotape]. Maryknoll, NY: Maryknoll World Productions, PO Box 308, Maryknoll, NY 10545-0308. Tel: 800-227-8523.

Ute bear dance. http://www.southern-ute.nsn.us/culture/bear.html

Walters, J., & Gardner, H. (1987, April). Managing intelligences (Tech. rep. no. 33). Cambridge: Harvard University, Project Zero.

We, the working children of the Third World, propose . . . http://www.oneworld. org/ni/issue292/simply.html

Wiese, K. (1945). *You can write Chinese*. New York: Viking Press.

Wood, N. (1993). The circle. *Spirit walker*. New York: Doubleday.

The world through kids' eyes. (1997). [Videotape]. Maryknoll, NY: Maryknoll World Productions, PO Box 308, Maryknoll, NY 10545-0308. Tel: 800-227-8523.

Yankovich, A. (Performer). (1996). *Amish paradise* (Cassette Recording). Santa Monica, CA: Scotti Brothers.

Zoned for slavery: The child behind the label. (1995). Crowing Rooster Arts. Distributed by the National Labor Committee, 275 Seventh Avenue, 15th Floor, New York, New York 10001. Phone: 212-242-3002.

INDEX

Index of Activities for the Multiple Intelligences

ABOUT THE EDITOR

Jackie Glasgow, Ph.D., taught junior and senior high school English, speech, and drama for eighteen years. She is currently associate professor of English education at Ohio University, Athens. She teaches undergraduate and graduate courses including Young Adult literature, methods of teaching composition and methods for teaching literature, as well as English composition. She was named Outstanding High School Language Arts Educator by OCTELA (Ohio Council of Teachers of English Language Arts) in 1998. She was recipient of the Education Press Association of America Distinguished Achievement Award given for Excellence in Educational Journalism to International Reading Association for "Accommodating Learning Styles in Prison Writing Classes" *Journal of Reading*, Learned Article, 1994. She works with secondary teachers in Ohio on standards and assessment, literature instruction, and teacher research. She is a former EECAP Director (Early English Composition Assessment Program) in northeast Ohio. A frequent presenter at state and national conferences, she is author of numerous articles in state and national English journals. As co-editor with Ruth McClain, she wrote Competency-Based Education Assessment for English Grades 9-12 for the Ohio Department of Education.

About the Contributors

Allison Baer is a creative middle school language arts teacher for Warren City Schools, Warren, Ohio. She holds a M.A. in Reading from Kent State University. She is a Northeast Ohio Writing Project Fellow and recipient of the 1996 Sallie Mae First Class Teacher Award. Having graduated from Kent State University in 1995, she received Departmental Honors with Distinction in Elementary Education for the Gifted. Her Honors Thesis was: *Gifted Education in Transition: Service Delivery in the 21st Century.* Allison is a frequent presenter at NCTE (National Council of Teachers of English), OCTELA (Ohio Council of Teachers of English Language Arts), Trumbull Literacy Conference, and numerous Staff Development Workshops. Allison currently serves as President-Elect of the Ohio Council of Teachers of English Language Arts.

Rita Elavsky has been teaching eighth grade language arts at Roberts Middle School in Cuyahoga Falls, Ohio for 18 years. She holds a Master's of Education with a reading specialization degree from Kent State University, Kent, Ohio. Rita has received many awards: National Board Teacher Certification, Mandel Teacher Fellowship sponsored by the United States Holocaust Museum for in-depth study of the Holocaust, Ohio Governor Bob Taft's Educational Leadership Award, Summit County Impact II Disseminator Grant to purchase 130 Holocaust books for the school library, Summit County Six District Educational Compact Award for community and school service in the Cuyahoga Falls C.A.R.E. and D.A.R.E. programs and Compaq Teacher Lesson Plan Contest, First Place Winner for her lesson plan entitled "Using Newspapers Across the Curriculum." She is working with the City of Cuyahoga Falls to plant a Garden of Acceptance and Tolerance to be dedicated on April 19, 2001, Holocaust Remembrance Day.

Mary Hostetler currently teaches civics at Jefferson Area High School, Jefferson, Ohio. She graduated Valedictorian from Kent State University, Kent, Ohio and is active in both the National and Ohio Councils of Social Studies. Mary is currently researching the many sects of Amish in northeast Ohio and collecting oral histories, stories and literature from these various Amish sects.

Linda Rice is a National Board Certified Teacher. She earned her BA from Grove City College (PA) and her M.Ed. Admin. from Westminster College (PA). She is currently working on her doctoral dissertation on Performance-Based Assessments through Kent State University (OH). Linda was named Outstanding High School Language Arts Educator by OCTELA (Ohio Council of Teachers of English Language Arts) in 1998 and is two-time recipient of the A+ Teacher Award from *The Tribune Chronicle*. Linda has published in *Ohio Teachers Write* and the newsletters of EECAP (Early English Composition Assessment Program), OCTELA, and WROTE (Western Reserve chapter of Ohio Teachers of English). She is a frequent presenter at OCTELA, Trumbull Literacy Conference, and NCTE (National Council of Teachers of English). Linda has taught English Education majors at Kent State and Ohio University and has been teaching at Lakeview High School in Cortland, Ohio for the past 5 years where she is Lead Mentor and a *Pathwise* trainer.

Mari Lin Robinson has been teaching English at Newton Falls Junior and Senior High Schools for 18 years. She holds a Master in Classroom Teaching with a minor in Fine Arts from Rio Grande University, Rio Grande, Ohio. She is a National Board Certified Teacher, and a Martha Holden Jennings Scholar. She is a frequent presenter at NCTE (National Council of Teachers of English), OCTELA (Ohio Council of Teachers of English Language Arts), Trumbull Literacy Conference. She is a two time recipient of the A+ Teacher Award from the Warren *Tribune Chronicle* (1993 and 1998). Currently, she mentors for the Rio Grande University Graduate Program and the Youngstown State University's National Board Certification Program.

Joyce Rowland has been teaching middle and high school English at Bristol High School, Bristolville, Ohio, for 24 years. Joyce holds a M.S. in Educational Administration from Youngstown State University, Youngstown, Ohio. She is a Martha Holden Jennings Scholar and recipient of the Warren *Tribune Chronicle* A+ Teacher Award. She serves as Editor of *Touching Base*, a community newsletter from the Bristol Association of School Employees. Joyce has been a frequent presenter at NCTE (National Council of Teachers of English), OCTELA (Ohio Council of Teachers of English Language Arts), and Trumbull Literacy Conference. Because of her strong interests in curriculum development, she contributed to the Tech Prep Applied Communications Curriculum and many projects using Gardner's Multiple Intelligences.

Carolyn Suttles has been teaching English at Bristol High School for the last 18 years. She received her MA in English from Youngstown State University, Youngstown, Ohio. She has distinguished herself by receiving the A+ Teacher Award from *The Tribune Chronicle* and she was chosen as a Martha Holden Jennings Scholar. She has published in the *Ohio Journal of English Language Arts*, *Inside CEA* (Career Education Association Journal), and *Trumbull County Tech Prep Curriculum*. Carolyn's innovative teaching units

can be found in *English Journal*. She is a well-known presenter at OCTELA (Ohio Council of Teachers of English Language Arts), Trumbull Literacy Conference, and NCTE (National Council of Teachers of English). She is currently serving as OCTELA Vice-President. She, too, contributed to the Tech Prep Applied Communications Curriculum and many other projects using Gardner's Multiple Intelligences.